NOLO *and* USA TODAY

NOLO
YOUR LEGAL COMPANION

For more than 35 years, Nolo has been helping ordinary folks who want to answer their legal questions, create their own documents, or work with a lawyer more efficiently. Nolo.com provides quick information about wills, house buying, credit repair, starting a business—and just about anything else that's affected by the law. It's packed with free articles, legal updates, resources, and a complete catalog of Nolo books and software.

To find out about any important legal or other changes to this book's contents, sign up for our free update service at nolo.com/legalupdater or go to nolo.com/updates. And to make sure that you've got the most recent edition of this book, check Nolo's website or give us a call at 800-728-3555.

USA TODAY
The Nation's Newspaper

USA TODAY, the nation's largest circulation newspaper, was founded in 1982. It has nearly 3.9 million readers daily, making it the most widely read newspaper in the country.

USATODAY.com adds blogs, interactive graphics, games, travel resources, and trailblazing network journalism, allowing readers to comment on every story.

Retire Happy

What You Can Do NOW to Guarantee a Great Retirement

by Richard Stim & Ralph Warner

First Edition	FEBRUARY 2008
Editor	ILONA BRAY
Cover & Book Design	SUSAN PUTNEY
Proofreading	ROBERT WELLS
Index	ELLEN SHERRON
Printing	DELTA PRINTING SOLUTIONS, INC.

USA TODAY CONTRIBUTORS

Book Editor	BEN NUSSBAUM
Contributing Editors	JIM HENDERSON, FRED MONYAK, AND GERI TUCKER
Special thanks to	JULIE SNIDER

Warner, Ralph E.
    Retire happy : what you can do now to guarantee a great retirement / by Richard
Stim and Ralph Warner.
        p. cm.
    Includes bibliographical references and index.
    ISBN-13: 978-1-4133-0835-8 (pbk. : alk. paper)
    ISBN-10: 1-4133-0835-X (pbk. : alk. paper)
    1. Retirement--Planning. I. Stim, Richard. II. Title.
HQ1062.W373 2008
646.7'9--dc22

                                        2007035631

Acknowledgments

Bringing the voices of actual retirees into this book was a top priority for us. Still, we could never have imagined the different ways in which we would be inspired, educated, and surprised by their stories. Accordingly, we'd like to thank Ernest Callenbach, Afton Crooks, Rod Duncan, Bernie and Bob Giusti, Amy Ihara, Stan Jacobsen, Arthur Levenson, Babette Marks, Henry and Althea Perry, Hazel Peterson, Yuri Shibata, Cecil Stewart, Carol Thompson, and Peter Wolford.

Many thanks also to our editors, Ilona Bray (at Nolo) and Benjamin Nussbaum (at USA TODAY). And this book would be only a stack of paper were it not for Nolo's production and design team, including Jaleh Doane and Susan Putney.

About the Authors

Richard Stim is an attorney and Nolo editor and author who lives in San Francisco. His books include *Wow! I'm in Business: A Crash Course in Business Basics*, *Music Law: How to Run Your Band's Business*, and *Getting Permission: How to License & Clear Copyrighted Materials Online & Off*.

Ralph (Jake) Warner is an attorney, a widely recognized pioneer of the do-it-yourself law movement, and a popular speaker on retirement topics. After cofounding Nolo in 1972 and running the company for much of the past three decades, Jake tried retirement for three years—during which time he embarked on a new business venture, TallTales Audio, which produces audio books for children. Today he's back at Nolo, serving as chief executive officer. Jake has also authored or coauthored many books, such as *How to Run a Thriving Business* and *How to Buy a House in California*.

Table of Contents

I Will You *Really* Retire?_____1

1 Start Your Planning (and Dreaming) Now_____3
The Four Things You Need in Retirement_____5
Look Outward and Inward_____13

2 Invest in Your Health_____19
Four Conditions You Should Treat Now_____20
Exercise and Diet_____33
Three More Tips_____41

3 Strengthen Family Ties_____47
How Strong Are Your Family Ties?_____49
Five Ways to Improve Family Function_____50
Couples Power: The Tie That Binds_____62
If One Spouse Retires Before the Other_____64

4 Appreciate Friends, Old and New_____67
Friends: Many Concepts—One Goal_____69
Four Paths to Friendship_____70
Members of Couples: Find Friends Who Are Yours Alone___78
Those Furry Friends_____80

5 Develop Lifelong Interests and Activities Now_____83
Volunteer_____84
Do the Things You Always Meant To_____93
Educate Yourself_____94

6 Figure Out Your Number_____99
Using Online Retirement Calculators_____100
The Choices and Variables Underlying Your Number_____102
A Do-It-Yourself Retirement Calculator_____107

7 **Convert Debt Into Retirement Savings**_____115

Can You Avoid Car Payments?_____117

Heading Into Retirement With Credit Card Debt?_____119

Should You Prepay Your Mortgage?_____127

8 **Where Will the Money Come From?**_____133

It's Not Too Late to Begin_____134

What to Expect From Social Security _____137

Employer Pension Plans_____148

Individual Retirement Savings Plans: IRAs and 401(k)s_____151

Withdrawing Money From Your 401(k), IRA, or Annuity_____159

Savings and Investments_____164

Inheritances and Gifts_____164

Early Retirement Incentives and Buyouts_____169

Reverse Mortgages_____170

Immediate-Fixed Annuities_____173

9 **Growing and Protecting Retirement Assets**_____177

The Safe Withdrawal Approach_____178

What Are Your Investment Choices?_____184

Cash: Lowest Risk, Low Returns _____184

Bonds: Low to Moderate Risk, Low to Moderate Returns____186

Individual Stocks: High Risk, Varying Returns_____188

Mutual Funds: Varying Risks, Varying Returns_____190

Making Choices, and Sticking by (Some of) Them_____198

Investing in and Profiting From Real Estate_____201

Getting Help: Financial Planners, Advisers, and Brokers____204

10 **Working After Retirement**_____209

Start Planning Now_____211

Whether to Work and Collect Social Security_____221

Legal Rules Protecting Older Workers_____222

Index_____224

Will You *Really* Retire?

Birds *don't* do it. Bees don't do it, either. But humans—the only species aware of their own mortality—have created a final phase to their life known as retirement.

Retirement, we're told, is an inevitable event when you step away from the desk, the counter, or the time clock and retreat to your home where you will live off your 401(k) savings, pension, or Social Security (assuming it's still around).

But will it really happen to you? And how will you prepare for this sea change?

As for the first question, yes, retirement will *really* happen to you just as it happens to most people between the ages of 60 and 67. You will wake up one day and not go to your job. That doesn't mean you will stop generating income—many older people continue working in some capacity, some into their seventies, and even beyond. For example, as this book went to press, author Elmore Leonard, age 84, was busy at work on his 42nd novel.

It also doesn't mean that you will move from the office to a nursing home. If you make it to 65, you should expect at least two decades of activity—much of it at the same pace and intensity as earlier decades.

As retirement unfolds, you will also likely find yourself transitioning—if we can borrow a buzzword—into a new version of yourself. You may find yourself more reflective, more passionate, more appreciative, and more inquisitive. Or you may also find yourself more lonely, more bored, and perhaps more short on cash.

Which leads us to our second question. How can you prepare for retirement?

It's our opinion that you need four things to retire happily: money, health, friends and family, and engaging activities. (In this sense our book takes a different approach than retirement advisors who stress that the accumulation of money is the sole retirement goal.) The Catch-22 of retirement is that it's much harder to acquire these elements after you retire than before.

For that reason this book stresses that you begin your retirement preparations now, before you leave your job. Just as you will find it hard to save money after age 65, so too will you find it difficult to make new friends, mend family rifts, and begin new activities. For example, you may learn when you apply to be a volunteer at a local animal habitat at age 65 that the best volunteer positions go to those who have been volunteering at the organization for years. This book will help you to begin your preparations now.

We also believe it's best to get retirement advice from those who have already experienced it, rather than from organizations or institutions that profit from retirement fears. As you will read, much of the advice in this book is derived from interviews with retirees by coauthor Ralph (Jake) Warner, and this advice emphasizes a balance between savings and personal satisfaction, and between security and a strong social network. As you will learn, no matter what your age, or your financial situation, there are always ways to prepare now for a satisfying retirement later. ●

Start Your Planning (and Dreaming) Now

The Four Things You Need in Retirement_____5

    Money_____5

    Good health_____6

    A network of friends and family_____8

    Engaging and enjoyable activities_____11

Look Outward and Inward_____13

Picture your retirement. Do you see yourself swinging contentedly on a hammock, a great-grandchild smiling in your lap, your golf clubs nearby? Or do you see yourself counting off the hours on your new gold-plated watch, fearful that you'll outlive your savings?

In his book *Stumbling on Happiness*, psychologist Daniel Gilbert explains that when it comes to prospection (looking forward in time), humans have conflicting impulses. On one hand, we like to daydream about a future in which we're "achieving and succeeding rather than fumbling or failing." On the other hand, we have a tendency to create futures that are frightening. Our forecasts become "fearcasts," whose purpose is "not to predict the future so much as to preclude it."

USA TODAY Snapshots®

America's oldest age group

Estimated population of Americans 85 and older:

Men   1.5 million

Women   3.4 million

Source: Census Bureau   By David Stuckey and Karl Gelles, USA TODAY 2006

Neither of these approaches works well for retirement planning. If you want to retire happy, you'll need to put away the crystal ball and look in the mirror. That's because the true predictors of a satisfying retirement—money, health, social connections, and interesting activities—are controlled more by what you do today than what you think you'll do when you retire. Though it sounds like a cliché, retirement is truly a journey, not a destination. And by beginning your journey today, you'll be a seasoned and happy traveler when you finally pass through the retirement portal.

The Four Things You Need in Retirement

Let's look closer at those four factors that are so important for a happy and satisfying retirement:

- money
- health
- a network of friends and family, and
- engaging and enjoyable activities.

Where did we get this list? It's derived from common sense, scientific studies, and from the insights and reflections shared by many retirees who coauthor Ralph (Jake) Warner interviewed. We'll discuss each of these in more detail in later chapters, but first, take a closer look.

Money

You can't retire happily without money, right? Like financial guru Suze Orman says, "Nothing more directly affects your happiness than money." Or maybe rocker David Lee Roth said it better: "Money can't buy you happiness, but it can buy you a yacht big enough to pull up right alongside it."

Accumulating an appropriate amount of money for your retirement years is inescapably important. We'll discuss what's needed—your "Number," as it's referred to in the media—and ways to shield and grow your savings. We'll also discuss what to do if you can't seem to hit that magic number—a burden many eventual retirees are carrying.

But this book diverges from those financial experts and retirement advisers who believe that the accumulation of a giant nest egg should be your sole retirement goal. With a narrow outlook like theirs, you could find yourself like the insecure couple profiled in a 2007 USA TODAY article, unsure whether they had enough money to retire, even with nearly $2 million in assets, a monthly stream of income of $4,200 from Social Security and pensions, and a paid-off home and partial ownership of two rental co-ops.

Yes, money is important. But it's only one element of the retirement picture, and it's possible that you don't need as much as you think you do. It's best to approach the dire warnings about how much money you'll need in retirement with a dose of skepticism, keeping in mind that some of those warnings come from people who'd like to make money off your retirement planning. One of our interview subjects, Babette Marks, a retired teacher, expressed it succinctly: "Most people now in their 40s and 50s will have more than enough money if they will just adjust their lifestyle to what they have, which, of course, is already much more than most people in the world will ever have and probably far more than their own grandparents enjoyed."

USA TODAY Snapshots®

At what age did you start saving for your retirement?

18 to 24: 27%
25 to 34: 25%
35 to 49: 13%
50 and older: 5%
Have not started: 25%
Don't know: 5%

Source: Edward Jones Retirement survey of 1,008 adults 18 and older conducted by Opinion Research. Margin of error ±3 percentage points.

By Jae Yang and Veronica Salazar, USA TODAY 2006

You can start your financial planning now by following the advice in subsequent chapters (especially Chapters 6 through 9). Our goal is to provide clearheaded financial advice based on common sense, historical patterns, and financial discipline.

Good health

You may believe that by middle age, it's too late to reverse the damage created by an unhealthy lifestyle. Not true. Miriam Nelson, associate professor at the Friedman School of Nutrition Science, told USA TODAY, "All the research shows that what you do now is far more important than what you did when you were younger. We work with people well into their 80s and 90s. The body's capacity to get stronger and to be healthier and happier is still there." Still, old habits can be hard to break, so don't wait. Your health at age 65 is determined to a great extent by how you behave today.

Is It Too Late to Start Retirement Planning? Never!

It's possible that—like many Americans approaching retirement—you feel there's no way you can save enough money this late in the game, so why bother? Here are three answers:

Money is only one aspect of retirement happiness. With or without money, it's not too late to set the stage for a healthy, active, socially satisfying retirement. And with your health and happiness on an even keel, you may even cut your spending on doctors and therapists. So please keep reading no matter your current financial condition.

Many financial situations are reversible. Even if you're drowning in debt, there are approaches that may help to pull you out. We discuss some of these in Chapter 7. What we've learned from interviewing retirees is that financial discipline—the ability to constrict your budget when times are lean and expand it when times are good—is the key to weathering financial storms.

Work it through. For a lot of people, retirement will include some sort of part-time or full-time employment. In addition, many people are delaying their retirement from full-time jobs in order to build up a proper retirement nest egg. An analysis by the Center for Retirement Research at Boston College found that workers who had no retirement savings needed to work only about 3½ years longer to avoid a steep drop in their standard of living in retirement.

As Dr. Thomas Perls, the lead author of *Living to 100: Lessons in Living to Your Maximum Potential at Any Age,* explains, "Many people still believe the myth that 'the older you get the sicker you get,' when in fact our studies and those of other researchers are revealing that it is much more accurately the case that 'the older you get, the healthier you've been.'"

We've included a chapter on health, because we believe—and statistics verify—that by investing in your health now, you can improve your odds of both living to retirement age and enjoying it once you get there.

You can start improving your health now by reviewing the four most common and fixable health issues for retirees—high blood pressure, smoking, high cholesterol, and obesity—and making changes to your habits and diet. In addition, and perhaps more importantly, you can start an enjoyable exercise routine that will carry you into retirement, even if it's just brisk daily walks. We provide more health solutions in Chapter 2.

A network of friends and family

Studies have shown that the most powerful predictor of life satisfaction after retirement is the size of your social network. So, whether it's your family, your church, or your book club, maintaining a quilt of family and friends will be an essential and comforting aspect of retirement.

USA TODAY Snapshots®

Seniors split on next vacation and retirement

Which do you think about more? How to manage your financial assets for retirement or your next vacation?

Asset management 47%

Next vacation 46%

7% Don't know

Source: Lincoln Retirement Institue survey of 500 affluent seniors ages 60 to 69. Margin of error ±5 percentage points.

By Jae Yang and Alejandro Gonzalez, USA TODAY 2006

But how many of us are spending enough time with friends and family now, in order to develop or maintain that network? Just making a living and dealing with day-to-day events can easily absorb all our time. Yet ignoring social contacts at the expense of gathering your nest egg can backfire, and you may find that it's impossible to renew relationships that have atrophied.

You can start improving your social network now by assessing your current relationship with friends and, if possible, mending broken relationships with family members. In case you're out of practice, now may also be the time to relearn how to make new friends. We discuss family and friends in Chapters 3 and 4.

What's Your Retirement Age?

A few decades ago, the answer was 65. That's when people left their full-time job, began accepting "full retirement age" Social Security benefits, and applied for Medicare. But now the age at which people "officially" retire is not so clear.

With so many people contemplating working into their 70s— estimates range from 30% to 80% of baby boomers—many now claim that the actual median age of retiring (that is, leaving full-time employment) will soon move to 67 or 68. Whether this is a good idea depends on how much you like your job, how long you expect to live, and the size of your savings.

In addition, full retirement age for Social Security benefits for baby boomers—those born between 1943 and 1954—has been raised to 66. You can still retire at age 65 (in fact, as early as age 62), but the amount of your benefit check will be permanently lower than if you'd waited. And if you delay claiming benefits until you're 70, your benefit amount will increase by almost 30% over what you would have received at full retirement age.

Of course, not everyone is excited about working into their late 60s and 70s. At the other end of the spectrum are members of the "early retirement" movement, which encourages semiretirement for people in their 50s. The general principle is that you can retire from full-time work by combining solid investing, a 4% limit on withdrawals from your savings, part-time work, and sensible spending.

The table below looks at the ages that normally (or legally) trigger various retirement events.

The "Ages" of Retirement	
50–55	The period commonly associated with "early retirement," as recommended in books such as *Work Less, Live More*, by Bob Clyatt. Fifty-five is also the median age when most people begin seriously funding their retirement nest egg. As USA TODAY reporter Dennis Cauchon noted, "most wealth accumulation happens rapidly and late in life—after the kids leave, when income is high, debts drop, 401(k) accounts fatten, and home equity swells." Income typically peaks at age 57, and wealth (a person's net worth—assets minus debts) tops out at 63, according to the Fed's Survey of Consumer Finance. Some pensions may offer payouts at age 55.
59½	The age at which you can begin withdrawals from tax-deferred accounts (IRAs and 401(k)s) without paying the 10% early withdrawal penalty. (There are some exceptions permitting early withdrawals without penalty, as described in Chapter 8.)
60	If your spouse has died, you may be eligible for Social Security retirement benefits at this age.
62	The age when you can elect early retirement benefits from the Social Security Administration. If you claim benefits at this age, you will receive 20% to 30% less in Social Security annually than if you wait for full retirement age (and you may receive even less if your work income at the time exceeds government limits). For more on Social Security, see Chapter 8.
65	This age, traditionally associated with retirement, is when you qualify for Medicare. Some people during their 65th year (those born before 1943) will reach full retirement age for Social Security benefits.
66	For baby boomers (born 1943 through 1954), this is the "full retirement age" for Social Security retirement benefits. (For those born after 1954, the full retirement age moves from 66 to 67 and remains at 67 for those born after 1960). If you don't claim at full retirement age, each year you wait, your benefits will increase by 8% annually until age 70.
67	This is the median age at which baby boomers are expected to leave full-time employment.
70½	At this age, IRA and 401(k) withdrawals become mandatory and you can no longer make contributions to an IRA or 401(k) (with the exception of Roth IRAs, see Chapter 9).
84/87	These are the median ages of death for men/women who have lived to 65. Another way to look at it: 28% of men who reach 65 will live to 90, 11% will live to 95, and 2% to 100. 40% of women who reach 65 will live to 90; 19% will live to 95; and 5% will live to 100.

Engaging and enjoyable activities

In 2006, USA TODAY reporter Mindy Fetterman wrote that when life spans were shorter, social scientists and financial planners saw two phases to retirement: "Go" and "No Go." "In the first phase you took maybe a couple of vacations, visited your grandkids, and messed around in the a) garage or b) garden. Then your health declined, you slowed down and, well, you know the rest."

Now that we're living longer—20 or 30 years longer than previous generations—the time between "Go" and "No Go" has extended to two or three decades. When asked what they plan to do with this time, potential retirees usually respond with vague lists of activities. The problem is that attempting to narrow in on and start up these activities after you retire can prove frustrating.

You can begin staying active and connected now by assessing your interests and determining whether, and in some cases exactly where, you'd like to work, volunteer, travel, study, or pursue personal projects. In Chapter 6, we explain how to begin.

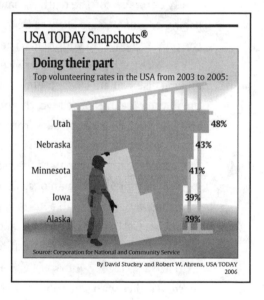

USA TODAY Snapshots®

Doing their part
Top volunteering rates in the USA from 2003 to 2005:

Utah 48%
Nebraska 43%
Minnesota 41%
Iowa 39%
Alaska 39%

Source: Corporation for National and Community Service

By David Stuckey and Robert W. Ahrens, USA TODAY
2006

Ernest's Retirement Tips:
Connect, Create Space, and Stay Healthy

Coauthor Jake Warner's interview with Ernest Callenbach demonstrates why you should begin your planning well before retirement.

Ernest retired at age 62. Before that he worked as editor of a respected film magazine and the *Natural History Guide* series, and also authored books, including the best-seller *Ecotopia*. Jake asked Ernest to imagine that he was to give a lecture entitled "What I've Learned About Retirement." Ernest listed three things:

Stay connected. "The truth is," says Ernest, "even if you love fishing or golf, you are likely to become quickly bored if those are the only activities on your plate. The key is to find useful ways to connect to the world—otherwise you'll drive your spouse or anyone else you are close to nuts. Men, especially, often suffer a big dip in their feelings of self-worth once they are no longer working and don't get all those strokes from colleagues or subordinates. Often this means having to start from scratch to reconstruct one's self esteem. Fortunately, there are a number of ways to do it—for example, turning an occasional hobby into a small business. Providing service through a nonprofit organization is another good approach. Getting involved in local politics to try and improve the way your community works is a third."

Create a space for yourself. "When you retire, assuming you're married or live with someone else, you must share space in a way you never have before. And I mean all types of space, including even using the telephone. Especially for men, who have typically seen the home as being more a woman's environment, this can be a huge problem. Whether it's in the basement, attic, spare room, or out of the house altogether, everyone needs their own defensible space. And I would add that once a domestic partner retires, a spouse who mostly managed the home also feels his or her space has been invaded, so by creating a space for the recently retired person, the spouse also minimizes conflicts created by the change."

> **Ernest's Retirement Tips:**
> **Connect, Create Space, and Stay Healthy, cont'd.**
>
> **Stay healthy.** As with all of his retirement tips, Ernest recommends starting now. "If you don't, you may not even live that long. Not only will paying attention to your physical well-being likely result in your living longer and feeling better, it will also save you a pile of money in expensive medical care. But in addition to eating better—less salt, fats, and sugar—you need to be active, to exercise every day. Whether you join a gym, ride a bike regularly, or just walk briskly doesn't make a big difference as long as you really do it. Also, look at your life and find ways to accomplish your daily rounds more actively. For example, instead of getting in the car to drive to the neighborhood market or a friend's house, walk or bicycle."
>
> Check out Chapter 10, Listen to What Retirees Have to Say, for more interviews.

Look Outward and Inward

Your retirement years are likely to consist of a number of messy—and sometimes scary—personal transitions, beginning on the very day you retire. Some changes will be unpredictable, such as a stock market downturn, a rise in your blood pressure, or financial requests from a pregnant granddaughter. If these prospects worry you, think back and remind yourself how many major changes you've already weathered: perhaps leaving home for the first time, marrying (or forming another close relationship), parenting, changing jobs, or dealing with the death of a loved one.

To deal with life's curveballs, you'll need to look outward and inward. An outward view means looking at how people you admire have aged, grown, and changed to meet the challenge of living well in later life.

Start this process now, and when you find older people you admire, arrange to spend some time together. If one of them is so busy that it's hard to make an appointment, you know you've found someone worth talking to. Don't be afraid to ask tough questions, whether they're about experiencing loneliness, poverty, a decline in sexuality, boredom, or death itself. We've found that most successful retirees have developed strategies to cope with all of these issues—and probably a bunch more you haven't thought of—and will be pleased to pass them on to you.

The first country with more than one-fifth of its population over 65? Japan, starting in 1993.

But more importantly, they will almost surely provide you with a positive vision of the excitement and growth possible at a time of life when there are fewer day-to-day responsibilities.

At the same time, you'll need to look inward. A successful retirement doesn't result solely from a plan; it results from your ability to adapt and modify as things change.

Do some soul-searching about who you are now and who you want to be in retirement. Some people do this sort of thinking by themselves, alone in their car or on a hike in the woods. As part of this exercise, try to ask and answer one essential question: Is the inner me well-prepared for the final one-third of my life?

You may be tempted to answer, "How would the inner me know? It's never retired before." But retirement is simply another life transition. So, look at how the inner you coped with previous difficult life transitions. If you didn't do very well—except perhaps to fool others that you were fine—think about how you could improve your coping skills, maybe by talking to someone about any anxieties and demons.

Breaking through your sense of isolation can be the first real step toward surmounting huge problems. Listening to and learning from the insights and experiences of people you respect is also valuable. Then you'll be ready to incorporate this knowledge into a new version of yourself— one with a little more humility, flexibility, and hopefully wisdom.

For Women Only

In 2006, USA TODAY highlighted some of the ways that women preparing for retirement are—unlike their male counterparts—hit with a double whammy: Not only do they typically have smaller retirement savings than men, they also live longer. Here are some of the ways this plays out:

Women quit working earlier than men. The average woman retires at age 62, the average man at 63. Married women tend to stop working once their husbands retire, even though the average woman is younger than her husband and will outlive him and have a longer retirement. But by working longer, women could contribute more to retirement savings plans and boost their Social Security benefits.

Divorcing women too easily give up shares in their husband's pension plan. Some women's number one priority in a divorce is keeping the family house—but they often give up valuable shares of their ex-spouse's pension or retirement savings in exchange. If done wisely, there's nothing wrong with that decision. But before signing off on the divorce decree, obtain as much information as possible from your husband's employer about the pension plan, to make sure it's a fair trade. You have a right to this information, but many pension plans won't provide it without a letter from your lawyer, according to the Women's Institute for a Secure Retirement. (You should also tell the pension plan administrator that you're in the process of getting a divorce. That will prevent the plan from paying out your share to your husband before the divorce is final.) Bottom line: In some cases, the financial benefits of the pension may outweigh the home equity. If you do choose the pension, you'll need a separate court order—called a qualified domestic relations order—which recognizes your right to part of your ex-husband's pension.

For Women Only, cont'd.

Women invest timidly. Because women tend to have less money to invest, they're often more fearful of taking losses. But they live longer than men, which means they have longer retirements—and more time to ride out the market and take full advantage of riskier investments, which typically return more over the long term. Because most women can expect at least 20 years in retirement, at least some of their assets should be in stocks.

Women rent instead of own. Women approaching retirement are more likely than male counterparts to rent housing. But there's a good reason to aim toward owning your own home in retirement: It's cheaper. For women, who typically have less retirement income and live longer, that's essential. Housing eats up 33.6% of the income of the seniors who rent and are in the lowest 25% income bracket, according to the Joint Center for Housing Studies at Harvard University. But those who own their own homes use an average of only 18.3% of income to pay housing costs. The reasons are fairly simple. If you rent, your rent is likely to rise year after year, and you have no chance of recovering any of that money. If you own, your mortgage will probably be a fixed amount, and, over time, you could pay it off entirely. Even if you're buying just a small condo, you'll build up equity over time, which you may eventually tap using loans or a reverse mortgage. The trick is finding a house or condo you can afford. To do that, you might have to move to a part of the country where housing prices are lower, or settle for a smaller living space.

For Men Only

Why do so many more men than women seem to have a tough time dealing with retirement? Easy. When work stops and physical limitations make it more difficult to participate in recreational sports, many men do not have good family relationships to fall back on. We know men whose careers were highly successful and who are nevertheless lonely and isolated, in significant part because children to whom they paid little attention earlier in life are now returning the favor.

One reason why women, on average, may live substantially longer than men is that so many men—in addition to being members of the more violent and accident-prone sex—are social misfits after they retire. By contrast, women, who have typically developed better social and family skills earlier in life, adjust far better. Many older women seem too engaged in life to be ready to quit it early.

One of the best ways for men to increase their chances of enjoying a fulfilling retirement is to spend more time becoming close to their families during midlife. If there is one key to a man's ability to really be part of his family, it's to get involved in day-to-day activities. Intimacy must be earned by reading bedtime stories, helping with homework, driving carpools, volunteering in the classroom, coaching Little League, and even helping a seven-year-old make a new dress for her favorite doll. Children, of course, aren't the only family members who need your caring involvement. Taking the time to be truly part of the lives of parents, siblings, nieces and nephews, and cousins will benefit all of you, both now and after you retire.

Finally, don't disregard (or take for granted) the power of a spouse. A married man has 2-1 odds of outliving a never-married man and 3-1 odds of outliving a divorced man, according to the National Center for Health Statistics (NCHS).

USA TODAY'S Retirement Corner

Start your retirement planning by bookmarking USA TODAY's helpful "retirement" Web page at www.money.usatoday.com. Under the "Managing Your Money" drop-down menu, click "Retirement." You'll find timely investing advice, planning tips, and many relevant retirement articles.

Invest in Your Health

Four Conditions You Should Treat Now_____20

    Stop smoking_____20

    Maintain a healthy weight_____25

    Control your blood pressure_____28

    Control your cholesterol_____30

Exercise and Diet_____33

    Exercise often_____33

    Clean up your diet_____38

Three More Tips_____41

    Prevent brittle bones_____41

    Manage stress_____42

    Schedule medical tests_____43

Our goal is to help you reach retirement with wealth and health intact. If you retire in poor physical condition, you will have achieved little, except to provide a comfortable nest egg for your heirs. Without making too many sacrifices—you may not need to throw out that Häagen-Dazs just yet—we've come up with some suggestions to help you minimize your health risks and maximize your retirement enjoyment.

Four Conditions You Should Treat Now

We start with four health conditions—smoking, obesity, high blood pressure, and cholesterol—that, if left untreated, have the potential to ruin your golden years, or prevent you from even reaching them. The good news: They're not hard to manage and the positive results are often immediate.

USA TODAY Snapshots®

Where smoking is not cool
States with lowest percentage of smokers ages 18 and older:

Utah   10.5%
California   14.8%
Idaho   17.5%
Connecticut   18.1%
Massachusetts   18.5%

Source: American Cancer Society

By David Stuckey and Karl Gelles, USA TODAY
2006

Stop smoking

No single act of retirement planning will have a greater positive influence on your retirement than kicking the habit. Smoking will shorten your life (most smokers can subtract a decade from life expectancy) and make your final years miserable, as you possibly battle cancer, emphysema, heart disease, and dementia. Michael Fiore of the University of Wisconsin, who headed the efforts to create Public Health Guidelines recognizing nicotine addiction as a chronic disease, told USA TODAY, "Few diseases kill 50% of the people who have it. This one does."

You may already know these facts and still have a hard time quitting. Below we provide some suggestions.

What to do now. Experts suggest that smokers approach quitting as if training for a marathon. USA TODAY reporter Liz Szabo consulted the American Cancer Society for ways to help smokers weather the physical and mental stress of kicking the habit and came up with these tips:

- **Pick a "Quit Day,"** perhaps two or three weeks in the future. Research shows it's more effective to go cold turkey than to try to taper off. Be patient. Smokers may spend all of Quit Day just trying not to light up.

- **Ease your burden.** Take care of errands or chores before you quit so that your first few days as a nonsmoker will be less stressful.

- **Clean house and stock up.** Throw away all ashtrays, lighters, and matches. To combat hunger pangs on Quit Day, keep foods at home, in your car and at work. Try carrot or celery sticks, licorice, lollipops, hard candies or mints, herbal tea, orange sections, raisins, seeds, popcorn, or sugarless gum. We wouldn't normally recommend keeping stocks of lollipops close at hand, but the damage to your health from these sugary treats is less than the damage from cigarettes—and remember, we're just talking about Quit Day.

- **Build your team.** Tell your friends and family about your Quit Day, so you'll be less likely to put it off. Ask for their support. Ask other smokers to neither smoke in the house nor around you, and to never offer you cigarettes, nor give you one if you ask. Find a few friends to agree to talk you out of smoking if you feel the urge, such as by reminding you of the vacation you'll take with the money you save by not smoking.

- **See a doctor.** A doctor can prescribe products to help you quit and help craft a personalized plan. Research suggests that using an antidepressant along with a nicotine replacement is more effective than either product alone.

- **Find a support group.** The most effective groups meet for about 30 minutes for at least four to seven total sessions. Nicotine Anonymous, local hospitals, and even some employers sponsor such groups. Telephone counseling from the cancer society (877-YES-QUIT), the National Cancer Institute (877-44U-QUIT), or the CDC (800-QUIT-NOW), can provide information and motivation and connect you with a local support group. The American Lung Association (www.lungusa.org) offers an online smoking-cessation program.

- **Create "flashbulb moments."** Write down brief but powerful reminders to "stop you in your tracks" when you have the impulse to smoke—for example, "I don't want my kids to see me in the hospital." Post them in all places where you typically smoke. Promise to reflect on these reminders before smoking. The urge to smoke might decline by the time you're done reading.

USA TODAY Snapshots®

At a healthy weight
Percentage of men and women ages 20 to 74 considered to be at a healthy weight[1]:

Men
31.8%

Women
35.3%

1.– Healthy weight is measured by BMI (body mass index), body fat level calculated by weight and height. Healthy BMI ranges from 18.5 to 24.9.
Source: Weight-control Information Network

By David Stuckey and Sam Ward, USA TODAY
2006

- **Practice how you'll respond to stress or offers to smoke.** Decide how you will fight cravings and excuses such as "I'll just have one." Say phrases out loud to yourself like, "Thanks, but I'm serious about quitting this time, and could use your help."

- **Exercise.** Consider walking or beginning some other physical activity, which will help prevent weight gain. (See "Exercise often," below.) Some smokers gain no weight at all after quitting; those who do typically put on five to ten pounds. A smoker would have to gain 100 to 150 pounds to undo the health benefits of giving up cigarettes.

What Doesn't Work

According to the American Legacy Foundation, certain strategies such as acupuncture, hypnosis, and antismoking diets have been shown generally ineffective for quitting smoking. The American Cancer Society warns consumers to beware of programs that promise instant success, charge a high fee, or use "secret" ingredients.

You might be able to avoid relapses if you:

- **Wait it out.** Cravings will go away whether you smoke or not. The urge to smoke typically passes in five minutes.

- **Avoid triggers.** Certain foods are more likely to make you want to light up, including coffee, caffeinated and sugary soda, and alcohol.

- **Occupy your hands.** To avoid reaching for a cigarette, try holding a pen, a straw, a soft stress ball, nail file, or a piece of paper that you can fold and refold.

- **Avoid hunger.** Eating small meals throughout the day regulates blood sugar levels, which can relieve the urge to smoke. But don't overdo it with the sugary and spicy foods, which can trigger cigarette cravings.

- **Don't smoke even one.** Nicotine is so addictive that former smokers who smoke even one cigarette can quickly relapse into a two-pack-a-day habit.

If you do relapse, don't give up. Tell yourself, "I'm still a nonsmoker." Perhaps it's time to try one of the many antismoking products approved by the Food and Drug Administration. Using one of these products doubles the odds you'll quit successfully, according to the U.S. Department of Health and Human Services. You've got your choice of a patch, gum, nasal spray, lozenge, inhaler, and pills. (But read the warning labels before using; all have side effects or contraindications.)

The potential payoff. Everyone likes to see results from their efforts. But with quitting smoking, the results can be subtle—you won't necessarily look in the mirror and see a new you. Still, important changes will be happening under the surface:

- **After one day:** Within hours of quitting, oxygen and carbon monoxide levels in your blood will return to normal. Blood pressure should begin to drop.

- **After six months:** Your lung function will increase and your circulation improve. You'll have less fatigue and shortness of breath.

- **After one year:** Your risk of heart attack will have been cut in half. Consider that in Helena, Montana, the number of heart attack patients admitted to the hospital fell by 40% during a six-month period in 2002, when the city curbed smoking in workplaces. Also, you should have saved at least an extra $1,850 after one year if you were a pack-a-day smoker.

  The leading cause of death from residential fires? Careless smoking. (And adults over 65 are twice as likely to die in those fires.)

  The American Cancer Society's website (www.cancer.org) allows smokers to quickly calculate how much their habit costs.

- **After a decade:** Your risk of stroke and heart disease will get closer to that of a nonsmoker. Your risk of lung cancer will have fallen substantially.

- **After 15 years:** Your risk of stroke or coronary heart disease will be the same as that of a nonsmoker.

- **Lifetime benefit:** Depending on when you quit, you may extend your life by a decade or more.

Spouses Copy Good Health Habits

A 2007 Yale School of Public Health study of 20,000 people over the age of 50 found that when one spouse improves health behavior, the other spouse is likely to do so as well. For example, smokers were five times more likely to give up cigarettes or alcohol if their partner quit as well. So when you change your unhealthy habits, it's possible you'll help your spouse to do so.

Maintain a healthy weight

When Miriam Gittelson, 5' 10" and 200 pounds, moved into the assisted-living wing of a retirement home in Jamesville, New York, she expressed regrets. If she could live her life over again, she told USA TODAY's Nanci Hellmich in 2006, "I would have tried to lose weight a long time ago." Ms. Gittelson lamented that if she hadn't been overweight much of her life, she might still be in her own home, not using a wheelchair, and not suffering from type 2 diabetes, arthritis, and impaired mobility—she's had knee and hip replacements.

Obesity is a relatively new issue for retirees. Due to a sedentary lifestyle and a change in diet, the number of obese Americans increased by 60% between 1991 and 2000.

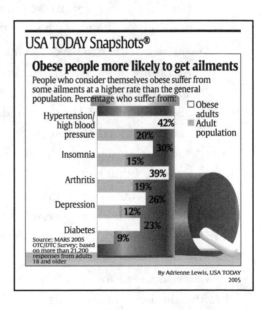

USA TODAY Snapshots®

Obese people more likely to get ailments

People who consider themselves obese suffer from some ailments at a higher rate than the general population. Percentage who suffer from:

☐ Obese adults
■ Adult population

Hypertension/ high blood pressure: 42% / 20%

Insomnia: 30% / 15%

Arthritis: 39% / 19%

Depression: 26% / 12%

Diabetes: 23% / 9%

Source: MARS 2005 OTC/DTC Survey; based on more than 21,200 responses from adults 18 and older

By Adrienne Lewis, USA TODAY 2005

(Obesity generally means being overweight by about 25% of the normal body weight for someone of that height.) Today, three out of five Americans are either overweight or obese, and at increased risk for heart attack, cancer, stroke, and diabetes (the latter two diseases also greatly increase your chances of suffering from dementia).

The number of calories you must burn in order to lose one pound? 3,500.

A 2002 RAND study reported that being obese is the equivalent of aging two decades. It increases your chances of acquiring chronic conditions by 67%, and raises your medical expenditures dramatically; obese individuals spend 36% more on health services and 77% more on medications than the general population.

How else can obesity affect your retirement?

- **You're more likely to end up in a nursing home.** According to a study by Barry Popkin, a nutrition professor at the University of North Carolina at Chapel Hill, extremely obese people—those who are 80 or more pounds over a healthy weight—are 2.3 times more likely than normal-weight people to stay in hospitals longer or to end up in nursing homes after an illness.

- **You're more like to have high blood pressure and bad knees.** According to Sharon Brangman, a geriatrician in Syracuse, New York, and a board member of the American Geriatrics Society, "People who are 30 or 40 pounds overweight are more likely to have high blood pressure, type 2 diabetes, and lots of joint pain and problems. Osteoarthritis of the knees is probably the biggest problem I deal with."

So although you may not want to hear it, plenty of evidence indicates that being even moderately overweight (pleasantly plump, if you will) is a major negative health factor and potential life-shortener. Now is the time to shed those extra pounds.

What to do now. You can't lose it all overnight—that wouldn't even be healthy. But here's how to start:

- **Concentrate on not gaining more weight.** The editors of the *New England Journal of Medicine* suggest starting with a hold-steady approach, focusing on halting any further weight gain. Did you know that you can gain ten pounds in one year just by eating 100 more calories a day than you burn off? Harvard University obesity expert George Blackburn offers a related approach. He says that overweight people who want to slim down should begin by aiming to lose 10% of their weight and then "try to maintain that weight loss permanently."

  The percentage of American women trying to lose weight at any time: 33% to 40%. Men? 20% to 24%.

- **Say goodbye to sugary drinks.** According to a study from the Obesity Society, dieters who replace sugary drinks with water lose an extra five pounds a year, and those who drink a couple of cups of water a day increase weight loss by two pounds a year. Try herbal teas or lemon in your water for variety.

- **Get moving now.** The most effective exercise program for keeping weight off is one that you like, adopt early, and increase gradually. If you hate the treadmill, try swimming or dancing. Cardiovascular and strength exercise are both essential. USA TODAY sponsors an annual weight loss challenge each spring. In 2007, members of the registry (about 5,000 people who lost an average of 66 pounds and kept off at least 30 pounds for more than six years) walked an average of an hour a day or burned the equivalent calories.

Atkins Has the Edge, But Most Diets Do Little for Weight Loss

A 2007 Stanford University study compared persons on the Atkins diet, The Zone Diet, The LEARN diet, and Dean Ornish's "Eat More Weigh Less" Diet. Women on the Atkins diet lost an average of ten pounds over a year and had slightly better improvements in blood pressure and HDL (so-called good cholesterol) than the others. The message from researchers, however, was that all of these diets roughly worked about the same and none of them, by themselves, offered substantial weight loss potential.

The potential payoff. Every pound you lose represents important progress, even if it just means you're not carrying that weight around:

- **Lose 11 pounds.** Losing as few as 11 pounds can cut the risk of osteoarthritis of the knee by 50%. And new research suggests that people who already have arthritis might get some pain relief by shedding extra weight.

- **Lose 5% to 10% of body weight.** Exercising just half an hour a day, along with losing 5% to 10% of body weight, can lower your chances for developing heart disease or having a stroke. In addition, according to the American Diabetes Association, it can reduce your risk of diabetes by nearly 60%.

Control your blood pressure

Two-thirds of retirees have high blood pressure, also known as hypertension. When the blood pressure cuff reading hits 140/90 or higher, you've got it. Millions more have slightly lower levels, between 120/80 and 139/89, a condition known as prehypertension. Like smoking and obesity, both hypertension and prehypertension make you more susceptible to chronic illnesses, increase your chances of needing assisted care, increase your medical expenses, and can shorten your life. Many health care professionals believe that the single most important thing you can do to improve your long-term health is to maintain healthy blood pressure levels.

What to do now. You can take effective steps to lower your blood pressure and, by doing so, reduce your chances of experiencing brain-damaging strokes. How? The short answer, according to the National High Blood Pressure Education Program (NHBPEP), is to:

- **Reduce your salt intake.** An average U.S. adult consumes two teaspoons of salt a day, much of it in processed foods or restaurant meals. Hypertension expert Rose Stamler says that if, starting at age 25, we reduced this amount of salt by half, it could mean a 16% drop in coronary heart disease deaths and 23% fewer stroke deaths at age 55.

- **Lose weight and quit smoking.** Both factors are discussed above.

- **Exercise.** The U.S. government now recommends 30 minutes of aerobic exercise per day. More is definitely better, especially after age 50 (see "Exercise often," below).

- **Get DASHed.** The National Institute of Health (NIH) supports the Dietary Approaches to Stop Hypertension diet (DASH), an eating plan rich in fruits, vegetables, and low-fat dairy products, and low in saturated fat, total fat, and dietary cholesterol. DASH has been shown to lower blood pressure; learn more at the NIH website, www.nih.gov.

  The future's so bright, you'll definitely need shades: By the time you reach age 60, your eyes will have been exposed to more total light than would be released by detonating a nuclear bomb.

- **Take medications.** If taking the steps above fails to counter your rising blood pressure, consult with your doctor about taking one of the 100-plus blood pressure medications on the pharmaceutical shelf. But you should still follow the other recommendations above, both to help your medication work better and potentially to reduce the amount of it you need.

- **Breathe.** Breathing exercises and meditation have been shown to lower pressure, although scientists can't yet explain why. (A device that debuted in 2006, RESPeRate, may also guide users to that goal.)

Don't just assume your blood pressure is okay because you've taken steps to improve your health. High blood pressure is called the silent killer; you can have it and still feel fine. So have regular physicals, attend a blood pressure screening, or get a home test kit and find out your level. If it's elevated (or even at the high end of the normal range), promptly take steps to lower it.

The potential payoff. Unfortunately, only about half the people with high blood pressure attempt to modify their lifestyle. This creates a vicious cycle: Reducing the damage caused by high blood pressure becomes more difficult the longer you delay. During the years of hypertension, fatty and other substances build up in the inner lining of an artery (known as atherosclerosis), leading to even higher blood pressure, and so forth. That's why diagnosing and treating hypertension early provides the most benefits. A study conducted by the National Heart, Lung, and Blood Institute (NHLBI) concluded that men and women with elevated blood pressure who make healthy lifestyle changes and sustain them for up to 1½ years can substantially decrease their heart disease risk.

Your time has not come: Less than a third of people admitted to emergency rooms believing they've had a heart attack have had one. (But don't let that stop you from heading to the hospital to make sure.)

Control your cholesterol

Despite all its bad press, cholesterol is an essential (and self-produced) substance for our bodies. Cholesterol has gotten a bad rap because elevated levels of a form of cholesterol known as low-density lipoprotein (LDL) causes fatty and other substances in the inner lining of an artery to build up. LDL is referred to as bad cholesterol because an undesirable level of it is associated with heart attacks and heart disease.

There's also good cholesterol, high-density lipoprotein (HDL), which carries away LDL from the walls of the arteries and returns it to the blood stream. According to a 2007 study, elevated levels of HDL can help prevent heart attacks. The race is on among pharmaceutical companies to create drugs that raise HDL levels.

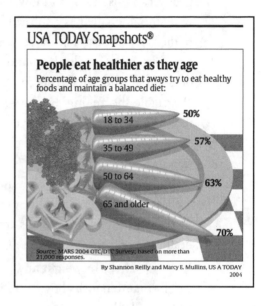

USA TODAY Snapshots®

People eat healthier as they age

Percentage of age groups that aways try to eat healthy foods and maintain a balanced diet:

18 to 34 — 50%
35 to 49 — 57%
50 to 64 — 63%
65 and older — 70%

Source: MARS 2004 OTC/DTC Survey; based on more than 21,000 responses.

By Shannon Reilly and Marcy E. Mullins, US A TODAY 2004

What to do now. As the American Heart Association points out, cholesterol is one of the major controllable factors for coronary heart disease, heart attack, and stroke. Much of what we advise about cholesterol mirrors our advice regarding obesity and blood pressure. For more information on cholesterol and its treatments, review the National Cholesterol Education Program website sponsored by the National Institute of Health (www.nhlbi.nih.gov/about/ncep/index.htm).

- **Know your numbers.** Schedule a cholesterol screening, and follow that with periodic monitoring. Act quickly to reduce elevated LDL levels. What are the desirable numbers? Cholesterol is measured in three levels:

  - **total blood (or serum) cholesterol,** for which a measurement of 200 mg/dL or lower is desirable and over 240 mg/dL is considered high risk

  - **HDL (or "good" cholesterol),** for which a measurement below 40 mg/dL for men and below 50 mg/dL for women is considered a risk, while a measurement above 60 mg/Dl is desirable, and

  - **LDL (or "bad" cholesterol),** for which a measurement of 100 mg/dL or less is desirable and over 160 is considered high risk.

- **Change your oil.** Studies have shown that trans fats, often found in foods such as French fries, doughnuts, and commercial baked goods, can raise LDL and lower HDL levels. (Curiously, trans fats were initially hailed as a substitute for the vilified saturated fats in the early 1980s.) Saturated fats—like those found in coconut and palm oil—are also bad, and the American Heart Association does not consider them acceptable substitutes for trans fats. (Vegetable shortening, by the way, is probably one of the single most toxic grocery products you can put in your body.) Other research has shown that total cholesterol can be lowered when trans fats and saturated fats are replaced with oils that are high in monounsaturated and polyunsaturated fats, such as canola, corn, soybean, sunflower, and olive oils. Whatever oils you use, avoid fried foods; the frying process creates unhealthy fats and other health concerns.

- **Maintain a healthy weight and exercise regularly.** We discuss weight maintenance above, under "Maintain a healthy weight"; and we talk about how to choose and implement an exercise regimen, below, under "Exercise often."

- **Consult your physician.** Some people cannot lower cholesterol even by modifying their lifestyle—for example, those who inherited a predisposition to cholesterol problems. Talk to your physician, who may prescribe a cholesterol-lowering drug in addition to diet and exercise.

The potential payoff. Here are some positive incentives to get those bad cholesterol numbers down:

- **One percent gets you two percent.** For people in midlife with a high LDL cholesterol level, a drop of 1% reduces the risk of heart disease by 2% or 3%.

- **Back to normal levels.** Maintaining desirable cholesterol levels can lead to a 23% reduction in coronary-related mortality, a 24% reduction in the need for coronary revascularization (bypass surgery), a 17% reduction in the fatal or nonfatal stroke rate, and a 30% to 40% reduction in cardiac events (heart attack, heart disease).

Exercise and Diet

Look at the trend of your general health and fitness over the last few years. Are you satisfied with it? If not, then unless you make a determined effort to change, this trend will very likely continue or accelerate. For example, if you're significantly heavier and less aerobically fit than you were a decade ago, you're on your way to being in even worse shape by the time you retire.

Get outta bed! A person who is immobile loses about one fifth of muscle strength during the first three days of immobility.

You may say to yourself that once you retire, you'll be more active and energized. But unless you're retiring tomorrow, such resolutions won't do you any good if your current lifestyle leaves you in such poor physical condition that you'll spend your retirement on a couch. And if your joints hurt because you've ignored your health, enjoying your retirement leisure activities, not to mention any exercise at all, will be a lot harder.

Exercise is not difficult, it will save you money, and you'll feel better for it. Here's what to do.

Exercise often

If you're not already on an exercise program, beginning one now will let you transition seamlessly into retirement. Virtually every one of the successful seniors we've talked to followed a structured exercise program. Many either walked or ran as many as four or five miles a day or swam laps, sometimes supplemented by fairly strenuous upper-body calisthenics.

The best news about exercise is that it's never too late to start. "One of the keys to preserving your body is exercise—a combination of strength training, aerobic activity, and stretching," says William Evans, author of *Biomarkers: The 10 Keys to Prolonging Vitality*. According to Evans, exercise programs "allow people to live independent lives with dignity for as long as they choose. Nothing holds that promise like exercise."

Exercise Is Good for Your Mind, Too

Exercise doesn't just prepare your body for retirement, it also prepares your mind. Here's how:

Look in the mirror. Regular exercise provides a sense of vitality that you can see in your reflection. How you look will influence how you feel about yourself just as much at age 75 as it did at 25.

Frailty leads to fear. Older people who don't maintain their strength often become frail, which can result in their becoming afraid of physical attack; so fearful in some cases that they're reluctant to venture out of their houses.

Weakness leads to dependence. Seniors who can't do things for themselves (carry groceries to the car, twist off a bottle cap, or move a piece of furniture) become overly dependent on others and less inclined to try anything new.

Mitigate depression. Estimates vary, but experts suggest that as many as 20% of people over 65 suffer from depression. Lack of exercise is one factor. Vigorous exercise—like many antidepressant drugs—increases production of a brain chemical called serotonin. For people who are severely depressed, this information isn't likely to be of much help. Nevertheless, regular exercise, along with other treatments, can go a long way toward mitigating the effects of temporary or mild bouts of depression.

Make the commitment. Most everyone can think up endless reasons not to exercise, lack of time being the most common. For example, if you have a full-time job plus a long commute, or you must care for and support a disadvantaged child or senile parent, or you are a single parent, finding enough time to go jogging or take a brisk walk will be a challenge. And even if your life isn't quite so full, there will always be plenty of reasons to put off exercising.

What if you got out of your chair right now and went out for a brisk 30-minute walk? Yes, we mean it—just put down this book (unless you're in a bookstore; then take it to the counter and buy it), and slip into some comfortable shoes and start. As you stride along, think positively about what kind of life you envision after you retire, and what you can do to get there with health intact.

During your search for time to begin a daily exercise program, keep two other things in mind:

- **Exercise is addictive.** Overcoming the initial inertia is the hardest part of an exercise program. Once you get into the groove, your energy and desire to exercise increases, and will replace the time periods when you were too exhausted to do anything but collapse with a DVD. According to a study reported in *Behavioral Neuroscience*, joggers may become as addicted to running as other people do to alcohol, tobacco, or drugs.

USA TODAY Snapshots®

Joint pain by gender
People in the USA with doctor-diagnosed arthritis (in millions):

Women 25.9

Men 16.8

Source: Arthritis Foundation

By David Stuckey and Adrienne Lewis, USA TODAY 2006

- **Where there's a will ...** Can you join an exercise facility near work and go during your lunch hour? Can you share child care with other parents, so you each have a free hour or two several times a week? Can you put off shopping for clothes, and instead work on fitting into those clothes at the bottom of the drawer? You may have to be inventive, but if you're committed to exercise, there's always a way to fit it into your routine—especially when you consider that 40% of the average American's free time is spent in front of the TV.

Arthur Cuts Back

Arthur Levenson retired in 1974 after a long and successful career in the U.S. defense security services—during World War II he was part of the team that broke German codes. Jake Warner talked to Arthur about his exercise regimen.

JW: *Arthur, when I called you this morning, you were out running five miles. Do you do that every day?*

AL: *When I turned 80, I cut back to six days a week.*

JW: *Do you work out in other ways?*

AL: *I do various stretching exercises after I run, and 100 push-ups per day to keep my upper body in shape.*

JW: *Is exercising something you began doing when you retired?*

AL: *No, I started running about age 50, when I read a book by the Yale swimming coach advocating exercise. It was easy for me to do because I quickly found that running was enjoyable. Running just makes you feel good all over.*

JW: *You obviously enjoy life. Do you attribute that to getting lots of exercise?*

AL: *Well, to stay healthy, you should follow the advice of the medical profession—don't smoke, moderate drinking, watch your weight, and eat sensibly, avoiding too much fat. But beyond that, yes, I'm a great believer in exercise. It has enormous benefits, both psychological and physical.*

JW: *You mean it has benefits besides keeping your body fit?*

AL: *Certainly. Among others, it's a great tranquilizer, and one of the best ways to relieve stress. By contrast, a sedentary lifestyle is a risk factor perhaps as dangerous as smoking. Incidentally, I once participated in a study at Johns Hopkins that compared older athletes with younger athletes and older sedentary people. It turned out that, by most measures, older athletes were much closer to younger athletes than they were to older sedentaries.*

Arthur Cuts Back, cont'd.

JW: *Do you believe people in their 40s and 50s ought to be jogging, swimming, biking, or doing something else to work up an aerobic sweat so they will be in decent shape later on?*

AL: *Yes, but it's hard for many people to find the time when they are working. It takes some determination and commitment. I used to get up at 5 a.m. to run, and it was worth it. If you wait until 65, it's not easy to reverse a poor physical condition, but it's not impossible.*

How much is enough? Peter Jaret, writing in *Health* magazine, concluded that every hour of an activity like fast walking will add an hour and a half to your life. This fits with many studies concluding that even moderate exercise, such as taking a walk a couple of times per week, can significantly reduce the risk of heart attack and therefore increase the length of your life. Exercise doesn't need to be formal—anything that gets you up and moving (like playing hide-and-seek with the grandkids) counts, and a little exercise is better than none at all. But for maximum benefits, both mental and physical, many experts recommend working out at least five days a week. A complete workout includes:

- **30 minutes of cardiovascular exercise.** Pick your favorite: perhaps daily swimming, dancing, jogging, or another aerobic activity such as fast walking. According to Miriam Nelson, an exercise scientist at Tufts University in Boston and one of the authors of *Strong Women, Strong Hearts,* cardiovascular exercise is "the real sledgehammer" when it comes to burning calories. "If you go out for a brisk walk for 30 to 45 minutes, you are going to burn 150 to 200 calories during that time." Other research indicates that exercisers burn three times as many calories in 30 minutes of walking and biking as they do in the same amount of time strength training.

- **30 minutes of strength and endurance.** The average person loses about 6.6 pounds of lean muscle mass a decade, and the rate of loss accelerates after age 45. To begin an at-home strength and weight program, go to your local sporting goods store and buy weights. You'll need a variety to accommodate the increasing amount of weight you'll be lifting. Homemade weights are also fine—like soup cans or containers filled with water—but for safety's sake, experts advise using containers with handles for upper-body workouts. Lifting weights is not the only method for increasing muscle strength; you can also do pull-ups and push-ups, as well as various calisthenics.

Muscles don't grow during exercise, they grow during sleep; exercise is the stimulus.

- **15 minutes of stretching and flexibility.** For people who are inactive, even gentle stretching can improve fitness. Yoga is one of several approaches to flexibility. We recommend it because it also offers strength and cardiovascular benefits—and it's a gentle approach to exercise that carries well into retirement. Researchers report that yoga can benefit people with asthma, arthritis, repetitive stress injuries, and high blood pressure and that it aids with balance and flexibility.

Clean up your diet

If you believe that French fries qualify as a vegetable, you've probably already got a dietary problem. Most of us understand that we should be eating far healthier meals and not consuming heavy doses of fat and calories. But how do we change old habits?

Nutrition professor Marion Nestle told USA TODAY reporter Nanci Hellmich that the basic principles of a good diet are so simple that they can be summed in ten words: "Eat less, move more, eat lots of fruits and vegetables." For an additional five-word clarifier, she added, "Go easy on junk foods."

The Biggest Exercise Mistake?

In 2007, USA TODAY reporter Nanci Hellmich interviewed three fitness movement stars and asked them what they considered to be most people's biggest exercise mistake.

Judi Sheppard Missett, Jazzercise's founder, said, "Not doing something that you like. You have to find something that you really like, otherwise you won't continue. The second mistake is thinking that exercise is the cure-all for everything. You have to eat right, too." Missett also offered advice on how best to motivate those who don't exercise. "You have to be unafraid to try different things. The second thing you have to do is find other people who will help you continue: Find a buddy in class, find someone to walk with in the evening or bike with or go to a pool and swim with. You need a few friends who will keep you on track who are also interested in the same things."

According to fitness guru Kathy Smith, the biggest exercise error is what she called the "same time, same place" mentality. "Sometimes an exercise routine becomes an exercise rut: same treadmill workout, at the same pace, at the same time of day, for the same amount of time. The body adapts and plateaus, and frustration sets in. Mixing up speed, intensity, and type of exercise is key to getting results."

Tamilee Webb, star of the *Buns of Steel* videos, said that the biggest mistake was, "[d]oing too much too fast, and not finding something that inspires them to make it fun and motivates them to keep at it."

 "They still have all the moves," by Nanci Hellmich, July 3, 2007.

There's plenty of great diet information available online and off, and you've probably heard most of it already. But here are three simple and relatively painless adjustments that will pave your road to retirement.

- **Eat out less.** Restaurant servings have increased dramatically in the past three decades. According to one study, most restaurant chefs are now serving portions that are two to four times bigger than the government's recommendation and that contain more than 60% more calories than the average meal served at home. (The chefs don't expect you to finish your plate: When 300 chefs were surveyed, 58% reported that if a diner is served a huge amount of food, it's the diner's responsibility to eat the appropriate amount. Take home the leftovers!) In addition, at many traditional Chinese, Mexican, and Italian restaurants—and virtually every hamburger, chicken, pizza, and hot dog establishment—most foods are prepared with unhealthy quantities of saturated fats and carbohydrates.

- **Avoid products with trans fats and saturated fats.** On this one, everyone seems to be in agreement. The over-abundance of trans fats (which now must be labeled) and saturated fats has been a key factor in our nation's growing obesity and clogged-artery problems. Probably the most important step you can take is to avoid, or at least limit, trans fats, hydrogenated oils, vegetable shortening, fried foods, and margarine. (According to health guru Andrew Weil, you're probably better off eating butter than margarine or similar products made from a hydrogenation process.)

- **Shop the perimeter.** When USA TODAY reporter Nanci Hellmich interviewed nutrition professor Marion Nestle, author of *Food Politics*, Nestle's tip had to do with supermarket shopping. "If you want to eat a fairly healthful diet, shop the perimeter and pick up produce, fish, meat, low-fat dairy products, and fresh-baked bread, and stay out of the center aisles, which often are loaded with processed foods." Nestle recommends carefully reading the nutrition-facts panel and ingredient lists. If the ingredient list is several inches long and has additives you've never heard of, then put the product back. One other tip from Nestle: Don't be misled by labels. A meat package that reads "80% lean" actually means the meat contains 20% fat by weight, and this fat makes up more than two-thirds of its calories. So a serving from this package has 200 fat calories of its total of 280 calories. Yikes!

Three More Tips

Here are three additional health suggestions that can lead to a more robust retirement.

Prevent brittle bones

Twenty-five million Americans, 80% of them women, suffer from osteoporosis, a disease that is as preventable as it is horrible. This debilitating disease results in 1.25 million skeletal fractures annually, of which 300,000 are hip fractures. The good news is that osteoporosis—and the height loss, pain, and high risk of bone fracture it causes—can largely be prevented. The keys are to get enough vitamin D and calcium and to engage in regular weight-bearing exercise.

The most natural way to get adequate vitamin D is to expose your skin to sunlight for a few minutes several times per week without first covering it with sunscreen. Consult your physician regarding the potential for skin cancer, but generally, as long as you carefully

The most commonly broken bone for people under 65? The wrist.

limit the time you spend in the sun without sunscreen, the dangers are minimal compared to those posed by osteoporosis. In addition to vitamin D, you need plenty of calcium, which can be found in nonfat milk products, green leafy vegetables, and a variety of supplements. People over 50, especially women, should have their bone density checked as part of their regular medical checkup.

Manage stress

Many experts believe that reducing stress can decrease the likelihood of heart attack. Dr. Dean Ornish, director of the Preventive Medicine Research Center, puts people with coronary artery disease on a strict, low-fat, vegetarian diet, and prescribes stress-management techniques such as yoga and meditation for an hour per day. Older people who attend religious services regularly also appear to be healthier than others, quite possibly because their stress levels are lower.

A number of studies have failed to produce clear evidence that for healthier people, stress is linked to heart and other diseases. Some people actually seem to thrive on stress—they call it excitement.

USA TODAY Snapshots®

Treating ailments with diet, exercise
Percentage of people within age groups who treat ailments with diet and exercise:

18-24: 22%
25-44: 25%
45-54: 30%
55-64: 37%
65-74: 32%
75 and older: 24%

Age group

Source: 2005 MARS OTC/DTC Survey; based on more than 21,200 responses from adults 18 and older

By Shannon Reilly and Sam Ward, USA TODAY 2005

Because the causes of stress, and the ways we handle it, vary so much from one person to the next, you're probably the best judge of whether you are experiencing too much stress too often. If you're drinking too much, overusing legal or illegal drugs, sleeping poorly, or are chronically tired and depressed, warning flags are flying.

You can start dealing with this tonight, by getting to bed on time. Although adult sleep needs vary considerably from about six to ten hours, one thing seems clear. If you regularly get too little sleep, the resulting stress can harm both your health and feelings of well-being. Even short-term sleep deprivation results in loss of energy, irritability, memory loss, and becoming more accident-prone. A 2002 survey by the Washington, DC-based National Sleep Foundation reports that nearly two in ten drivers say they have actually fallen asleep at the wheel in the past year. No wonder many thousands of traffic accidents each year are attributed to sleeping drivers.

Can't sleep no matter how hard you try? Although there is no one-size-fits-all cure for insomnia, substantially increasing your daily ration of physical exercise and occasionally using one of the newer and safer sleep medications should help. Also see Dr. William Dement's classic, *The Promise of Sleep*.

Schedule medical tests

Nowadays, many invisible but life-threatening problems can be discovered early, with the high likelihood of being eliminated or contained. For example, sigmoidoscopies and colonoscopies may discover polyps and other suspicious growths, which can then be quickly removed years before turning cancerous. Although the value of some tests has been debated, as a general rule, you'll benefit from cholesterol testing, pap smears, bone density scans, prostate exams, and blood tests. Your doctor may recommend further periodic testing. If problems are spotted and corrected early, your chances of enjoying a healthy retirement will be greatly enhanced.

More than 60% of Americans ages 50 to 64 report having at least one of six chronic conditions (hypertension, high cholesterol, arthritis, diabetes, heart disease, cancer), but that number shoots up to 80% for those 65 and older, according to the American Hospital Association.

Should You Buy Long-Term Care Insurance?

A long stay in a nursing home is many retirees' worst nightmare. The expense can ruin nearly anyone's finances. (The average cost of nursing home care is upwards of $60,000 a year.) Should you buy long-term care insurance to protect against these uncertainties?

Actually, your odds of winding up a long-term resident in a nursing home are long, probably longer than you think, according to attorney Joseph Matthews, author of *Long-Term Care: How to Plan and Pay for It*, from Nolo. The key word is "long-term," meaning more than six months. Many people will have short stays in nursing homes after major surgery, for example. Long-term care insurance typically doesn't cover that.

Nevertheless, you might wish to get long-term care insurance as a safety net. The insurance shouldn't cost more than 5% of your income. (That's your retirement income, not your income now.) The amount of your premiums will depend mainly on these factors:

- The waiting period before it starts to pay. A long waiting period—say, six months—will get you a lower premium than a policy with a three-month waiting period. But you'll have to be able to afford the six months you wait.
- How much it pays.
- Your age. The older you are, the more expensive the policy.

Be sure to get a rider that increases your payments with inflation. "If you get a policy that pays $100 a day, that won't buy a candy bar in 30 years," Matthews says. And make sure the policy covers assisted living or home health care, or you might be forced to go to a nursing home.

Bonnie Burns, policy specialist with California Health Advocates, told USA TODAY, "Spend some time researching policies. Long-term care insurance policies offer a bewildering array of choices, and it's hard to determine what kind of care you'll need in 30 or 40 years."

Should You Buy Long-Term Care Insurance?, cont'd.

"Some policies cover assisted living, a popular choice for older Americans who need some help but don't require full-time nursing home care. But such policies sometimes limit their coverage to facilities licensed by the state where the policy is issued," Burns says.

Some insurers sell policies that restrict coverage to home health care. Premiums for these policies may be lower, but for most people, "that's a dangerous product," Burns says. "If you buy a home-care-only policy and you can't stay at home, the policy will do you no good, and you'll have no protection for any institutional care."

Sandra Block writes, "The younger you are when you buy a policy, the lower your premiums, but you'll have to pay them for a longer period."

Although most people won't need long-term care insurance, it does provide peace of mind. "I just bought a policy not too long ago, and I feel good about it," says Vern Hayden, a 67-year-old financial planner in Westport, Connecticut. "It's enough to get into a good home if I need it."

To learn more about long-term care, check out the National Clearinghouse for Long-Term Care Information (www.longtermcare.gov).

 "10 questions you should ask yourself now about retirement," by Sandra Block, John Waggoner, and Mindy Fetterman, June 9, 2005; and "If you're in your 50s, it's time to plan how you'll pay for long-term care," by Sandra Block, January 9, 2007.

Strengthen Family Ties

How Strong Are Your Family Ties?_____49

Five Ways to Improve Family Function_____50

   Make time to be with your children_____50

   Forge links with extended family_____54

   Be ready to take on a family leadership role_____57

   Help create a family that makes everyone feel welcome___59

Couples Power: The Tie That Binds_____62

If One Spouse Retires Before the Other_____64

Should retirement mean saying goodbye to family and friends and migrating to Arizona or Florida, golf clubs in hand? Not necessarily. The American Association of Retired People (AARP) found that nine out of every ten Americans 60 and older actually live in the same county they lived in approximately five years prior, and more than three-quarters have even stayed in the same house.

The top reason given for not moving is that retirees want to stay close to family. Or as Lawrence Davidow, a former president of the National Academy of Elder Law Attorneys, told USA TODAY, "[These retirees] don't want to [lose out on the] experience of seeing their grandchildren grow up."

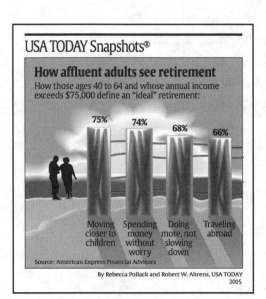

USA TODAY Snapshots®

How affluent adults see retirement
How those ages 40 to 64 and whose annual income exceeds $75,000 define an "ideal" retirement:

75% Moving closer to children
74% Spending money without worry
68% Doing more, not slowing down
66% Traveling abroad

Source: American Express Financial Advisors

By Rebecca Pollack and Robert W. Ahrens, USA TODAY 2005

Of course, if the kids have already moved far away, staying put yourself isn't going to do much for family togetherness. That's why a small but growing number of seniors, especially those with medical problems, move near their adult children. USA TODAY reporter Marco R. della Cava wrote in 2007, "Relying on adult children for care and monitoring will only increase as the number of Americans 65 to 84 nearly doubles to 65 million by 2050 and overall life expectancy continues its gradual rise for both sexes."

For many of us there is no substitute for the ties that we were born with, and retirement is a great time to enjoy them. In this chapter we'll discuss the relationship between retirement and family and suggest methods of strengthening and improving family ties.

But before we jump to any conclusions: We realize that not everybody wants to spend time with their family after retirement. You may—for reasons that are complex and even painful—prefer to see your family in the reflection of a rear-view mirror. You may simply not feel a need to be surrounded by blood relatives. Or you may have substituted your biological family (if you have one) with a network of friends who love you for what you are. If any of this describes you, you may not have much need for this chapter (though we hope you'll take a look at the section on mending family ties, below).

How Strong Are Your Family Ties?

With life expectancies getting longer, you might live a quarter, or even a third, of your life after retirement. Four-generational families are now commonplace. It's easy to see why the many positive influences of a supportive family—or the negative influences of a dysfunctional one—can have an enormous impact on your retirement experience. Your psychological and practical need to be part of a loving, supportive group will grow as you age, just as your ability to create or solidify these relationships is likely to decline.

Take a minute to assess the health of your own family by asking yourself these questions:

- If you are married, do you get along well with your spouse?
- Do you feel that your relationship with your spouse is built to last?
- If you are a parent, do you feel emotionally close to your children— that is, do you look forward to hearing from or seeing them?
- If your children are married, or living in long-term committed relationships, do you communicate with their spouses or partners often?
- If you have grandchildren, have you made yourself an important part of their lives?
- Are you meaningfully connected to your brothers, sisters, nephews, nieces, cousins, and their families?

- Have you maintained close bonds with key family members who live far away?
- Have you taken steps to repair broken relationships with other family members?
- If your own family is very small or absolutely incapable of giving you support, have you been able to join a new one—either a biological family or a "family" of friends?

If you're mostly answering "No" to these questions, consider whether you want to make your family functional. By functional, we mean relatively strong and unified, with the capacity to love and, if necessary, care for its older members.

In a family, what goes around, comes around. If you do a good job caring for the young and nurturing the old during your middle years, your chances of being similarly helped later in life will be excellent. But if you pay little attention to your family during youth and midlife, these crucial relationships are likely to atrophy. The good news about families is that for most, it's never too late to fix things.

Five Ways to Improve Family Function

Despite hours of watching Dr. Phil, we're not so naïve as to believe that a quick fix or pop psychology will magically correct family dysfunction. But the suggestions below—spending more time with children, strengthening extended families, seeking family leaders, accepting lifestyle differences, and reconnecting with black sheep—are all simple concepts that offer great potential rewards.

Make time to be with your children

In his book, *Dinner with Dad: How I Found My Way Back to the Family Table,* Cameron Stracher cites polls showing that less than one third of U.S. children sit down to dinner with both parents on any given night. Stracher told USA TODAY that nearly all the working parents he spoke to while writing his book "told me they never ate dinner with their families except on the weekend."

Togetherness at the dinner table is just one piece within the mosaic of family life, but its absence can also serve as a warning sign. A widely quoted survey by Columbia's National Center on Addiction and Substance Abuse suggests that eating dinner with your children is an important factor in keeping them away from substance abuse.

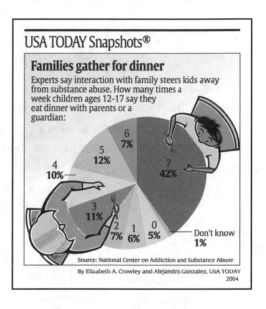

Studies aside, how do you realistically carve out more time to be with your kids? If you're like most parents, the biggest barriers are the hours you spend either at your job, commuting there and back, or on business trips. But if you're lucky enough to work for a family-friendly employer—one that helps employees achieve a work-life balance by offering staggered hours, flextime, shared jobs, child care, and other options—take advantage of it! It's not just altruism that guides companies in this direction. According to a National Institute of Mental Health study, companies with family-friendly policies report lower rates of absenteeism, illness, and employee turnover.

Oddly, baby boomers—the people now on the verge of retirement—are the furthest behind the curve when it comes to achieving a work-life balance. A study by the Families and Work Institute (www .familiesandwork.org) verifies this: Generation X and Generation Y workers (those younger than 40) are more likely than boomers to say they put family before jobs. Here are some ways to correct the balance:

- **Reduce your commute with flextime.** Tweak your work schedule so you work nontraditional hours (referred to as flextime). The trends are in your favor. Up to 40% of workers can now select their start and quit times within a range of core operating hours set by employers (according to a survey by the Families and Work Institute). Flextime can also mean rearranging your hours into a compressed workweek, perhaps consisting of three or four long days instead of five.

Are You an Extreme Commuter?

According to the Census study *Journey to Work,* 3.4 million of us are "extreme commuters," traveling more than 90 minutes each way to work. Extreme commuters are also the fastest-growing segment of commuters. They spend almost three times more than the average commute of 25.5 minutes each way. With a schedule like that, it's no wonder so many parents can't eat dinner with their kids.

- **Telecommute.** Could you do your job from home, either full- or part-time? Desk jobs are the easiest to do remotely, requiring mostly a computer and telephone. You don't even have to feel like you're asking your employer for a big favor. Telecommuting benefits employers by cutting operating costs (especially costs associated with real estate) and by bringing some workers (especially salespeople) closer to customers. It has become an acceptable part of doing business—over a quarter of U.S. businesses allow it on a part-time basis. (Note: Most of the 23.6 million Americans who telecommute work only a day or two per week at home.)

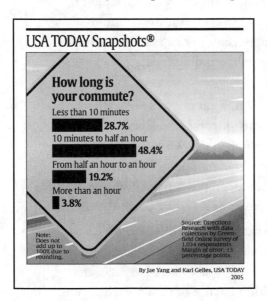

USA TODAY Snapshots®

How long is your commute?

Less than 10 minutes
28.7%
10 minutes to half an hour
48.4%
From half an hour to an hour
19.2%
More than an hour
3.8%

Note: Does not add up to 100% due to rounding.

Source: Directions Research with data collection by Greenfield Online survey of 1,034 respondents. Margin of error: ±3 percentage points.

By Jae Yang and Karl Gelles, USA TODAY 2005

- **Reduce your business travel.** Flying around the country just doesn't seem as necessary or desirable as it used to. Nearly 50% of male senior executives say they're more likely to ask for less travel during their job negotiations than they were five years ago (according to a 2007 study by the Association of Executive Search Consultants). "Employers are slowly, slowly getting on board with this," author and work-life consultant Amin Brott told USA TODAY.

- **Cut your hours.** One contradiction about U.S. workers is that when asked by survey takers, they say they'd trade more time for more money. But when actually faced with that choice in the workplace, most choose money over time. What about you? Would cutting the size of your paycheck seriously conflict with your attempts

  Most common telecommuting jobs? Programmer, lawyer, customer-service rep, salesperson, accountant, manager, writer/editor, and artist/designer.

  to build a nest egg for retirement? Cameron Stracher says, "I have no easy answers. But I would remind [parents] that ten years from now, they may not miss the extra money but will definitely miss their children." As work-life guru Bob Clyatt—author of *Work Less, Live More* (Nolo)—has shown, reducing your paycheck can provide a rewarding life, but requires planning and discipline.

- **Look for a new job in a family-friendly company.** If all else fails, talk to your friends about which local employers walk their pro-family talk. At job interviews, ask questions about the employer's family-friendly policies. If it's a large company, you can also check annual surveys published by magazines such as *Working Mother*, *Fortune*, *Business Week*, and *Fast Company*.

Get Help Making Your Request

Don't be dismayed if your employer is not offering flexible work-life options—yet. You may be able to convince your boss to change course. There are books, career counselors, and websites devoted to helping you achieve that goal. For example, *The Work From Home Handbook*, by Diana Fitzpatrick and Stephen Fishman (Nolo), offers help with preparing a proposal and presenting it to your boss, dealing with common objections, and taking advantage of relevant tax deductions. Armin Brott, a partner in Fathers at Work (www .fathersatwork.com), provides workshops tailored to dads dealing with work-life balance dilemmas.

Forge links with extended family

It may come as no surprise to you that nearly half of U.S. children live apart from one or both parents or with people outside their immediate family. Although the nucleus of such families may be broken, the eventual result is often a larger extended family or a blended family.

Unfortunately, this broadening means not only bigger families but less connected ones, in many cases spread out by sheer geography. So start gathering those phone numbers now, not only of your parents and siblings, but of your nieces and nephews, grandchildren, and cousins, as well as the step-variants of each. A sense of belonging to a good-sized clan can be particularly important to your children, but it's almost guaranteed to pay huge dividends as all family members age. Unlike so many American seniors who are close to only one or two family members, your phone and doorbell will ring regularly.

For many people, even figuring out who is really part of their family isn't easy. Divorce, death, remarriage, and nontraditional relationships all play a part in redefining the very term "family." You may have to bond with people whose place in the family you don't approve of, like a child's former spouse or partner (for the sake of the grandchildren).

Trudie to Family: Make My Dinner

Trudie, now in her mid-80s and still living in her own home, is the mother of three, grandmother of seven, and just recently became a great-grandmother. In addition to doing a few key things to help her children, like lending them money for first-home down payments, and helping when grandchildren are born, Trudie has always made time for little acts like clapping at innumerable school plays, cheering at athletic events, and helping every toddler in the family blow out birthday candles.

Less typically, Trudie has also made a consistent effort to be an active part of the lives of her four nieces and nephews and, more recently, their children. Since Trudie gains happiness from showing others kindness, she expected no payback. Widowed for a number of years and resigned, if not happy, to live alone, Trudie was as surprised as she was pleased when ten years ago her oldest granddaughter, Miya, asked if she could move in while attending college. Seeing how well "hanging with grandma" worked as a transition from home to full independence, three other young adult grandchildren and a niece followed Miya's example and bunked with Trudie for six months or more. Obviously pleased, Trudie says, "My only rule is that they make me dinner twice a week—I don't care if it's a sandwich, as long as someone else puts it on the table."

The Barber Family in Action

Here's how one retired couple created and strengthened its family ties.

John and Emily Barber, in their early 80s, are at the center of a family consisting of their own three children—Katherine, Brian, and Sabina—as well as June, a high school friend of Sabina's whom the Barbers adopted (emotionally, not legally) as a teenager. In addition, the Barbers have two sons-in-law, a daughter-in-law, and eight grandchildren. Most of the members of this 19-person family live around San Francisco, which allows for frequent group get-togethers, including about eight large yearly holiday or birthday gatherings and many smaller ones. Obviously, the geographical proximity of many of its members makes it easier for the Barbers to function as a meaningful group. But it's interesting to note that this didn't happen accidentally; John and Emily, realizing that distance is no friend to the maintenance of close family ties, relocated from Los Angeles at their own retirement 20 years ago.

While the Barbers have fun together, they are at their best when one or another family member quietly helps another cope with day-to-day concerns. Here are just a few of many ways John and Emily have helped their children:

- When grandchildren—and now the first two great-grandchildren—were born, they were always there with loads of TLC and, in a few emergencies, an open checkbook.
- They followed up with much-needed babysitting and after-school child care.
- They loaned money to all their children to help them purchase their first homes.
- They handed down their old cars to the children who needed them most and quietly paid for the occasional plane ticket when one of the kids couldn't quite afford a family reunion.

With examples like these, it's no wonder later generations have gotten into the spirit and help each other out with things like summer jobs in their businesses and tutoring for those with bad math genes.

But a family almost always becomes stronger when its members are inclusive, and weaker when members erect barriers to admission. In addition, the experience we gain in welcoming outsiders into our family may prove invaluable later in life should unforeseen circumstances, such as the premature death of a spouse, mean that we suddenly find ourselves alone and hoping to bond with someone else's family.

Be ready to take on a family leadership role

Many extended families are headed and defined for many years by a charismatic person or couple. Other families stay in reasonably close touch because a small group works together (two sisters, for example) to make it happen. Being a family leader requires little more than good people skills, including the ability to notice and respond when a family member needs an extra measure of nurture, support, or coaching.

If you haven't yet played a leadership role, don't get complacent: A vacuum may some day open up. Longtime family leaders may become very old or ill, die, or, for some other reason, no longer play their familiar role. In that case, one or preferably several of the people who have been going along for the ride must start to pedal, as in the story "On Golden Blog," below.

On Golden Blog

For years, Frank Carroll's parents, Tim and May lovingly—and sometimes autocratically—headed their brood of nine children and 15 grandchildren. Even though the Carroll children settled all over the United States, they, together with their spouses and grandchildren, gathered every summer at their vacation cottage in the Adirondacks and every Christmas at Tim and May's home in New Jersey.

Then Tim died one October. May, in her mid-80s and feeling her age, made no plans for the next summer. Frank, the middle child, now in his 40s, became increasingly bothered by the family leadership vacuum. His first solution was to do what he'd always done as a child: call in his older sisters, Maureen and Kathy. He hoped to talk them into playing their traditional roles as junior parents and organize the August reunion. But when Maureen pleaded job problems and Kathy said she and her husband were having a tough year emotionally and wanted to go to Europe by themselves, Frank got angry. Didn't any of his siblings care enough about the future of the family to do even a little work?

A few days later, it occurred to Frank that he was asking something of others that he was in a position to do himself. So he took a week off work and organized the reunion. For the first time in years, everyone came—even Kathy and her husband, who had patched up their relationship—and Maureen, who'd decided her demanding boss could stuff her job if he objected. Best of all, Frank's commitment prompted a family meeting at which his siblings volunteered to take turns organizing future get-togethers. Plans were even made to have several teenagers coordinate a family Internet site or "blog." Using Blogger (www.blogger.com), a free service from Google, they created an easy-to-use Carroll Family website, allowing members to post comments, photos, stories, links, and jokes. It quickly served to link and strengthen the family ties.

Help create a family that makes everyone feel welcome

Many families have been torn apart at some point in the past. Addictions, disputes over money or business, personality conflicts, issues of religion, or disagreements over lifestyle can all stress or even sever family bonds. If your family is in this situation, now is the time to consider reconnecting, even if it's painful—or even if you think you're in the right. Few things are harder than reaching out to people you feel have judged you, mistreated you, or turned their backs on you. But remember that they are probably as hurt as you are.

Consider one family (let's call them the Martins). When John, the oldest of three children, announced he was gay, his mother dissolved into nearly perpetual tears and his father disowned him. June, the second child, sided with John and voluntarily removed herself from the family. Tim, the youngest child by eight years and still in high school, was so traumatized by the family rift that he lost much of his self-confidence, and with it his good grades and active social life. Eventually, he dropped out of high school and did poorly at a series of dead-end jobs. It wasn't until his mid-20s, after a stint in the army and marrying a loving woman, that Tim enrolled in college and began to put his life back together.

How is the Martin family doing today? It barely exists. John died a lonely death of AIDS in San Francisco a few years ago, still estranged from his parents. June and Tim, both fortunate in their marriages, have been welcomed into the families of their respective spouses. The senior Martins have retired and live in Florida. They haven't seen or talked to either of their surviving children in years. Each year June sends them a Christmas card with a picture of her children. Tim doesn't.

What will you do if a close family member chooses a way of life that clashes with your ingrained moral values? Choosing between core values and family ties is an epic decision and only your own conscience can guide you. But keep in mind that sometimes, if you open your arms and heart wide—perhaps wider than you thought possible—you can find a middle ground that allows you to retain your beliefs and your love for blood relatives. Be prepared; this kind of resolution may require a few tears, a lot of talking, and a good sense of humor.

Family Support for Gay and Lesbian issues

If your family members are dealing with the gay or lesbian relation-ship of a close family member or friend, an organization called Parents and Friends of Lesbians and Gays (PFLAG) may be helpful. It provides a warm community that encourages acceptance. For a chapter near you, check out www.pflag.org.

When it comes to keeping your family together in times of trouble, here are some ideas you may find helpful:

- **Try to prevent family dropouts.** Family members who are socially awkward, or who judge themselves as unsuccessful or unwanted, often begin to avoid family get-togethers and ceremonies. If you see a person starting down this self-isolating path, it's important to quickly find ways to prevent a complete exit. If a family member has already dropped out, do everything possible (and then some) to recover him or her.

- **Don't give up on substance abusers.** One common reason for excluding a family member (or for that person excluding himself) is a serious drinking or drug problem. You should not condone or support the destructive habit, but you also should not give up on the troubled person. Many organizations and publications can show family members how to intervene constructively, such as *The Recovery Book*, by Mooney, Eisenberg, and Eisenberg.

- **For past hurts, forgiveness can be the best path.** Stanford University psychologist Carl Thoresen has found that the act of forgiveness often results in substantial emotional and even physical health benefits for the forgiver. Letting go of grudges, even righteous grudges, can be a great gift to yourself. And as

Thoresen points out, you don't have to condone or even forget bad behavior in order to forgive it. Instead, forgiveness "means giving up the right to be aggravated and the desire to strike back."

- **Get quick, effective help if someone in your family becomes physically abusive or seriously neglectful.** A child who has been neglected or abused will carry emotional scars for life, and may even withdraw from the family. A person found guilty of neglect or abuse is ostracized. Either way, family cohesiveness suffers, and the family may fall apart. There are no easy solutions to the gut-wrenching situations caused by abusive behavior. Start by accepting the fact that without outside help, neither the perpetrator nor the victim—nor, for that matter, the rest of the family—is likely to return to anything approaching healthy functionality. A wise and determined family member (or a small group) must insist on, and, if possible, arrange for, long-term counseling or therapy for both the abused and abuser. Sometimes, of course, a particular person may be beyond redemption. Even in the worst cases—the blackest of black sheep—try not to lose touch with that person's children or grandchildren, in the hopes that you can keep them within the family fold.

- **Don't let divorce be a family wrecker.** Statistically, chances are good that if you are in midlife, you have already experienced at least one divorce. If so—and especially if you were already a parent—you know just how tough postdivorce family relationships can be. We're not here to meddle in your family. But if you can—no matter how unpalatable it is—occasionally spend time with your ex at family social events (making it a rule never ever to criticize him or her). You owe it to your kids to make the effort.

The Divorcing Lees

When the Lees' son and daughter-in-law divorced, the parents were at first shocked, and then angry, fearing that their grandchildren would be emotionally scarred and that they might lose their close relationship with them. They blamed their son, who had precipitated the break-up by becoming involved with another woman, and even considered barring him from upcoming family Christmas activities. But on the advice of good friends, the Lees decided to keep their judgments to themselves and try to steer a neutral course, even though the first two years after the divorce involved staging two Christmas parties, so their son and his ex wouldn't have to meet. Three years later, with both their son and former daughter-in-law now married to nice people—and even willing to attend the same holiday event—the wisdom of this approach is apparent to all.

Couples Power: The Tie That Binds

"A good marriage at age 50 predicted positive aging at 80," concludes George Vaillant in his book *Aging Well*, based on the Harvard Study of Adult Development. Historian Will Durant, at age 90, offered this perspective: "The love we have in our youth is superficial compared to the love that an old man feels for his old wife." Comedian Jack Benny had perhaps the most down-to-earth view of a long and successful marriage: "Mary and I have been married 47 years and not once have we had an argument serious enough to mention the word divorce—murder, yes, but divorce, never."

Six in ten people age 55 and over are married and living with their spouse.

Two people living together—no matter how the relationship is officially categorized—are usually in a better position to survive longer than those who face the future alone. But surviving doesn't mean that a couple's "happiness" quotient is higher than single counterparts. That depends on you and your mate. There are several ways to increase your chances of enjoying your retirement years with a kindred spirit.

- **Talk about your relationship.** How long has it been since you sat down and asked your mate how he or she really feels about you and your relationship, or what could be improved? If you're reluctant to ask so direct a question, maybe it's because you fear you won't like the answer. This makes it all the more urgent to start communicating.

- **Stop fighting about the same stuff.** Approximately 70% of the time couples quarrel, they're arguing about the same old thing. Couples reach a gridlock and eventually become emotionally distant, says University of Washington psychologist John Gottman. According to Gottman's research, couples who solve conflicts successfully have a few things in common: husbands let wives influence them and wives let husbands influence them; wives started an argument "softly" rather than harshly, which reduced escalation; and both partners attempted to repair damage while an argument was in progress. Some problems cannot be solved, and couples would do best to stop trying to "solve" them and instead come to some acceptance of their partner's position.

USA TODAY Snapshots®

Luxury isn't just about expensive things

What is luxury?

Happiness and satisfaction from being with family or friends and enjoying good times — 44%

Having enough time to do whatever you want and being able to afford it — 37%

Finer things in life that provide supreme comfort, beauty and quality — 19%

Source: American Express Platinum

Survey of 770 respondents with household incomes of $125,000 and over. Margin of error ±4 percentage points

By Darryl Haralson and Dave Merrill, USA TODAY 2005

- **Do things together.** It's a big help if mates share at least some day-to-day enthusiasms. So whether it's bridge, bird-watching, cooking, or doing volunteer work, look for and build on common interests. Just be patient when you first approach your partner with your desire to skydive or square dance. Finding things to happily do together may require a spirit of openness that neither spouse has exhibited for years.

- **Keep yourselves in good physical condition.** Everyone benefits from an exercise buddy, especially if it means you can enjoy activities like hiking or playing tennis together. For more on exercise, see Chapter 2.

- **Admit it when you're wrong.** The simple statement, "I made a mistake," is a magical way to cut short arguments.

- **Be responsible for your own happiness.** At a time when millions of Americans live into their 90s, marriage—even a second or third marriage—can last a long time. To succeed, each spouse must take responsibility for finding his or her own roads to fulfillment.

If One Spouse Retires Before the Other

Several generations ago, when a man retired, his typically nonworking mate often considered herself to be retired as well (despite the fact that she was still almost surely responsible for cooking and housework). Today, there is less certainty that spouses will retire simultaneously. This means that many couples now in midlife may soon find that their day-to-day lives are out of sync.

That creates some practical and psychological issues. According to a 2001 study in *Current Directions in Psychological Science*, newly retired men tend to have increased morale—but more marital conflict—if their wives remain employed after they retire. Married women who retire first face increased rates of depression and marital conflict. Of course, no two couples face the same situation, and the studies done in this area are few.

Among people 85 and over, 58% of men, but only 12% of women, are married and living with their spouse.

Here are a few ways couples have dealt with their mismatched retirement schedules. Note, these suggestions are not for everyone; they're just to get you thinking.

- The retired spouse goes back to work part time.
- The retired spouse gets deeply involved in nonprofit volunteer activities.
- The first spouse to retire enrolls in school full- or part-time.
- The retired spouse travels widely, alone. (Note: long separations aren't for everyone.)
- The retired male spouse becomes a house-husband, with an occasional day on the golf course.
- Both spouses move to a part of the country the retired spouse is yearning to explore.

The Little Pleasures ...

Bernie and Bob Giusti first met over 60 years ago, when Bob was 11 and Bernie 9.

"For us, putting our family and each other first has been important," Bernie said. "For example, 45 years ago, Bob's career as an up-and-coming business executive almost guaranteed that we would be asked to transfer to a new area every few years. But we jointly decided that we would rather live near family and good friends. So Bob just said no to leaving the area. As it turned out, even better career opportunities for Bob became available where we wanted to live. But more important, our commitment not to move allowed us to nurture a lifetime's good relationships with our family and friends.

"We always eat dinner together, light a candle, and say a prayer," Bernie explained. "You know, it's often the little pleasures you share in life—not big, complicated, expensive events—that truly bring pleasure. Instead of exhausting your energy, as can happen with a huge event, smaller activities allow you to grow in intimacy and sharing."

Appreciate Friends, Old and New

Friends: Many Concepts—One Goal_____69

Four Paths to Friendship_____70
    Relearn the art of forming friendships_____70
    Engage in virtual social networking _____73
    Make some younger friends_____75
    Make friends outside of work_____77

Members of Couples: Find Friends Who Are Yours Alone_____78

Those Furry Friends_____80

efore we begin, let's acknowledge that not every retiree is looking for friends. Some have had it with the chattering masses and are looking for happiness in solitude, nature, or the German shepherd lying at their feet. If this describes your retirement dreams, skip this chapter and get on with your retirement planning.

People who desire solitude, however, shouldn't be confused with those who find themselves on a "loneliness treadmill." Researcher Louise Hawkley explained to USA TODAY that this occurs when people "become less trustful and more suspicious of others." They convince themselves that they aren't going to get along with people, so why bother befriending anyone? Their prophecy becomes self-fulfilling, as they stay at home and become progressively more lonely and depressed. To avoid such a situation, you'll need to see it coming and take action using the techniques described in this chapter.

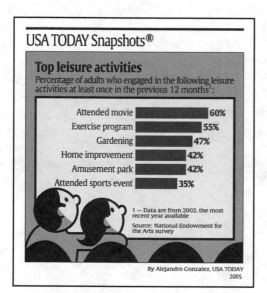

USA TODAY Snapshots®

Top leisure activities
Percentage of adults who engaged in the following leisure activities at least once in the previous 12 months[1]:

Attended movie	60%
Exercise program	55%
Gardening	47%
Home improvement	42%
Amusement park	42%
Attended sports event	35%

1 — Data are from 2002, the most recent year available

Source: National Endowment for the Arts survey

By Alejandro Gonzalez, USA TODAY 2005

Most of us need friends. They make us feel connected and alive, and in retirement they break down the sense of isolation that results as we shed our jobs. Friends help us live longer—studies have shown that people who are isolated and lonely are more likely to become ill and die prematurely. Joseph Coughlin, Director of MIT's Technology for Healthy Aging Laboratory, says, "The greatest risk of aging is not necessarily disease. It is loss of social connectivity." Friends may even help us lower our blood pressure. In other words, there's real truth to the saying that a faithful friend is the medicine of life.

But if that sounds at all selfish, remember that friendship does more than provide us with benefits; it's a two-way street. We help and counsel those whom we've befriended. And it's within that altruistic side of friendship—giving to our friends—that many of us attain that elusive thing known as "happiness."

Friends: Many Concepts—One Goal

What is a "friend," anyway? The word has many meanings. In its deepest sense, as one writer put it, a friend is someone who knows all about you and still likes you.

Many worthwhile friendships don't involve deep life-lasting bonds. We all have friends-lite, a social network of people who provide pathways to other ends. For example, if you're trying to stop drinking or lose weight, you may have a network of friends built around supporting you toward that goal. Social networks may also be built around religious or political affiliations or social engagements, like a regular Friday night poker game. Exchanges of information or materials can also form the basis for social networks, as with a book club or group of neighbors who share information about local bird sightings.

All of these friends are important. It doesn't matter that the depth and richness of your friendships may vary—from childhood best buddies to fellow knitters. Studies have shown that the most powerful predictor of life satisfaction after retirement is the size of your social network. In a study of 100 retirees, those who expressed greatest satisfaction with life had social networks of 16 people or more. (Those who were less satisfied had social networks of fewer than ten people.)

Can Affluence Lead to Loneliness?

Loneliness for the elderly is actually a recent phenomenon, having appeared during the last century. Scholars believe that affluence is partly responsible. Unlike 19th century retirees, those living to-day—particularly those in suburban and rural areas—have enough money to maintain separate living spaces well into old age. And it is this very independence that sometimes isolates them.

Four Paths to Friendship

With any luck, you're less shy today than you were back in high school. Still, you may need to brush up on your social skills, or at least try strengthening your existing social network. We offer four suggestions for immediate action: relearn the art of making friends; learn about virtual social networking tools; make some younger friends; and make friends outside of work. And when making new friends, keep in mind Ralph Waldo Emerson's advice, "The only way to have a friend is to be one."

Relearn the art of forming friendships

Most of us find it easier to make friends during the first three decades of our life than after age 30 or 40. There are lots of good reasons for this—work, marriage, and children being the most common.

How can we reinvigorate our social relationships in midlife and later, so that our retirement years will be enriched by new human contacts? Start by understanding that the ability to make new friends after age 40 is a skill each of us needs to nurture—or in some instances, relearn. Here are some simple refreshers on how new friendships are typically made and maintained:

- **Finding common interests.** Friendships formed around real interests, whether they be surfing at Malibu or surfing the Internet, are more likely to last than those that grow out of more casual contacts.
- **Sharing.** Honest friendship is achieved by listening, giving support, and being open to talking about your real interests and worries.
- **Committing.** To convert friendly acquaintances into real friends takes effort sustained over a long period of time. It means keeping your eyes open for times and opportunities to meet or talk, and sometimes initiating contact even when you're feeling hesitant.
- **Reconnecting with old friends.** Close friends from our childhood and young-adult years know us in ways that no one else ever will. If you've fallen out of touch, chances are it was unintentional on both sides. Old friends will probably be delighted if you invest some time and energy getting and staying in touch once again—something that ever-cheaper travel and communications technologies facilitate. Next time you get an invitation to a reunion (class, workplace, sport, or other), overcome your shyness or your cynicism and get yourself there. Better yet, why not track down a few of your long-forgotten buddies and organize your own minireunion? You have more friends than you think.
- **Working part-time.** For socially isolated (or socially awkward) individuals, it may make sense to find friendships in a part-time working environment. For example, Tanya, a retired teacher, hasn't needed to work for years. But she still puts in three days a week as a designer at a small ad agency. "Not only does working keep my mind sharp, being part of an organization provides loads of social contacts I wouldn't otherwise have. Just going out to lunch a couple of times a week with my coworkers is something I look forward to."
- **Joining groups.** America used to be a country of joiners—everything from church, Grange, and Lion's Club to garden society, PTA, and Moose Lodge. All this joining has slowed down. Televisions, computers, and other technologic devices are among the culprits, having privatized leisure. Rather than going

fishing with our neighbors, we watch professionals fish on TV. Don't wait until after retirement to become involved with group activities—you'll only become more reluctant to insert yourself into unfamiliar circumstances. (Don't discount this possibility just because you have been gregarious all your life.) Join something now and you'll enjoy the benefits throughout your life.

Hilda the Hiker

Hilda, an older hiker who lives in Southern California, is a good example of how we can combine our deepest personal interests with our need for companionship. When she was in her early 50s, with her kids off to college, Hilda found she had time on her hands but few confidantes to spend it with. Having immigrated from Germany as an adult, she had no friends from her school or young adult years to fall back on. Confronting both her loneliness and the issue of what she really wanted to do with the rest of her life, Hilda realized that she was happiest when exercising outdoors. She decided to try to overcome her natural shyness and make some hiking friends.

She started by inviting her two good friends to spend a day on the trail. Both begged off, one claiming a bad leg and the other because she had a full-time job and cared for an infirm parent. Hilda next invited a couple of acquaintances, but again ended up with excuses.

At this point Hilda realized she needed to be more organized. She knew about the Sierra Club and decided to join and get involved in local chapter activities. Although it was an act of some courage for her to go on her first group hike, she was quickly reassured by how friendly and welcoming people were. From that day on, Hilda has never hiked alone. Instead, she happily participates in many day, weekend, and occasionally even international hiking trips with what has quickly become a large circle of new acquaintances and some real friends.

Engage in virtual social networking

Your social network need not be defined by the people who can ring your doorbell. Many potential retirees have created friendships via the Internet that have proven as rewarding and satisfying as flesh and blood contacts.

The great thing about virtual social networking is that it doesn't require getting dressed (or even getting out of bed). In fact, you can do it in the middle of the night when you're having trouble sleeping. Get up and post a few choice thoughts at the Rock From the Sixties chat room? Or make some comments at the Boston terrier blog, one of hundreds of websites detailing the activities of favorite canines? Or check out what happened to one of your high school friends at Classmates.com? The possibilities for social interaction online are endless. Once you enter discussion groups, engage in chat-room banter, or begin serious email threads with like-minded souls, you may find that virtual socializing is what you've wanted all your life—honest communication without having to comb your hair.

USA TODAY Snapshots®

Part-time job might make retirement better
Percentage of respondents who said retirement is better than expected because of:

- 34% Not working
- 45% Working part time
- 35% Working full time

Source: 2005 Merrill Lynch New Retirement Study of 2,189 respondents 88 and older. Margin of error ±2 percentage.

By Jae Yang and Keith Simmons, USA TODAY 2006

A computer and Internet connection can liberate shy and isolated people with easy-to-use email, chat rooms, and blogs. Many retired people have established their own websites or blogs (www .blogger.com lets you set one up easily, for free) sharing their opinions or knowledge about a particular subject—for example, hiking the Grand Canyon, helping new businesses get off the ground, or playing better tennis after 70. Others facilitate communication about a particular interest—for example, staying healthy while traveling to difficult places or coping with Parkinson's disease.

And best of all, you don't need your own computer to explore the online world. Many public libraries and other public institutions offer free Internet access. If you're new to networking, one site that's a good portal for midlifers is ThirdAge (www.thirdage.com), which says it's "rewriting the rules for getting older."

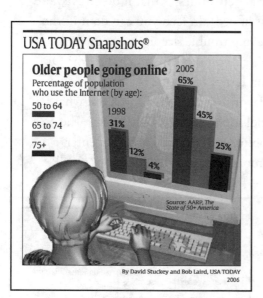

USA TODAY Snapshots®

Older people going online
Percentage of population
who use the Internet (by age):

50 to 64
65 to 74
75+

1998
31%
12%
4%

2005
65%
45%
25%

Source: AARP, The
State of 50+ America

By David Stuckey and Bob Laird, USA TODAY
2006

Posting a profile at a social networking site may also be your cup of tea. Sites such as MySpace (www.myspace.com) and Facebook (www.facebook.com) began as networking tools for youth but have quickly grown to accommodate all ages. Generally, you post a profile, invite and attract friends, and communicate within the network about shared subjects of interest. Another possibility is Gather (www.gather.com), a social networking site geared to adults and the exchange of ideas about culture and politics. There are also social networking sites for living green (www.care2.com), business contacts (www.linkedin.com), finding old friends, family, and classmates (www.reunion.com), and even for those who like Web-surfing (www.stumbleupon.com).

Seniors can expect more and more networking sites in the next few years. Silicon Valley has realized that baby boomers—who outnumber teens three to one—are more "sticky" than their younger counterparts, meaning they're more loyal to particular social networking sites. If you'd like to join a network of your peers, check out sites such as Eons (www.eons.com), Rezoom (www.rezoom.com), Multiply (www.multiply.com), Boomj (www.boomj.com), and Boomertown (www.boomertown.com).

Not on the Net? Get on, Now!

If you've managed to stay computer illiterate, and for reasons of pride, obstinacy, or insecurity, you're hoping to continue that way, we strongly recommend that you reconsider. Do not be intimidated by computers and the Internet. You'll soon realize that a high I.Q. is not a prerequisite for participating. And once you learn the ropes, it will make a zillion parts of your life easier. Sign up for a local computer course, ask your local librarian, have a friend or relation show you, or pay someone. Do it today. Get a free email account. Learn how to use a search engine. If you get online, one site that's sure to help you is SeniorNet (www.seniornet.com), by a nonprofit organization that has provided older adults with technology access and education for over two decades.

What does it cost to get on the Internet at home? Some seniors who don't want to deal with computers pay $200 for an MSN TV box (formerly known as Web TV) and then pay $21 a month to hook into a phone service. It's easy and requires no computer skills and provides you with Internet surfing and email basics. For not much more—say $400 or $500 for a computer and $30 a month—you could get a much faster connection with the ability to do much more—for example, download and save pictures of your grandchildren.

Make some younger friends

As George Vaillant, director of Harvard's landmark Study of Adult Development, states, "Learning to gain younger friends as we lose older ones adds more to life's enjoyment than retirement income." In other words, as we age we cannot rely solely on friends our own age (see "How Many Friends Will You Lose?" below).

How Many Friends Will You Lose?

Michael Phillips and Catherine Campbell, authors of *Simple Living Investments for Old Age*, analyzed the loss of friends in terms of actuarial tables: "As we age, the names listed in our personal phone books will slowly be crossed out. To sense the extent of the problem, we can imagine a party to which a large number of long-time friends are invited. Now picture the same guest list when we are 65: 25% of our male friends and 15% of the females will be dead. By the time we are 85, only one out of five men who were our friends at age 35 will still be alive, and only two out of five women...."

Although your tastes in music and clothing may differ, many younger people are attracted to the knowledge and experience of a person who has resided on this planet a little longer. And older people are commonly drawn to the energy, fresh ideas, and vivacity of people who are many years younger.

If deliberately setting out to make younger friends sounds calculating, try an experiment: Make an effort to befriend someone who is older than you are. You may soon see the benefits of an experienced friend who can provide guidance on confronting life's big transitions. And you can fill the same role for someone younger.

USA TODAY Snapshots®

Holiday party animals
How many holiday parties between Thanksgiving and New Year's we attend each year:

1-3 **55%**
None **10%**
2% More than 10
7-10 **5%**
4-6 **28%**

Lactaid and Opinion Research Corp. poll of 1,004 adults, 18 and older, living in U.S. households, Aug. 4–7. Margin of error ±3 percentage points

By Mary Cadden and Suzy Parker, USA TODAY
2005

Make friends outside of work

Do you think of your coworkers as your friends? Unfortunately, relatively few workplace social relationships survive retirement for long. The shared experience that brought you together will no longer be there. See "George Turns the Taps Back On," below, for how one retiree planned ahead.

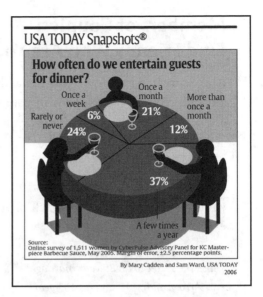

USA TODAY Snapshots®

How often do we entertain guests for dinner?

Once a week 6%
Once a month 21%
More than once a month 12%
A few times a year 37%
Rarely or never 24%

Source: Online survey of 1,511 women by CyberPulse Advisory Panel for KC Masterpiece Barbecue Sauce, May 2005. Margin of error, ±2.5 percentage points.

By Mary Cadden and Sam Ward, USA TODAY 2006

George Turns the Taps Back On

George Miller, a retired mutual fund executive, says: "After 35 years in the investment business, I knew quite a bit about it, and quite a few people who worked in it. But well before I retired, I guessed that most of my knowledge would have a shelf life of about six months. Sure enough, when the big day came, it was as if someone had closed the taps and opened the drains on my bathtub—both my knowledge and most of my business acquaintances quickly disappeared (it took about 90 days, not six months)!

But fortunately, I had already found new interests—lobbying to change California water policy, improving public education, and working with microcredit projects in the Third World. After retirement, I had the opportunity to spend more time in each of these areas. And as I did, I met lots of interesting people, some of whom have become good friends. In short, by starting early I was able to figure out how to get the taps back on and the stopper back in my personal bathtub."

Members of Couples: Find Friends Who Are Yours Alone

Make a mental list of your close friends. Now, if you are a member of a couple, count up how many of your friends are also coupled. If the answer is "lots" or "most," ask yourself whether most or all of your activities are done as a foursome. If you are typical, your answer will probably be yes.

A social life that's essentially based on double dating leaves you or your mate—depending on which of you survives the other—at risk of being lonely later in life. When the first member of the couple dies, the other very often and very quickly tends to lose close social contact with close friends who remain coupled. The dynamic feels off kilter, and everyone is conscious of the empty seat at the table, regardless of how hard the couples work to include the newly single person in their activities. Other common reasons that these friendships falter include:

What's the secret to an 80-year marriage? Percy Arrowsmith, 105, and his 100-year-old wife of England, attributed their eight decades together to (1) never going to sleep on an argument and (2) always kissing each other and holding hands before going to bed.

- **New directions.** The newly single person may cope with loneliness by embracing new activities and otherwise keeping busy, while the long-settled couple is content to move more slowly, following old habits.

- **Lack of empathy.** A widow or widower needs to be around people who can truly understand and empathize with the pain and loneliness. No matter how caring and kind, people who haven't lost a beloved mate simply can't fill this role.

- **Jealousy.** Meanwhile, whether they admit it or not, many members of long-time couples become jealous of the newly single person's freedom and new romantic adventures.

Whatever the cause, many people who lose their spouses find that just when they need them the most, they have also lost many of their old friends. What can you and your spouse do to avoid finding yourself in this situation? One retiree, Afton Crooks, told coauthor Jake Warner: "No matter how close you are to your spouse, you also need your own good friends, at least a couple of people you are really close to. I don't mean business colleagues or acquaintances, but intimate friends who you truly care about. Obviously, this is particularly true for women, who usually outlive their husbands by a number of years. In addition, it's also wise to keep up a good network of other people whose company you enjoy, people who share your interests."

Creating and maintaining separate friendships without offending your spouse can sometimes be problematic. A member of a couple that has always socialized as a duo may feel threatened if the other suddenly wants to pursue more personal friendships. The best approach is to discuss the problem with your mate and, if possible, ask an older widow or widower for insights. Chances are, you and your mate will be told two things:

- When one of you dies, the other will rely primarily on his or her own close personal friends for comfort and support, and much less on friends who are members of couples.

- As we age and the years we have spent with our mates add up, it's important for each of us to reinvigorate our lives with new experiences and thoughts. One excellent way to do this is to make and maintain our own friendships outside of our marriage. It will ultimately make the marriage stronger, too.

But how do you go about making new friends? You can join groups that share similar intellectual pursuits or hobbies, volunteer with a nonprofit group working for a cause, join a social group or club, become active in a church or other spiritual group, get a part-time job you enjoy (even if it doesn't pay much), or try any of the suggestions under "Four Paths to Friendship," above. We also discuss volunteering, in Chapter 5, and working, in Chapter 10.

Those Furry Friends

There's another kind of friend we haven't yet discussed. It's the furry, scaly, or feathered one who you have to feed daily. (Many retirees have become so attached to these friends that we gave some thought about including pets in the chapter on family!)

Studies have found that people who live with animals tend to be healthier and happier than those who don't. And as we conducted interviews for this book, we saw firsthand how many active, interested older people—especially those who live alone—have a close relationship with one or more animals. Cats and dogs, especially dogs who need a lot of exercise, figure prominently in the lives of a high number of fulfilled retirees we interviewed.

Hold the phone?! 33% of dog owners admit that they talk to their dogs on the phone or leave messages on an answering machine while away.

Babette Marks, a retired schoolteacher who Jake interviewed, put it this way: "As you get older, this spirit of caring helps you cope. Face it, most people need something to be responsible for, or to. My dog plays this role for me. Every day, whether I feel good or awful, I need to walk my dog, so I do it. A relationship like this is obviously particularly important if you are single."

Carol Thompson, a retired social worker, told Jake, "Our dog—I love her. Walking with her and talking with friends along the way gives me a connection to the community that makes me feel good."

Not only does a dog serve as a friend and companion, but it helps the older person in several other important ways, including getting exercise and making friends. Owners of dogs talk to each other quite naturally, whether at the dog parks or on walks.

Some more fun furry facts: Dog owners go to the doctor 21% less than others, as found by UCLA professor Judith M. Seigel, author of a study of 1,000 elderly Californians. She surmised that the dogs were a "stress buffer," lessening the need of their owners to seek out physicians in times of psychological unrest.

If you do get sick, a pet can help you get better faster. One study compared postcoronary survival of pet owners versus nonowners. Among the pet owners, 50 of 53 lived at least a year after hospitalization, compared to 17 of 39 non-pet-owners. (The study included all pets, not just dogs—so the results couldn't be solely attributable to the exercise people got from walking their dogs.) In a follow-up study, the same researcher found that pet owners' worry about their animals actually speeded their convalescence by providing "a sense of being needed and an impetus for quick recovery." ●

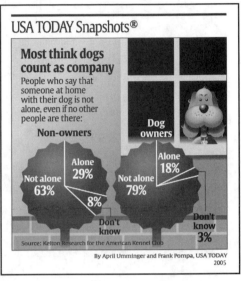

USA TODAY Snapshots®

Most think dogs count as company

People who say that someone at home with their dog is not alone, even if no other people are there:

Non-owners
Alone 29%
Not alone 63%
8%

Dog owners
Alone 18%
Not alone 79%

Don't know
Don't know 3%

Source: Kelton Research for the American Kennel Club

By April Umminger and Frank Pompa, USA TODAY 2005

Develop Lifelong Interests and Activities Now

Volunteer_____84

Do the Things You Always Meant To_____93

Educate Yourself_____94

And now, for a disheartening dose of reality: The typical female retiree (according to a Harris poll) spends half of her free time watching TV and a good chunk of the rest doing housework. If this doesn't sound fulfilling to you, you're not alone. Most of the same people polled complained of feeling less useful after retirement than before.

You can avoid a similar fate. However, as Afton Crooks, a retired college administrator told us, "Don't wait until your mid-60s to discover new interests. If you do, you may find you have forgotten how to become interested in new things." Afton's other tip: "Make sure at least some of your interests are your own and not tied to your spouse. You absolutely need to be an independent person."

Below, we focus on some activities that many retirees find satisfying, which you can become involved in now.

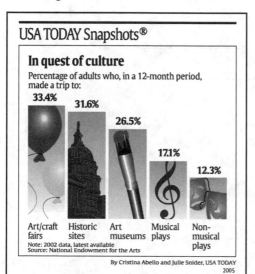

USA TODAY Snapshots®

In quest of culture

Percentage of adults who, in a 12-month period, made a trip to:

33.4% Art/craft fairs
31.6% Historic sites
26.5% Art museums
17.1% Musical plays
12.3% Non-musical plays

Note: 2002 data, latest available
Source: National Endowment for the Arts

By Cristina Abello and Julie Snider, USA TODAY 2005

Volunteer

It's almost a cliché that Americans will organize to support almost any good cause and more than a few slightly wacky ones. As a result, about 11% of the nation's economic activity takes place in the nonprofit sector, much of it dependent—at least in part—on the unpaid work of volunteers. "Senior power" is one reason why so many nonprofit groups achieve so much. If you doubt this, take a look at any local educational, religious, environmental, or health care group—even the volunteer fire department. You'll probably see that much of the behind-the-scenes leadership, as well as the bulk of volunteer help, is provided by retired people. Below are some benefits you might reap from volunteering.

Why Not Just Wait?

It's possible you're already too busy to take on anything new. That's fine; we don't want to burden you with another responsibility. But be aware that it's sometimes hard for seniors to find new, stimulating activities. Our interviews suggest the following reasons:

- **You lack know-how.** If you've never, for example, showed any signs of having a green thumb or an artistic touch, joining your local garden or painting club might not seem like the obvious thing to do.

- **You're shy or insecure.** Aging and no longer having a job sometimes brings a dip in self esteem and self worth ("Who would want me?"), making some retirees more introverted and less likely to try something new.

- **You're less agile.** Retirees who have relied on their participation in sports both to feel good about themselves and as a way to make friends are vulnerable to becoming depressed and isolated, should physical limitations mean they can no longer play.

- **You're bored and unable to find a use for your skills.** Some retirees are surprised when their planned activities are not as interesting as they'd expected. By the time you finish your third cruise, you may never want to see another margarita. And many retired people find that the volunteer work they've chosen is menial and unsatisfying.

- **You're overwhelmed by family issues.** Some retirees find they're drawn back into dysfunctional melodramas—ranging from dementia in elderly family members to child care expectations on the part of grown children.

If you're a busy, outgoing person in your 40s or 50s, it's probably hard to believe that factors such as these will ever severely limit your retirement horizons. But one has to spend only a short time with people in their 70s for the blinders to fall off.

- **Doing interesting work.** Nonprofits often allow retired people to do work that they find more interesting and satisfying than would be possible working for a company busily trying to make money. For example, Carol Thompson, a retired social worker, initially volunteered as a docent in a university botanical garden and then graduated to the garden's propagation program, working with unusual and endangered plant species.

- **Looking to the future.** Working with an organization dedicated to making at least a little slice of the world better helps some participants cope with the looming inevitability of their own death. The fact that your good work will live on after you can provide comfort. Or as Henry Perry, a retired postal worker, explained, "All your life, you're writing the speech someone will give at your funeral. If you have been concerned about helping others and making the world a little bit better, that speech will be about how your deeds will live on in the hearts of others." (For more from our interview with Henry, see "The Pied Piper of Bikes," below.)

USA TODAY Snapshots®

European countries we most want to visit

United Kingdom 56%
Ireland 42%
Germany 41%
France 45%
Italy 59%

Note: Respondents could choose more than one country.
Harris Interactive online survey for SideStep of 3,078 adults (Jan. 17-19). Margin of error ±3.8 percentage points.

By Mary Cadden and Sam Ward, USA TODAY 2006

- **Honoring those who have helped us.** We all know and cherish the memories of people and groups who did something extra to enrich our own lives or help us achieve something that might otherwise have been out of our reach. Maybe it was a grandparent, teacher, older friend, or helping organization. Helping others lets us pass on the love and support that they gave us.

- **Meeting interesting people.** Working with nonprofits may lead to more rewarding friendships than you're likely to find in the private sector. That's because nonprofit groups, by definition, tend to attract like-minded people. For example, one researcher found that, among older volunteers with the U.S. government's Foster Grandparents and Senior Companions programs, 71% reported they "almost never" felt lonely, compared with 45% of the waiting-list group.

USA TODAY Snapshots®

Prayer most pleasing

Nearly half of Americans 45 or older say they are somewhat religious. Those surveyed cite their most satisfying spiritual or religious experience:

Prayer	20%
Living a good, moral life	19%
Helping others	19%
Being with family	13%
Attending religious services	10%

Source: International Communications Research for AARP

By Cristina Abello and Robert W. Ahrens, USA TODAY 2005

Also, 83% of participants reported being "more satisfied" with their life, compared with 52% of those waiting to become foster grandparents.

At first you may think it's silly that you have to plan ahead to serve as a volunteer—after all, you're not asking to be paid, only to help out. The unfortunate fact is that retired volunteers who don't have a history of working in a particular field may have a difficult time finding satisfying work. The situation gets worse if the volunteer is a little shy or insecure or has physical limitations.

Another problem is that many nonprofits are overworked, underfunded, and—as much as they could use some help—just not ready to make room for volunteers. A 1998 study by the UPS Foundation found that 41% of people who regularly volunteered stopped because the nonprofit organization did not make good use of their time and talents. Close to 60% reported they would volunteer more hours if their time were better used.

Ted Almost Strikes Out as a Volunteer

Here's a real-life example of how a poorly planned volunteering episode threatened an otherwise sensible retirement plan.

After a busy and fairly prosperous career as an electrician, Ted retired a little early, at age 60. Ted planned to fill up his time volunteering with local youth groups that sponsored kids' sports. And during the school day and evening hours, when there would be no kids to teach, he saw himself working behind the scenes with like-minded adults dedicated to improving kids' sports opportunities.

After some difficulty getting a coaching assignment, Ted finally was assigned to help coach a ten-and-under baseball team. On the first day of practice, Ted was shocked and dismayed that the kids didn't respond to his heavily structured approach, flocking instead around the other coach—a 19-year-old college freshman who wore his clothing three sizes too large and kept his hat on backwards. Nor did anyone in the community center seem to be particularly interested in Ted's repeated offers to contribute his organizational skills to the nonprofit corporation that ran the youth softball and soccer programs. Before long, he stopped coaching the baseball team, explaining to his family, "Kids just don't want to listen these days. I'm not going to be ignored or treated like an old fool." Later that summer, Ted tried helping with a summer recreational program for low-income kids and again felt unappreciated by the kids and undervalued by the program coordinator.

In less than six months, Ted's retirement dream had crashed and he decided to start up his business again, if for no other reason than to get out of the house and stop driving his wife nuts.

Ted Almost Strikes Out as a Volunteer, cont'd.

At this point, Ted's adult son, Peter, figured out that something was badly wrong. Guessing that his dad had simply lost touch with how to relate to kids in the almost two decades since he'd coached, Peter took a week off from work and accompanied ("dragged" might be a better word) Ted to a well-organized weeklong coaches' clinic. Ted loved the clinic, which was based on the theory that from the first moment, teaching and learning the fundamentals of baseball should be a positive experience. And although he never quite admitted it, Ted quickly saw the flaws in his drill-sergeant-type approach, which focused too much on telling kids what they were doing wrong. Armed with his new positive coaching approach plus a small library of state-of-the-art skills videos and drills, Ted again signed up as an assistant Little League coach. This time, the kids were much more responsive, and Ted began to look forward to every practice and game. His success with the kids and his willingness to take on lots of extra tasks, such as lining the field and coordinating equipment, quickly led to a position as head coach, and then to running spring baseball and the summer tennis and soccer programs. Eventually, Ted was also asked to coordinate the entire countywide under-ten soccer program.

Somewhere along the line, Ted bought a bright red hat, complete with prominent floppy ears. The kids, by whom he was now increasingly surrounded, started calling him "Teddy Ears." A few years later, when the commissioners of the local kids' basketball program voted him coach of the year, he was given a plaque that read, "To Coach Teddy Ears, the one man we couldn't do without."

Social Innovation Pays Off

Your altruistic desires may receive some unexpected rewards. For example, Gordon Johnson, a 74-year-old retiree, received a $100,000 award from Civic Ventures, a group that gives five such grants each year for people over 60 who tackle challenging social problems. Johnson spends 40 to 60 hours a week running Neighbor to Family, a program he founded to fix the foster care system. For more on the Civic Ventures program, check www.civicventures.org.

Volunteering well before you retire gives you time to look for a group that will make good use of your existing skills. It also lets you find out whether you're really suited for a particular type of work, and gives you a chance to look elsewhere if you aren't. You may discover that you need additional education or training to do volunteer work that will be truly satisfying.

Another reason to start volunteering before you retire is that finding a good nonprofit you can truly bond with is sometimes harder than you might guess. For example, one friend, Joan, who had planned for years to help out with a marine animal rescue project, retired early so she could begin this exciting work. She was hugely disappointed to discover that being around cold saltwater caused her arthritis to flare up so badly that she couldn't continue. Her efforts to volunteer with several other wildlife organizations also didn't work out. After consulting the staff at a local volunteer center, Joan finally found a good match—helping out in, and eventually running, the animal lab at a children's science museum. Looking back at her experiences, Joan said, "I was lucky to get inspired help from our volunteer center—otherwise my lack of preparation might have doomed my whole plan."

The Pied Piper of Bikes

Henry Perry, a retired postal worker in Oakland, California, explains to coauthor Jake Warner how he started volunteering.

JW: *You're a bike rider?*

HP: *Let me tell you about that, because you'll see a little of how I work in the community. I was 52 when I got my first bike. Black kids just didn't have bikes when I was young. At any rate, when I rode my bike, I saw all the neighborhood kids watching me enviously. I had been thinking about how to approach them about such things as why it's important to do well in school, but until that moment, I hadn't figured out how to get their attention.*

JW: *It's useless to just go up to a kid and give him good advice, isn't it?*

HP: *That's it. I needed a gimmick, a way to break the ice, and I saw right away that the bike was it. But to make my idea work, I needed more bikes. So I talked to a family on my mail route who had an old bike they weren't using, and they let me have it. Later, I bought a few old banged-up bikes from a guy at a bike store. Soon after, I was able to get a truckload of broken bikes someone was taking to the dump for free. I bought some bike books and taught myself how to fix them.*

JW: *So you became a sort of Pied Piper of bikes?*

HP: *Yes, kids came from everywhere. I taught them safety, formed drill teams, and did all sorts of other things. Many of the kids were from the housing projects and were just hungry to get on those bikes. It gave me a chance to really communicate the important things I wanted to talk to them about.*

JW: *Were all the bikes in your backyard?*

HP: *Yes, at the start, but not for long. The media heard about what I was doing and I was interviewed for some newspaper and radio stories. The result was that bikes came in from everywhere. The City Recreation Department and the Oakland Police Department began to help me and provided an old warehouse. By then we had 435 bikes.*

Similarly, Rob, a law librarian, thought that after retirement he'd like to help people learn legal survival skills. But a few years before retirement, when he volunteered at a legal aid office, he found that dealing with lots of anxious, impatient people caused him too much stress. He looked for other places to volunteer and after a couple more near misses, found a group of volunteer lawyers who needed someone to organize their library and help research legal issues. Rob was so excited about embracing what he now jokingly calls "my second career" that he retired from his first one a few months early.

Don't try this at home (or in Pamplona): John Dreelin, a retired London pharmacist, became—at age 77—the oldest known person to run with the bulls in the final 100-yard dash of the eight-day Spanish fiesta. He was bruised, but not gored.

To start your volunteering efforts now, go to Volunteer Match (www.volunteermatch .org), sponsored by the Ford Foundation, which helps match volunteers with various positions, some for just a few days, others permanent. You can also check out the federal government site www.volunteer.gov and the United Way's Volunteer Solutions (www.volunteersolutions.org). Another good resource is Retired Brains (www.retiredbrains.com), which connects older workers with charitable and nonprofit volunteer opportunities.

"Where Two or Three Come Together in My Name, There I Am with Them"

Songwriter Brian Wilson of the Beach Boys once wrote of "a place where I can go and tell my troubles to..." Though Wilson was describing his room, for at least 60% of Americans, that place is their house of worship. Churches, temples, and mosques in America serve as the all-purpose community center, places where you can recharge your spiritual batteries, meet and greet friends, volunteer to help the less fortunate, and perhaps win a game of Bingo.

Do the Things You Always Meant To

For many people, retirement offers a chance to finally do the interesting things they've put off all their lives. If, like many people in midlife, you haven't had time to follow up on old interests or develop consuming new ones, but plan to do both after you retire, then you're at high risk of having a difficult retirement. The unfortunate fact is that middle-aged people who allow too many years to pass without developing new interests or renewing old ones may never again be able to tap into their creativity. Or put another way, if currently you do little more than consume passive types of entertainment while fantasizing that you'll become more active when you retire, your fantasies are likely to turn out to be just that.

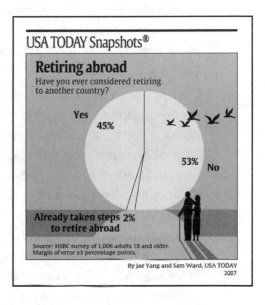

USA TODAY Snapshots®

Retiring abroad
Have you ever considered retiring to another country?

Yes 45%

53% No

Already taken steps 2% to retire abroad

Source: HSBC survey of 1,006 adults 18 and older. Margin of error ±3 percentage points.

By Jae Yang and Sam Ward, USA TODAY 2007

If at any time during your life you thought of yourself as a creative person (painter, musician, poet, or whatever else), we urge you to make a real effort to rediscover or enlarge upon these impulses now. The reason is simple: Art takes both skill and inspiration, and you don't want to be relying on rusty skills while experiencing the sustained burst of creativity that many people enjoy after age 65. Also, artists, musicians, and craftspeople tend to remain vital and purposeful in their own eyes, which of course is one of the keys to continuing to be respected by others.

Of course, artistic activities aren't your only possibility. You might also start a business, become your family's genealogist, or set up websites for your friends. Finding personal interests is a personal decision. But to get some inspiration, consider Brett's annual challenge, below.

Brett Skates to Success

Brett Davis is a successful, middle-aged, college-educated American in his 40s, with an executive-level job, a wife and two teen-aged sons, and a house in the suburbs. But one habit sets him apart. Each year, Brett challenges himself to master a significant new skill. Brett's list of recent accomplishments includes learning to ice skate, play the guitar, and scuba dive. He also started a Toastmaster's chapter to engage in an organized program of public speaking. He explains:

"It's easy to get so comfortable with life that you forget how to ask new questions or do new things. To stay open and interesting, it's my goal to periodically get outside my comfort zone, even if it means looking foolish. In fact, I believe we humans learn best and have the most fun when we give ourselves permission to be dumb. For example, several years ago I attended our company's annual skating party. As a nonskating son of Texas, I nevertheless took to the ice and predictably flopped, fell, and clowned to everyone's delight. Over the next year I had the fun of being the butt of lots of friendly ribbing. But without telling any of my coworkers, I also enrolled in a skating class. At the next year's event, I didn't just surprise my colleagues with my newfound ability to stay on my feet—they nearly fell down themselves when I started skating backwards. The look on their faces was worth every bump and bruise it took to get there."

Educate Yourself

Here's one of the great benefits of being a senior: You've got the time to take classes on any topic that interests you, whether it's how to sculpt, read Latin, teach autistic children, or design a Japanese garden. And you'll probably be welcome everywhere from your local college to community center. Against this background, it's fair to ask why today's typical American retiree watches 26 hours of TV each week and takes advantage of few, if any, learning opportunities.

But here again, it's best not to wait. Although neuroscientists and others who study aging can't conclusively tell us why older people seem so resistant to learning, evidence is accumulating that it has a great deal to do with how we use—or, in too many cases, underuse—our brains throughout our lives. The old workout mantra "use it or lose it" seems to apply to our brain just as much as it does to the rest of our body. Or as writer Sean O'Casey said, "If you've never read a book in your life, you won't start at age 60."

A brain that's not challenged to learn new things for an extended period will actually

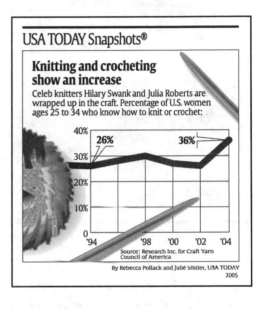

USA TODAY Snapshots®

Knitting and crocheting show an increase

Celeb knitters Hilary Swank and Julia Roberts are wrapped up in the craft. Percentage of U.S. women ages 25 to 34 who know how to knit or crochet:

26%   36%

40%
30%
20%
10%
0
'94   '98   '00   '02   '04

Source: Research Inc. for Craft Yarn Council of America

By Rebecca Pollack and Julie Snider, USA TODAY
2005

become smaller and less capable of learning in the future. At the same time, continuing to be an active learner throughout your life may contribute to a larger, healthier brain. Underlining this point, one doctor reported that adults over age 70 with brain-stimulating hobbies were two and a half times less likely to suffer from the effects of Alzheimer's later in life than were those whose main leisure activity was watching TV.

Think about how you can challenge your brain to stay active every day from now on. Things as simple as learning to operate your computer mouse with your left hand or taking a walk in an unfamiliar area are small and easy steps we can all can take.

Better yet, challenge yourself to learn a new subject—one that uses the lazier cells in your brain. For example, if you're already fluent in three languages, don't just master another one. You'll likely stimulate more brain-cell growth by learning to paint, play a musical instrument, take apart a car engine, or wrap your mind around basic physics.

USA TODAY Snapshots®

Stressing relaxation in wellness
How important adults think relaxation is to health and wellness:

76%

21%

Not too important
1%

Very important

Somewhat important

Source: EXCEL Omnibus by ICR telephone survey of 1,000 adults taken Dec. 9–13 for Brookstone. Margin of error: ±3.1 percentage points.

By Cindy Clark and Alejandro Gonzalez, USA TODAY 2006

Anything that's both new to you and challenging will work; it doesn't have to involve formal schooling. A classics professor might do better to learn how to prune fruit trees, line car brakes, or even solve difficult jigsaw puzzles than to write a scholarly essay parsing Plato's logic. Activities that combine physical and mental challenges, such as square dancing or juggling, are particularly good, because they simultaneously challenge two parts of the brain.

RESOURCE
Where to go. Contact local community and state colleges to ask about adult education options. Also check the learning and technology section of the AARP website (www.aarp.org); click the "Learning and Technology" tab and check out the "Lifelong Learning" section as well as the message boards. You can also search online using terms such as "continuing education" and "adult education."

What, Me Work?

Another great way to stay active and involved is to work, either part- or full-time, whether at your current job or a new one. We talk about ways that retirees stay employed and offer other postretirement work strategies in Chapter 10.

Figure Out Your Number

Using Online Retirement Calculators_____100

The Choices and Variables Underlying Your Number_____102

A Do-It-Yourself Retirement Calculator_____107

   How much will you need during retirement?_____107

   How much extra will you need to save?_____110

Your "Number," according to USA TODAY writer Michelle Archer, is "that elusive, ephemeral, magical dollar digit that will last from the moment you say sayonara to work, to the moment you simply say sayonara." In other words, your "Number" is the total amount of money needed to guarantee safe passage through retirement.

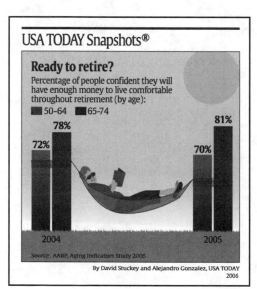

USA TODAY Snapshots®

Ready to retire?
Percentage of people confident they will have enough money to live comfortable throughout retirement (by age):
■ 50-64 ■ 65-74

72% 78% 70% 81%

2004   2005

Source: AARP, Aging Indicators Study 2005

By David Stuckey and Alejandro Gonzalez, USA TODAY
2006

In this chapter we'll help you calculate this figure. As you proceed through the math, you may begin to understand why the majority of Americans haven't bothered figuring out their Numbers. There are many variables, assumptions, and ambiguities involved in this formula, and the end result can seem as if it emanated from a Ouija board rather than a calculator. Although the exercise is ultimately worthwhile, keep in mind that:

- **Your Number is, at best, a very rough guess.** At worst, it's pure hocus-pocus. No one can know for sure how long you will live, at what rate inflation will grow, or how high a return you'll get on your investments. You can't even be sure whether you'll want to live the same way in retirement—with the same rate of consumption—as you do today. In the absence of a crystal ball, the best you can do is to make a ballpark estimate—or guesstimate—of things to come.

- **Some online retirement calculators are skewed toward the retirement industry's goals, not yours.** The Internet offers a multitude of retirement calculators, which you'll no doubt want to take a look at. But watch out for ones sponsored by companies with a vested interest in getting you to buy retirement services or products. By exploiting ambiguities, these calculators may put you on an unrealistic financial treadmill. They may, for example, default to longer-than-average life spans or higher-than-average inflation rates. Take a second look at the calculator's built-in assumptions and default settings, and make reasonable changes where you can.

- **You have the power to change your Number.** Your Number reflects you—your hopes, plans, and needs—and can be adjusted accordingly. For example, many people are shocked to find that their initial calculation seems hopelessly out of reach. For those who are deeply in debt, this can be a warning to pay down your debt as soon as possible. (See Chapter 7 for more information on debt reduction.) Consider the calculations you make in this chapter as an offer you're making to your future self—the person that you will actually be in retirement. In other words, if the amount you must save seems out of reach, then play out "what if" scenarios until you can settle on a Number that's reasonable and acceptable. You may find that you'll need to cut back on some retirement expenses or work longer before retiring, but this internal negotiation is an essential part of retirement planning. In fact, you can continue readjusting your Number after retirement, allowing you to accommodate blips on the financial radar.

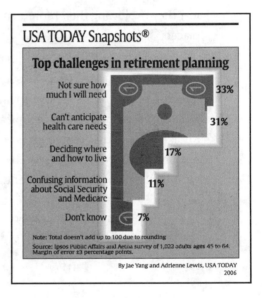

USA TODAY Snapshots®

Top challenges in retirement planning

Not sure how much I will need — 33%
Can't anticipate health care needs — 31%
Deciding where and how to live — 17%
Confusing information about Social Security and Medicare — 11%
Don't know — 7%

Note: Total doesn't add up to 100 due to rounding
Source: Ipsos Public Affairs and Aetna survey of 1,022 adults ages 45 to 64. Margin of error ±3 percentage points.

By Jae Yang and Adrienne Lewis, USA TODAY 2006

Is It Possible to Save Too Much for Retirement?

If you think it's impossible to save too much, think again. Sandra Block reported in USA TODAY that a group of economists at the University of Wisconsin found that many families are in better shape for retirement than they think. This is not to say that people should stop saving for retirement, explains one of the study's co-authors, John Karl Scholz. But if families who have already saved diligently for years are "delaying a lot of gratification because of the fear they're blowing their retirement, maybe that anxiety is mis-placed," he says.

Laurence Kotlikoff, an economics professor at Boston University, told Block that his research also suggests that a "significant fraction" of Americans are oversaving, largely because they're getting misleading and self-serving advice from financial advisers. Kotlikoff argues that retirement savings calculators offered by most financial services firms often grossly overstate how much individuals will need for retirement.

 "Are you saving too much for retirement; Group says it's possible some put away more than needed," Sandra Block, March 8, 2007.

Using Online Retirement Calculators

As with all matters financial, there are automated (and sophisticated) means of calculating your Number online. Type "retirement calculator" into your search engine and you'll see a lengthy list of these programs. Some are easy to use and others require more work at your end. In addition, you'll find that different calculators tend to arrive at starkly different results. *The New York Times* tested several calculators and found that—with the same set of numbers—one calculator concluded that a hypothetical investor would wind up $1.1 million short of a comfortable retirement, another put the shortfall just under $200,000, and a third calculator concluded that the same investor would end up with over $669,000 more than she needed.

There's no perfect solution; we recommend that you search out and try several calculators. The four online calculators described below are generally easy to use and free of common financial biases and unrealistic default settings.

- **FINRA (www.finra.org).** FINRA is an organization that oversees brokerage firms. Its calculator is probably the easiest one we used.

- **AARP (www.aarp.org).** AARP is the nonprofit group for people 50 and older. Two nice features of the AARP calculator are its ability to combine information from two people and to change your projected investment rate of return over time.

- **EBRI's Choose to Save Ballpark Estimate.** EBRI, the Employee Benefit Research Institute, is a nonprofit research group. Like AARP, it offers a detailed financial questionnaire and it lets you include wages after retirement.

- **T. Rowe Price.com.** T. Rowe Price, a mutual fund company, offers an easy-to-use calculator that it calls a Retirement Planning Worksheet.

If you don't have Internet access, a pencil-and-paper method of calculating your Number appears later in this chapter.

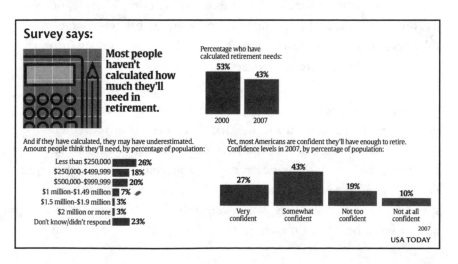

Survey says:

Most people haven't calculated how much they'll need in retirement.

Percentage who have calculated retirement needs:

53% (2000)
43% (2007)

And if they have calculated, they may have underestimated. Amount people think they'll need, by percentage of population:

Less than $250,000 — 26%
$250,000-$499,999 — 18%
$500,000-$999,999 — 20%
$1 million-$1.49 million — 7%
$1.5 million-$1.9 million — 3%
$2 million or more — 3%
Don't know/didn't respond — 23%

Yet, most Americans are confident they'll have enough to retire. Confidence levels in 2007, by percentage of population:

Very confident — 27%
Somewhat confident — 43%
Not too confident — 19%
Not at all confident — 10%

2007

USA TODAY

A Financial Planner's View of Calculators

Sheryl Garrett, founder of Garrett Planning Network (www.garrett-planningnetwork.com), reviewed all four of the calculators discussed above for USA TODAY. She noted that because they rely on different assumptions, it's hard to assess their accuracy. Still, Garrett favored EBRI's Ballpark Estimate for its "best real-life projections" and flexibility (it allows for factors such as postretirement job income). If you're young and haven't saved much for retirement yet, she suggests starting with one of the easier calculators (such as the FINRA) or trying different calculators. Though the assumptions won't be identical, they'll give you a range for how much to save.

The Choices and Variables Underlying Your Number

Here's a heads up on the meaning of variables commonly used to calculate your Number. Many online calculators will ask you to enter or make choices about the following:

Current income. Some calculators seek your after-tax income, others use pretax income and calculate based on your tax bracket. Some calculators combine spouses' income, some divide this money into two income streams (if there are spouses).

Postretirement expenses. You'll be asked to estimate your postretirement living expenses or—as it's sometimes calculated—the percentage of your current income that you'll need after retirement. This may be the single most important estimate that you make. Lee Eisenberg, author of *The Number*, calls this percentage the "Satisfaction Factor," because you'll need to decide what percentage of your current spending lifestyle will satisfy you in your 60s, 70s, and beyond. We believe you'll be safe estimating in the 70% to 80% range—that is, you'll spend 70% to 80% of what you spend now. These diminishing expenses may be attributed to a paid-off mortgage, children who've left the nest, or the end of your commuting or business-wardrobe expenses. Or you may just become more frugal, as you become more philosophical and less interested in keeping up with the Joneses.

Of course, not everyone agrees with our estimates. Some financial planners recommend using a much higher multiplier—that is, they suggest your future spending will equal 100% to 120% of your current spending. "Our experience," a San Francisco financial planner told USA TODAY in 2006, "is that, when couples retire, they spend as much or more than what they were spending while they were working." Perhaps these planners know something we don't, but their advice doesn't jibe with what many retirees have told us—that they commonly spend less than they did before retirement. However, one of the biggest unknowns here is your future medical costs, as discussed under "The Future of Health Care Costs," below.

Annual income after retirement. Here you estimate the income you expect (or hope) to receive after retirement. This includes Social Security, a pension, royalties, rent, part-time jobs, and other income. (For a summary of these income sources, review Chapter 8.)

If you haven't received an annual statement from the Social Security Administration summarizing your expected payout, you can request one, or estimate your Social Security benefits using the calculator provided by Social Security Online (http://ssa.gov/OACT/quickcalc).

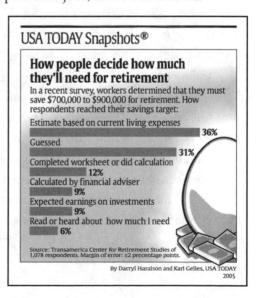

USA TODAY Snapshots®

How people decide how much they'll need for retirement

In a recent survey, workers determined that they must save $700,000 to $900,000 for retirement. How respondents reached their savings target:

Estimate based on current living expenses
36%

Guessed
31%

Completed worksheet or did calculation
12%

Calculated by financial adviser
9%

Expected earnings on investments
9%

Read or heard about how much I need
6%

Source: Transamerica Center for Retirement Studies of 1,078 respondents. Margin of error: ±2 percentage points.

By Darryl Haralson and Karl Gelles, USA TODAY 2005

If you have doubts whether you'll get your government retirement benefits—that is, you consider it "Social Insecurity" rather than Social Security—some financial advisers recommend that people currently under 50 halve their estimate of Social Security. As we discuss in Chapter 8, we believe that Social Security will survive, although we expect some necessary tweaks, particularly for wealthier Americans. If you disagree and see the whole system crashing, calculate accordingly.

Current savings. How much have you already set aside for retirement, including all stocks, bonds, mutual funds, 401(k)s, IRAs, and the like? All of this information is available from your financial institutions.

Yield/rate of return. This is the percentage of annual return you expect for your investments over the course of the investment. In some instances, this will be a fixed rate—for example, with certificates of deposit. But in other cases, your expected return will be less predictable, for example with mutual fund returns. Some calculators simplify matters and ask you to estimate one rate of return for all your investments; others break out individual investment sources and tabulate rates of return separately. Historically, the stock market has returned around 8%, though in recent years the gains have been higher. However, Sheryl Garrett told USA TODAY that any estimate more than 7% is too high. Says Garrett, "You only want to be surprised on the upside."

Inflation rate. The inflation rate determines the value of today's dollars in the future. In the last 15 years, inflation has averaged approximately 2.65% per year—meaning that what you bought for one dollar at the start of the year would cost approximately $1.03 at the end. (Or put another way, a dollar in January is worth around 97¢ at the end of December.) Since nobody can predict the rate at which inflation will rise, you have the difficult task of choosing a ballpark figure from within the official guesstimates, which range from 1.8% to 3.8%. The financial industry suggests an average of 3% per year. At that rate, a 2007 dollar will be worth 54¢ by 2027.

7% +
3% inflation

The Future of Health Care Costs

It's hard to avoid spending more for health care as you age. Although the federally sponsored Medicare program will provide some of your care for free, many retirees who are now in their 60s and 70s and are in decent health need to supplement Medicare coverage by buying a "medi-gap" insurance policy. And prescription drug costs are a separate item, although you'll also receive some federal help with this. Bottom line: You'll spend more for medicines and unreimbursed medical care than you do now. And if you or your spouse needs long-term care or in-home skilled nursing, your expenses will go up farther.

Fidelity Investments—in a widely-quoted study—has estimated that a 65-year-old couple retiring today will need an additional $215,000 to cover medical costs throughout retirement. (This assumes the couple has no employer-sponsored retiree health coverage and that the husband lives 17 more years and the wife 20.)

Does that mean a couple will spend in the neighborhood of $10,000 a year for over 20 years for health care? That figure is merely an educated guess and, at best, a median figure. If your health has been good, you're in good shape, and your ancestors have aged without many medical problems, you can probably estimate far less for medical costs—for example, $1,000 to $3,000 per person per year.

And again, as with Social Security, if you have doubts about the future of Medicare, increase your estimated medical expenses accordingly when you calculate your Number.

same as 08-Deductible $3000=
08 $3600   Insurance $6000 ↑09

How long will you live? Here we come to the grimmest question in the calculation: How long do you expect to live in retirement? In other words, could you please forecast your own death? Obviously, unless you're on death row, you can't provide the date. And since you can't write in, "As long as possible," you'll need to pick a number. Financial industry calculators default to the high side—often estimating 30 years after retiring at age 65. Statistics don't back up those numbers. The average life expectancy in the United States is 78 years, according to the most recent preliminary data from the National Center for Health Statistics. This projection also differs from actuarial tables, which forecast that, for people who live past age 65, the average retired man can expect to live about 19 more years, and the average retired woman, 22. Since these predictions—related to medians and averages—seem difficult to apply personally, some financial experts, such as USA TODAY'S Sandra Block, recommend using one of the many Internet calculators that help you estimate your longevity (type "life expectancy calculator" into your Internet search engine). One of the most popular calculators is the "Living to 100" life expectancy calculator (www.livingto100.com), which asks a series of 40 questions based on human longevity research conducted by Dr. Thomas Perls, an Associate Professor of Medicine at Boston University.

> One person in 2 billion will live to the age of 116.

How much do you want to leave in your estate? For example, if you have children, you may be hoping to help assure their future comfort, or leave a legacy that allows your grandchildren to afford the college of their choice.

A Do-It-Yourself Retirement Calculator

If you're finding the online calculators too complex or if you prefer paper and pencil, here's a low-tech, two-part calculation you can use. The first part includes three steps for getting a rough idea of your Number. The second part lets you fine tune that Number by calculating any gaps between expected income and expected expenses (and adjusting accordingly).

How much will you need during retirement?

No higher math needed here. The following steps will help you add and subtract your way to an estimate of what you'll need each year after you retire, using the worksheet below. You can also attempt this simply by looking at your current income and guessing the percentage you'll need in retirement (see our discussion about "Postretirement expenses" in "The Choices and Variables Underlying Your Number" section above).

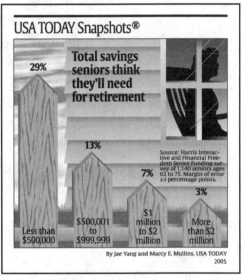

USA TODAY Snapshots®

Total savings seniors think they'll need for retirement

29%   Less than $500,000

13% $500,001 to $999,999

7% $1 million to $2 million

3%   More than $2 million

Source: Harris Interactive and Financial Freedom Senior Funding survey of 1,140 seniors ages 62 to 75. Margin of error ±3 percentage points.

By Jae Yang and Marcy E. Mullins, USA TODAY 2005

- **Step 1. Determine how much you spend now.** Start by pulling out last year's federal tax return and figuring out your after-tax income. (Any money you contributed to a tax-deferred retirement plan will already have been subtracted.) Then subtract any money you put into additional savings or gave away (to your kids or to charity, it makes no difference). Your total should more or less reflect what it costs you to live now. Enter this number on the right column in the worksheet.

- **Step 2. Subtract expenses you won't have by the time you retire.** Will the kids be done with college and living on their own? Great, that's one set of expenses done with. What about your home mortgage? Most householders over 65 own homes that are fully paid for. Enter the sum of your disappearing expenses on the column next to Step 2 and then subtract it from the running total in the right column.

- **Step 3. Add new postretirement costs.** If you've been dreaming of travel, add up how much you figure that will cost. Estimate your future health care expenses. If you have no idea, use the $215,000 figure (that's for a couple) cited above, annualized over a 20-year period. And think about whether your adult children may need some financial help, particularly with home buying or if one is disabled. Enter these sums in Step 3 of the worksheet and add them into the running total.

Your total gives you a rough idea of the amount of money you'll need each year after you retire.

Basic Expense Calculator		
	Amount	Running total
Step 1: Estimate current annual living expenses (after-tax income minus savings and gifts)	$ 2.0 misc 3.0 clothes	$ 100.0
Step 2: Subtract annual expenses you probably won't have after retirement	−$ 12.0 Mtg. 3.0 Rest.	$ 80.0
Step 3: Add additional expenses after retirement	+$ 4.0 Ins.	$ 84.0
Total Annual Income Required After Retirement	+	$ 84.0

Let's try an example so you can see how this simple calculation works.

Imagine that you currently spend about $67,000 annually. To arrive at your likely retirement spending (Step 2), you subtract the $16,000 per year you currently spend on your mortgage, having noted that it will be paid off eight years before you plan to retire. You subtract another $15,000 for costs currently attributable to your two teenage children. Finally, you subtract $5,000 for postretirement savings you expect to amass by driving less, eliminating work-related expenses, and taking advantage of senior discounts. To this total of $31,000, you add $5,000 to cover costs for increased travel

USA TODAY Snapshots®

Price of sickness rising
Average prescription-drug price (in dollars):

$46 $50 $55 $60 $64

2000   2001   2002   2003   2004

Note: Average of brand and generic drugs
Source: Census Bureau, *Statistical Abstract of the United States: 2006*

By David Stuckey and Marcy E. Mullins, USA TODAY
2006

and—since your family's vital signs are good—$3,000 for health care (Step 3). Your total annual anticipated retirement spending in current dollars is $39,000 per year.

Basic Expense Calculator Example: Married Couple with Children with $67,000 in Annual Spending	Amount	Running total
Step 1: Estimate current annual living expenses (after-tax income minus savings and gifts)		$67,000
Step 2: Subtract annual expenses you probably won't have after retirement	– $36,000	$31,000
Step 3: Add additional expenses after retirement	+ $8,000	$39,000
Annual Income Required After Retirement	=	$39,000

How much extra will you need to save?

Okay, now you have a rough idea of what you can expect to spend in retirement. But the challenging (and sometimes confusing) aspect of retirement planning is achieving the financial goals represented by that Number. For example, if you calculate that you need $60,000 per year (or $5,000 a month), and you know that you'll be receiving $2,000 a month in Social Security, where will you obtain the additional $3,000 per month? If you plan on tapping your $500,000 nest egg, how long will that last? You may begin wondering what good it is to estimate your retirement Number if you don't know how to fund it.

By retirement age (65), you'll have spent about 20 years of your life sleeping.

To bring it all into focus, you need to figure out the gap (or surplus) between your expected retirement income and your Number, and then factor in inflation. The result may require you to adjust your Number into a realistic zone, even if it means adopting a more frugal approach to retirement.

Here's how to do it:

Step 1. Calculate the monthly gap between income and expenses. To determine the gap between what you expect to spend each month and what you expect to receive, start by analyzing your postretirement income. The three traditional sources include:

- **Social Security.** Estimate this amount by reviewing your Social Security statement, or running some numbers at the Social Security website (following the instructions in Chapter 8).

- **Pensions and annuities.** If you have a pension, your plan's provider can help you determine your annual payouts. If you buy an annuity, your plan administrator can assist. (Annuities are described in more detail in Chapter 8.)

- **Periodic withdrawals from savings.** There are many systems you can devise for withdrawing from your accounts. For example, you can withdraw a fixed percentage of your retirement or savings accounts, or you can withdraw a fixed amount that you adjust each year to reflect the previous year's inflation rate. One increasingly popular approach is known as the safe withdrawal system, in which you withdraw 4% to 5% of your account— hopefully less than what it's earning annually in interest. Doing so should permit you to keep the principal intact, enabling you to live on it throughout retirement.

Total the various types of income you expect to receive (including from any other sources such as rental income or trusts) and then subtract that total from your annual expenses (the number you arrived at earlier in the first part of your calculations). This is your annual retirement income gap. When you divide this number by 12, you have your monthly gap.

By way of example, let's say you figured you needed $54,000 per year (in 2007 dollars). You expect to receive $20,000 annually from Social Security, $10,000 annually from a pension, and you currently have a retirement account of $250,000 that will generate $12,500 annually (at 5%). Your annual income gap will be $11,500, and your monthly gap $958.

Example: Calculating Annual Retirement Income Gap	
Total annual retirement expenditures	$54,000
Annual Social Security payments	– $20,000
Annual 5% withdrawal from funds	– $12,500
Annual pension payments	– $10,000
Annual retirement income gap	$11,500
	÷12
Supplemental monthly income (SMI) needed	$958

How will you bridge your monthly gap? You have a few choices—for example you might work part time, obtain a reverse mortgage (discussed in more detail in Chapter 8), or sell your home and downsize. You might receive an inheritance or gift that will bridge the gap. Or this may be the time for you to lower the bar for your retirement and recalculate your Number for a leaner lifestyle. In any of these cases, you've completed your calculation and you're prepared to make the necessary decisions.

Alternatively, you can simply save more for retirement. But how much more? To find out, proceed to Step 2.

- **Step 2. Recalculate your monthly gap to include inflation between now and retirement.** To figure the proper amount of savings you'll need to bridge your monthly gap in the future, you must consider inflation. Use the table below, "Inflation Factors," to pick a multiplier that will reflect inflation based on 3% per year. (This is a conservative estimate and a bit higher than the average yearly rate of inflation for the past 15 years.) For example, if you have ten years until retirement, your multiplier is 1.34. You would calculate the amount of your monthly gap times the multiplier. That number is the amount you will actually need to bridge the gap when you reach retirement age.

Let's go back to the previous example in which we determined that you had a monthly gap of $958. If you planned to retire in ten years, your adjusted-for-inflation monthly gap would actually be $1,284 ($958 x 1.34).

Example: Adjusting Monthly Gap for Inflation	
Years until retirement	10
Monthly gap in retirement income	$958
Inflation factor from table, below	x 1.34
Adjusted monthly gap in retirement Income	$1,284

Inflation Factors			
Number of Years to Retirement	Inflation Factor *	Number of Years to Retirement	Inflation Factor *
5	1.16	25	2.09
10	1.34	30	2.43
15	1.56	35	2.81
20	1.81	40	2.26

*Based on 3% annual inflation

In Step 3, you figure out how much you'll need to save by retirement age in order to bridge that monthly gap through retirement.

Step 3. Calculate how much you need to save before retirement.
Continuing with the example, you know you'll need to generate $1,284 every month to make your retirement plan come true. But for how many months will you need this amount—that is, how long will you live?

For example, if you need $1,284 a month and you expect to live 25 years in retirement, you could multiply that life expectancy against your needs, which comes to approximately $385,000 ($1,284 x 12 x 25).

However, that number doesn't factor in the possibility that your savings could be generating income during retirement (although they could also be losing value due to inflation). So here's a final calculation that factors in earning power and inflation. We've simplified this a bit in the table, below ("Calculating Required Savings"), which tells you how many dollars you'll need to put aside for each dollar you want to withdraw each month. But to use this table, you must make some assumptions about how long you'll live and when you'll retire.

For example, let's be conservative and assume you hope to spend 25 years in retirement, and expect to get a real (adjusted for inflation) annual return on your investments of 4% (that's a 7% return minus a 3% inflation rate). According to the table "Adjusted Savings Requirements," below, that would mean you'll need $190.08 in savings in order to spend $1 each month for the 25 years of your retirement. Since, for purposes of this example, you've already determined that you'll need $1,284 per month to fill the monthly gap, multiply $190.08 by $1,284 to arrive at a figure of $244,062.

Therefore, if you want to bridge your gap, and live within your original $54,000 annual budget, you'll need to save an additional $244,062 by the time you retire. If you can't save that sum (or don't want to), the alternative is to cut your predicted monthly living expenses by about $1,000.

Example: Calculating Required Savings	
Expected annual return on investments	6%
Expected annual inflation	– 2%
Expected real annual return	4%
Years of retirement	25
Amount from "Adjusted Savings Requirements," table	$190.08
Supplemental monthly income needed	x 1,284
Required savings	$244,062

Adjusted Savings Requirements

Dollars you need to put aside for each dollar you want to withdraw each month. (Choose your annual rate of return and number of years you plan to withdraw. Multiply the resulting number by the monthly supplemental income you need.)

Number of years you plan to withdraw $1 per month	Annual rate of return on investment					
	4%	5%	6%	8%	10%	12%
15	$135.64	$126.98	$119.10	$105.34	$93.83	$84.15
20	$165.57	$152.16	$140.28	$120.35	$104.49	$91.73
25	$190.08	$171.77	$155.98	$130.43	$110.96	$95.90
30	$210.16	$187.06	$167.63	$137.19	$114.90	$98.19
35	$226.60	$198.97	$176.26	$141.73	$117.29	$99.45

Convert Debt Into Retirement Savings

Can You Avoid Car Payments?_____117

Heading Into Retirement With Credit Card Debt?_____119

    Practical ways to break the credit habit_____122

    Adding up the savings_____125

Should You Prepay Your Mortgage?_____127

I f you live debt-free and never pay interest, you can skip this chapter. But if you currently pay interest on credit purchases—whether for household items, an automobile, or your home—there is a path to savings that you may have overlooked.

If you're willing to cut back on some consumption, pay off your debt, and invest the money you would have otherwise spent on interest, you may be able to amass a tidy sum.

Even the smallest commitments can pay off. For example, let's say you were to add $100 a month to your mortgage check. If you had a $200,000, 30-year mortgage payment at 6%, you could pay it off in a little less than 25 years and save almost $50,000 in interest. Once the mortgage was paid off, you could take the monthly amount you were spending on your mortgage and put it into a tax-free retirement plan, then watch as thousands of dollars accrue.

We talk more about prepaying mortgages in this chapter, but for now you get the idea. If you alter your spending habits a little and invest the money you currently pay out in the form of interest on credit cards, car loans, and mortgages, you can almost painlessly produce a comfortable retirement nest egg.

That's not to say that we're advocates of a bread-and-water budget to achieve retirement savings. Strict budgets, like strict diets, usually don't work for very long. And like diets, when many people abandon a strict budget, they go on a spending binge.

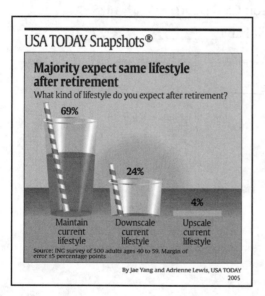

USA TODAY Snapshots®

Majority expect same lifestyle after retirement
What kind of lifestyle do you expect after retirement?

69% Maintain current lifestyle

24% Downscale current lifestyle

4% Upscale current lifestyle

Source: ING survey of 500 adults ages 40 to 59. Margin of error ±5 percentage points

By Jae Yang and Adrienne Lewis, USA TODAY 2005

Our strategy does require some belt tightening, and the more credit you carry, the tighter the belt. As a general rule—and there are financial advisers who may disagree—it's wise to eliminate debt.

Feathering your own nest, instead of those of banks and other credit grantors, requires you to do three things:

- **Change your credit habits.** Whether you go cold turkey or try to ease your way into it, you're going to have to avoid interest-bearing credit to pay for new purchases. This may include drastic measures like cutting up your cards, unless you can pay off the monthly balances. Obviously this "no-credit" rule will not apply when buying a house, although we'll recommend ways to reduce this type of long-term interest burden as well.

  U.S. federal debt, per capita, in 1900: $16.

  In 2000: $20,800.

- **Pay off all existing interest-bearing debts as soon as possible.** Again, we know this is easier said than done. But as you'll see, there are small steps you can take to make a difference, now.

- **Save and invest the money you were paying in interest.** Enjoy the satisfaction of watching money previously destined for financial institutions now socked away in your retirement funds.

This chapter will hopefully strengthen your willpower and provide some practical strategies to change your credit habits. Below we'll focus on three types of debts: auto loans, credit cards, and home mortgages.

Can You Avoid Car Payments?

What's wrong with buying a car on credit? You probably know the answer. Unlike a home, that shiny new Lexus begins losing value the day you drive it off the lot. And its value continues to drop as long as you own it. In other words, when you buy a car on credit, you're making substantial interest payments for a piece of property that's rapidly depreciating. And on top of that, you'll pay stiff costs to insure, register, and maintain an expensive new steed.

Leasing a Car Is Usually a Bad Deal

A car lease is like a high-interest car loan with a huge balloon payment at the end. When the lease runs out, you must either buy the car (often for more than it's then worth) or end up with no car and no money. And to make matters worse, many people, mesmerized by ads touting an "affordable monthly payment," end up paying significantly more for the vehicle than if they'd negotiated a good purchase price in the first place.

Why are nearly 20% of new vehicles being leased instead of purchased? Aside from the people who simply made a bad decision or felt they couldn't afford a car any other way, Jesse Toprak told USA TODAY that leasing makes the most sense if you drive less than 15,000 miles per year (more than that usually incurs a lease penalty) or you're fairly certain you'll be living in the same place for several years. It's difficult to get out of a lease contract before the term is ended, and as Toprak says, "If you have any uncertainty as far as your career or where you might be living, you're better off buying."

Still, many car-lovers are willing to take the loss and pay the interest, in order to buy or lease a pricey new vehicle. (See "Leasing a Car Is Usually a Bad Deal," just above.) If you believe you need to take out a car loan in order to have a decent ride, consider these tips to avoid overpaying on interest:

- **Shop for the lowest rate.** As of late 2007, the average rate for a five-year new car loan was just shy of 8%, and rates for three- and four-year loans were only slightly lower, according to Bankrate. com. The average rate for a used car was 8.72%. However, as Jesse Toprak, executive director of industry analysis for Edmunds. com told USA TODAY, dealers continually offer low-interest incentives to attract buyers.

- **Shop for the shortest term.** You're always better off keeping the loan for as short a time as possible—that is, three years or less.
- **What about used car loans?** The interest rates charged on used vehicle loans are almost always higher than for new ones. Try to scrape up cash for this one, or borrow from a friend or family member at a more reasonable interest rate (but one that still offers your lender a competitive return).
- **Avoid penalties for prepaying.** By reading the fine print, you can make sure your auto loan agreement permits you to pay off the loan principal if you come into some money, and thereby save a lot of interest.

Heading Into Retirement With Credit Card Debt?

Carrying even a relatively small credit card debt can pose a problem if you're trying to save for retirement. Consider the situation faced by Diane, a 55-year-old woman who charged $2,000 on a credit card carrying an annual interest rate of 19.8%. Feeling financially strapped, Diane begins sending in only $35 each month. At this rate, Diane will not fully pay off the debt until she is almost 70. The total cost of the $2,000 purchase will be more than $6,100.

Borrowing $2,000 diverts $4,000 from what could have been Diane's retirement savings. (And when she reaches age 70, she probably won't even remember why she borrowed that $2,000 those 15 years ago.)

Diane is not alone. Approximately 40% of U.S. households spend more than they earn. That gap between spending and earning is commonly filled by credit, or more specifically by the 1.2 billion credit cards in use in the United States.

Considering that 65% of credit card users don't pay their bills in full each month—the average payment is only about 15% of the outstanding balance—and that interest rates are often 13% to 24% (the average is 18.9%), consumer debt accumulates at a cost of tens of billions of dollars per year. No wonder the bankruptcy rate is ten times what it was during the Great Depression. (Some 1.48 million people filed for bankruptcy during the 12 months ending in June 2006).

The typical U.S. household that uses credit cards holds five different cards, owes over $14,500, and annually pays over $100 in late fees and other penalties. The average credit card debt among all households is $8,400.

Credit card interest rates are so high that many states have thrown up their hands and passed legislation to exempt revolving charge accounts from traditional usury laws, which prohibit most lenders from charging over 10% to 12% interest per year. Think about it: If your Uncle Harry charged as much interest for a loan as you probably pay to Visa or MasterCard, he would be guilty of a crime.

If, instead of paying high interest plus outlandish fees (over $42 billion last year) as well as penalties, Americans saved a portion of this amount, many could substantially increase their retirement nest egg. Yet nine out of ten Americans claim credit card debt has never been a source of worry. New Jersey debt counselor Kim Cole told USA TODAY, "There's a false sense of optimism out there that says, 'If I can't pay for it today, I probably can tomorrow.' A lot of people find out the hard way that that's just not true."

Perhaps people carrying substantial credit card debt hope that some intervening force will occur before they must pay it off—they'll win the Powerball Jackpot or write the next Harry Potter novel. We wish them the best. But the reality is that the only intervening force that can rescue you and your plans for retirement … is you.

What Happens If You Stop Paying Credit Card Interest?

Winston and Jennifer Lee are a middle-class couple who carry credit card debt that costs them $900 in interest a year. Your first thought may be that $900 a year isn't much—surely not enough to contribute significantly to the Lees' retirement savings needs. Think again. The table below illustrates what would happen if, instead of paying credit card interest, the Lees annually saved and invested this amount in a mutual fund, keeping the investment until they retire at age 65. It also assumes their money will grow at a rate of 8% per year, and that they reinvest all dividends and interest without paying tax, as would be possible if they put the money into a tax-sheltered retirement plan.

Age the Lees start to invest $900/year	Value at age 65	Age the Lees start to invest $900/year	Value at age 65
25	$233,151	45	$41,186
30	$155,085	50	$24,437
35	$101,955	55	$13,038
40	$65,795	60	$5,280

The Lees' potential savings are impressive. And they achieved them without working one more hour, earning one extra dollar, or making one less purchase.

That's fine for the solidly middle-class, but isn't buying on credit a necessity for many lower-income families, who simply can't afford to pay for needed items immediately? Buying on credit may be a convenience, a habit, and, for a few people, an addiction, but it's usually not necessary. The proof is in credit card statistics that demonstrate that most debt is incurred for clothing, jewelry, restaurant meals, recreational equipment, travel, and toys (both for kids and adults). These purchases could, in many cases, be put off until the cash necessary to purchase the item was saved. Similarly, a significant amount of each family's credit card total occurs just before the Christmas holidays. Yes, it feels good to give your loved ones nice gifts, but it also feels good not to be drowning in debt. Homemade gifts or services are often more appreciated anyway.

Practical ways to break the credit habit

"Never have Americans, who have always liked their toys, been faced with a situation where their impulses are so hard to control," Stuart Vyse, professor of psychology at Connecticut College and author of the book *Going Broke: Why Americans Can't Hold on to Their Money*, told USA TODAY. "If you want a new widescreen TV in your house in one day, you can do it. The effort involved in shopping has been reduced to nothing, and everyone is made to believe they can afford anything."

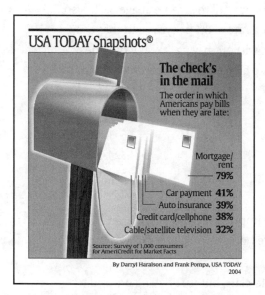

USA TODAY Snapshots®

The check's in the mail

The order in which Americans pay bills when they are late:

Mortgage/rent — **79%**
Car payment **41%**
Auto insurance **39%**
Credit card/cellphone **38%**
Cable/satellite television **32%**

Source: Survey of 1,000 consumers for AmeriCredit for Market Facts

By Darryl Haralson and Frank Pompa, USA TODAY
2004

It's unrealistic to expect that millions of credit-addicted Americans will suddenly stop purchasing things on credit. But that doesn't mean you can't commit to changing your own behavior.

In theory, you could simply lock up your credit cards for the months it will take to pay off the outstanding balance and get far enough ahead financially that you'll be able to pay cash for needed purchases. From then on, you could charge things only when you're sure you can pay your bill at the end of the month. Just say no to costly and largely bogus add-ons, such as credit card insurance.

Unfortunately, if you already have a large outstanding credit card balance, you've got some preliminary work to do—namely paying off your existing balances. Here are a few dos and don'ts to ease your task:

- **Do transfer balances to a card with a lower interest rate.** Make sure the new card lets you transfer your existing balance without a fee, and that your old card won't charge you a closing fee. Also watch out for cards that offer the lower interest rate only on the amount you transfer, but jack up the rate for new purchases. Learn which cards offer the best deals at www.cardweb. com or www.bankrate.com.

USA TODAY Snapshots®

Spending habits women find hardest to break

Eating out or getting takeout — 49%
Shopping for clothes — 28%
Daily coffee fix — 17%
Personal beauty products — 14%

Note: Respondents could select multiple answers.
Source: Harris Interactive QuickQuery of 1,202 women, Nov. 21-23. Margin of error ±4 percentage points.

By Mary Cadden and Julie Snider, USA TODAY 2006

- **Do pay off balances with a system.** You can't rely on the credit card companies to help you pay off debts— they'll keep recalculating your decreasing balance to maximize interest payments. You need to create a payment system and stick to it. The easiest way is to use an online calculator that helps you figure out how much you need to pay to get rid of outstanding card balances. Nolo (www.nolo.com/calculators) has one, as do many other sites, including www.bankrate.com.

- **Don't take out a home equity loan to pay off your cards unless you can definitely repay the loan within about two years.** If, like most people, you extend the home equity payments over a much longer period, you'll pay even more interest than if you'd taken a year to pay off your higher-interest credit card debt. And if you default, you could lose your house, which you'll have turned into collateral for the loan. On the plus side, the interest payments on home equity loans are tax deductible.

- **Don't take money from a retirement plan such as a 401(k) to pay off your debt.** Bad strategy, as USA TODAY's Sandra Block points out. You'll pay taxes on the withdrawal and a penalty if you're under 59½. In addition, you may never recoup your gains. Borrowing against the 401(k) also has risks, especially if you leave your job and will be required to pay it back within months or else face penalties and taxes. You'd be better off putting less into the 401(k) and using that money to pay off debts. (But put in at least enough to get your company's matching deposit, if any.)

And here are some additional ways to develop new habits around your use of credit cards:

- **Switch to a debit card.** As you probably know, debit cards, issued by many banks, immediately subtract the cost of a purchase from your bank account, at no added cost to you. This means if your bank account is empty, you'll be unable to make additional purchases. A similar strategy involves using a secured credit card, which allows you to charge only up to the amount you have deposited with the financial institution.

- **Talk about it.** As many as 47% of credit card holders refuse to tell a friend how much they owe. Don't be like them. Tell your friends—especially those who are also prone to pay with plastic—about your desire to pay off your current credit card balances and stop using credit for future purchases. They may be interested in joining you. If so, plan to get together or chat by phone or email regularly to compare progress. Just like losing weight or cutting down on drinking, a little support can make reaching your goal a lot easier.

- **Minimize your future use of credit cards.** Once you're on the road to recovery, keep one or two credit cards and use them only when you're sure you can pay your bill in full at month's end. To help you keep your resolution, put a piece of easy-to-remove tape across your credit card and use the card only after you remove the tape. This little reminder should slow you down enough to avoid unwise impulse buying.

Can't Stop Spending?

Kim Cole, financial counselor with debt-advice nonprofit Novadebt, prepared a list of statements. If you find yourself agreeing with these statements, you may be having trouble controlling your spending, and should seek help, for example by going to www .shopaholicsanonymous.org:

I can afford to make only the minimum payments on my credit cards.

I have to use my credit cards for necessity purchases such as groceries and utilities.

I have less than three months of salary in a savings account.

I have been turned down for credit in the past year.

I have nothing put away for retirement.

I have more than five credit cards with balances on them.

I run out of money before the end of the month, and I am not sure why.

Adding up the savings

To reiterate the point of this chapter—that excessive interest payments are a substantial hurdle on the road to a happy retirement—let's see what would happen if, over a 25-year period, an average couple (Tom and Elizabeth, both schoolteachers) committed to living as free of debt as possible. Instead of buying clothing, meals, gasoline, or a vacation on credit and paying interest for several months or more at a rate of almost 14% per year, they wait until they can afford to buy the same things for cash. (That doesn't mean they'll never use their credit cards, just that they'll use them only for things they know they can pay off by their next credit card statement.) Before, Tom and Elizabeth had been maintaining an average outstanding balance of $3,000 on their credit cards at 14% per year, paying $420 in interest yearly. It takes them less than 1½ years to pay off their outstanding balance at $200 per month.

Over Your Head in Debt?

Below, we list some of the common strategies you can employ to cope with overdue debts. For more information about these and other strategies, plus sample letters you can write to bill collectors, check the Nolo website or see *Solve Your Money Troubles: Get Debt Collectors Off Your Back & Regain Financial Freedom*, by Robin Leonard (Nolo). Other resources include books by popular financial gurus such as James Pond or Suze Orman.

- Pay them off gradually, concentrating first on those carrying the highest interest rates.
- Work with the nonprofit Consumer Credit Counseling Service or a similar group to help restructure your debts and reduce or stop ruinous interest payments while you pay them over time.
- Ask to have the debts rescheduled at a lower rate of interest if the debts are so high that you're contemplating bankruptcy.
- Negotiate with the creditor or collection agency to cancel the entire debt in exchange for one big payment that's considerably less than the total owed. If you're successful, ask a close family member or friend to lend you the money, interest-free.
- Declare bankruptcy, either Chapter 7, which wipes out most consumer debt but may require your giving up "secured assets" (possibly even your house), or Chapter 13, which allows you to reorganize your debts into manageable payments without losing any property.

Keeping track of the interest savings they achieve, our sensible couple first use this extra money to pay off other debts such as car and student loans. They decide not to purchase a new car right away, instead depositing half of their avoided car payments (about $150 per month) in what they label their new-car savings account. Their next priority is to fully fund their tax-sheltered 401(k) or other plans. After this is accomplished, they begin paying off their home mortgage early. They bought their house three years ago for $300,000, borrowing $204,425 on a fixed-rate mortgage with a 7% interest rate. Their payments are $1,360 per month.

By adding the $200 they've saved in credit card interest, plus the $150 they're saving on car payments to each month's mortgage check, they'll have the house paid off in less than 20 years.

Long before this happens, their new car account will be fat enough to allow them to trade in one of their old cars and purchase a new model. Once their house is paid off, they decide to put all the money they've been paying for their mortgage (about $1,635 per month) into a retirement savings fund. Over ten years, at an annual appreciation rate of 8%, this grows to over $299,000.

USA TODAY Snapshots®

Staying on track

Which is more challenging to stick to?

55%

A diet

45%

A budget

Source: Kelton Research for Medifast. Jan. 25-29 survey of 1,000 adults ages 18 and over; margin of error is ±3 percentage points.

By Cindy Clark and Julie Snider, USA TODAY 2006

Should You Prepay Your Mortgage?

The largest source of debt acquired by most households is a mortgage. No one expects you to pay the whole thing off at once. But prepaying even small but regular portions can produce substantial retirement savings, not to mention that owning your home is virtually a no-risk investment strategy. And paying off your mortgage while you're working means you'll have one less expense when you retire.

Is It Better to Invest Elsewhere or Prepay the Mortgage?

Although your house is a home, it's also an investment. So the question arises whether maxing out your real estate investment by prepaying your mortgage is the best use of your spare money—in other words, whether it wouldn't be better to take the cash and invest it in the stock market. The answer isn't cut and dried, but depends on your age, the success of your investments, and other factors.

In 2005, USA TODAY's Sandra Block, John Waggoner, and Mindy Fetterman wrote that paying off your mortgage while you're working is not a bad idea. Why? Simple. It's one less expense you'll have when you retire. This is especially true, they note, for homeowners closing in on retirement. "If you've been in your home a long time and have a lot of equity, you're probably not paying much interest, diminishing the tax benefits of a mortgage. And once you retire, you'll probably invest your savings more conservatively, making it more difficult to earn better returns than you'll get by paying off the mortgage."

If you're young, however, some financial planners advise against paying off your mortgage, since mortgage rates are low, and younger homeowners can theoretically earn better long-term returns in the stock market—assuming you have the wisdom, discipline, and luck to invest at a relatively high return.

There's one other strategy raised by some financial planners, who believe that instead of prepaying the mortgage, it may be wiser to invest extra money in a tax-sheltered retirement plan, such as a 401(k), an IRA, or a Keogh plan. This theory is based on the fact that the money you contribute to retirement-plan investments lowers your taxable income and therefore the amount of your income tax in the year you contribute it. Also, in case of emergency, you can borrow against the money in a retirement plan, paying interest to yourself, not a lender. Finally, if you have college-bound children who will be applying for financial assistance, it is also

Is It Better to Invest Elsewhere or Prepay the Mortgage?, cont'd.

important to know that money invested in retirement plans is not counted when judging aid eligibility, while money invested in home equity increases your family's net worth and therefore decreases the amount of financial help your kids qualify for. The obvious drawback to this strategy—you may be making house payments after you retire while your mortgage-free peers have no monthly housing payments.

RESOURCE
Find out how much faster you can pay off your mortgage with one of Nolo's online calculators. Go to www.nolo.com/calculator.cfm.

If you doubt whether this strategy can really free up significant amounts of cash, consider how much you could save if you didn't have to pay interest on your mortgage. Let's say you bought a house for $227,000, using a 10% down payment and a $204,300 fixed-rate mortgage at 6% interest for 30 years. Before you own the house free and clear, you'll pay more than $463,500. That's a lot of interest. Even allowing for the fact that inflation will mean that the dollars you repay in ten or 20 years will be worth less than they are today, that's still a remarkably large sum of money. If your house is more expensive and your mortgage bigger, you'll pay even more interest—as much as a half-million dollars on a house costing $300,000.

Why does paying a few extra dollars result in a mortgage being paid off so much faster? Simple. By paying down part of the principal of your mortgage now, you prevent interest from mounting up on that money for as many years as you have left on your mortgage. And the earlier you begin prepaying, the more you save. Below we've highlighted some common prepayment issues

What about prepayment penalties? Before you consider prepaying, check your mortgage agreement to make sure it doesn't charge you a fee for doing so (to compensate the lender for the lost interest). Most mortgages don't have a prepayment penalty, or the penalty runs out three to five years into the mortgage. Some adjustable-rate mortgages contain penalty clauses, but they're often limited to large paydowns early in the mortgage.

If your mortgage interest is tax deductible, why reduce it? It's almost always better to be out of debt than to claim the tax deduction. Paying $1 to a lender and getting back roughly 10¢ to 35¢ (depending on your tax bracket) at tax time is no bargain. In addition, the lower the tax rate—and tax rates are lower now than they were ten years ago—the less beneficial the deduction.

How much can you save? Plenty. By adding just $50 a month to your mortgage payment, you'd save $27,879 in interest over the life of the loan on a $200,000, 30-year mortgage at 6%. The table below shows how increasing your monthly payment on a 30-year fixed-rate mortgage will affect the time it will take to pay it off and the interest you'll owe. This table is based on the extra payments being made from the beginning of the loan. If you already have a mortgage, the earlier you start making extra payments, the sooner it will be paid off. Nolo (www .nolo.com/calculators) has a calculator that enables you to plug in the specifics to learn the advantages of prepaying your mortgage.

Goodbye Interest: Prepaying a 6%, Fixed-Rate, $200,000 Mortgage		
Amount of extra payment per month	Number of years in which you'll pay loan off	Interest saved over life of loan
$0	30	$0
$50	27	$27,789
$100	24.5	$49,138
$200	21	$79,800
$300	19	$101,106
$500	15	$129,142

How do you do it? If you plan to prepay, enclose a separate check with your regular mortgage payment. You may have to write "Principal only" or "Principal prepayment" on the check and enclose a note stating your purpose, unless your lender offers a box to check on its bill or a similar way to facilitate principal payments. This prevents the lender from later arguing that the extra money is really an early payment for next month. Some lenders will—for a fee—arrange to help with prepayments by having the money withdrawn from your bank account. A common way to calculate a reasonable prepayment is to add one more full monthly payment per year—that is, making 13 monthly payments a year instead of 12. In practice, you'd most likely want to spread this payment over the year, by taking the amount of one monthly mortgage payment, dividing it by 12, and adding that amount to each monthly payment. Some lenders permit biweekly mortgages, in which you pay half your monthly mortgage every other week. Over the course of a year, this also equals 13 rather than 12 monthly payments. Another strategy recommended by PBS financial expert James D. Pond is called "Doubling up the principal payment" in which, using a mortgage amortization table, you make the current month's payment of principal and interest and also pay the next month's principal. You cross out those two months on your table and 30 days later, pay the next two months, enabling you to pay off the mortgage in half the time.

When you prepay, why does the bank keep reducing your monthly payment? Monthly payments on adjustable-rate mortgages are commonly refigured once a year. A bank will take into account your lower principal and new interest rate to set a lower monthly payment. If your goal is to pay off your mortgage early, ignore what your bank says your minimum payment is, and keep making your original payment along with your monthly addition to it.

Isn't it better to pay off other debts than prepay a mortgage? Absolutely. Interest on credit card debt, personal financial loans, and car loans is not tax deductible. And chances are good that interest rates charged for these loans are much higher than for a home loan. It follows that before you prepay your mortgage, you should first pay off these other loans. One possible exception involves student loans, which often carry a relatively low rate of interest and can, in some circumstances, be rescheduled with no interest payments.

What else should come before prepayment of a mortgage? If your household doesn't have an emergency fund—enough to live on for six months—you're better off building that first. Similarly, if you lack adequate insurance, use the extra cash for those purposes. Finally, you may want to use extra cash to take full advantage of tax-advantaged retirement plans. (See "Is It Better to Invest Elsewhere or Prepay the Mortgage," above.)

USA TODAY Snapshots®

Retirees and outstanding mortgages
Percentage of retiree and near-retiree homeowners who have an outstanding mortgage on their primary home, in each group:

Just retired — 48%
Retired involuntarily — 53%
Expect to retire soon — 57%
Wanted to retire, but couldn't — 70%

Source: Prudential Financial survey of 1,023 workers ages 55 to 64 years old. Margin of error ±3 percentage points.

By Jae Yang and Adrienne Lewis, USA TODAY
2006

What about opting for a 15-year mortgage instead of a 30-year mortgage? Whether this is a good idea depends on your personal financial situation and who you ask. For example, if you trade in your current 6.8%, 30-year fixed-rate mortgage for a 15-year loan at 5.3%, you'll pay about 20% more per month, but of course you'll own your house much faster and at far less cost. Yet many financial experts consider it a better idea to stick with a 30-year mortgage, because of the flexibility. You can always pay it off in 15 years if you're flush with cash. Although 15-year mortgages usually have lower interest rates, they pose a challenge if your family cash flow gets tight and you find yourself hard-pressed to make the larger payments. ●

Where Will the Money Come From?

It's Not Too Late to Begin_____134

What to Expect From Social Security _____137

   Beyond Social Security's retirement program_____139

   Retirement benefits: How much will you receive?_____140

   When should you claim retirement benefits?_____141

   Are you a good candidate for early retirement?_____145

Employer Pension Plans_____148

   Basic questions to ask about your pension plan_____148

   Can you receive both a pension and Social Security?_____150

Individual Retirement Savings Plans: IRAs, and 401(k)s_____151

   401(k) and 403(b) plans _____152

   IRAs_____156

Withdrawing Money From Your 401(k), IRA, or Annuity____159

   Rules and penalties for early withdrawals_____159

   Withdrawal options at age 59½_____162

   Mandatory withdrawals at age 70½_____162

Savings and Investments_____164

Inheritances and Gifts_____164

   Planning for inheritances_____164

   Tax benefits of gifts_____168

Early Retirement Incentives and Buyouts_____169

Reverse Mortgages_____170

Immediate-Fixed Annuities_____173

S tephen M. Pollan, coauthor of *Die Broke*, once predicted that many baby boomers would never really retire; they'd need a paycheck, however reduced, as one of several income streams after turning 65. The other likely income streams, Pollan said, would be reverse mortgages (in which a bank pays you money in return for acquiring equity in your home); annuities; aggressive, smart investments; and the all-important 401(k) plan.

Pollan's prophecies have proven to be right on the money. Many boomers say they expect to continue working past retirement age, demand for reverse mortgages has grown exponentially, and nearly half of the ten trillion dollars now in mutual funds is held in 401(k) accounts.

In this chapter, we'll look at the nine common ways that potential retirees expect to fund their retirement, and the pros and cons of each. In the next chapter, we'll show you how to protect these assets and generate more income.

It's Not Too Late to Begin

If you're in your 30s, 40s, or early 50s and haven't saved much, don't fret. You still have time. As USA TODAY Reporter Dennis Cauchon noted, "[M]ost wealth accumulation happens rapidly and late in life—after the kids leave, when income is high, debts drop, 401(k) accounts fatten, and home equity swells. Income typically peaks at age 57 and wealth (a person's net worth—assets minus debts) tops out at 63, according to the Fed's Survey of Consumer Finance."

If you're already counting down the hours until retirement—perhaps you're in your early 60s— and you haven't done much planning, your job will be a bit harder, but don't panic. There are still ways of funding a livable, albeit more frugal retirement, including employment, Social Security, annuities, and reverse mortgages, as we discuss below.

How Baby Boomer Retirement Prep Is Going

If the government were grading baby boomer preparations for retirement, this generation would probably get a B. "[R]oughly half of boomer households are on track to accumulate enough wealth to maintain their current standard of living if the heads of those households retire when they now plan to," reported a 2004 Congressional Budget Office study.

"At the other end of the spectrum," the study said, "perhaps a quarter of the households—many of them low-income households with low-skilled workers—have accumulated very few assets thus far and are likely to find themselves largely dependent on government benefits in retirement.

"For some of those low-income households, Social Security benefits will be sufficient to let them maintain their working-age consumption (because Social Security benefits replace a larger share of previous earnings for low-income households than for high-income ones). Nevertheless, other households in the low-saving group could face a decline in their standard of living in retirement."

Nine Common Methods of Funding Retirement	
Social Security retirement benefits	The age at which you claim benefits—between 62 and 70—determines the fixed amount of your monthly retirement checks and whether deductions will be taken for continued employment.
Employer pension plans	Employees who work for corporations or federal, state, or local governments stand to receive significant employer pension income—in some cases over and above Social Security. The amount depends on the amount you earned, how long you worked, and how benefits are paid.
Tax-advantaged retirement savings plans—Keogh, SEP-IRA, IRA, 401(k), 403(b), and Roth IRA	These tax-deferred retirement plans let you accumulate money tax-free until you withdraw it. (Note: Roth IRAs are unique among retirement plans in that they provide for tax free distributions and—in some cases—investment earnings are not taxed on withdrawal, either.)
Savings	Savings generally refers to any non-tax-deferred accumulation of cash—whether in CDs, government bonds, or savings accounts.
Inheritances and gifts	Trillions of dollars in inheritances may change hands in coming decades. However, longer life expectancies, soaring health care costs, and high long-term care costs have chipped away at many of these nest eggs. Nevertheless, advantageous federal tax rules may motivate some affluent elders to make monetary gifts to their retiring family members.
Early retirement bonuses or buyouts	Cash, pension benefits, and enhanced health benefits are often offered by downsizing employers, providing seed money for retirement accounts.
Reverse mortgages	With a reverse mortgage, you trade some or all of your equity in the house for tax-free income from a bank or other lender. The payment can be in cash, monthly payments, or a line of credit you draw on as needed (or a combination of the three).
Annuities	An annuity is a gamble based on your life expectancy. You pay a lump sum to an insurance company, which pays you a guaranteed monthly income either for a fixed term, until death, or until your surviving spouse's death.
Working part- or full-time after retirement	Whether continuing at their present jobs, or "rewiring" for new part-time or full-time jobs, it's expected that at least half of people reaching retirement age will continue laboring in some capacity—often into their seventies. (We discuss working after retirement in Chapter 10.)

What to Expect From Social Security

First, let's address the elephant in the corner. Will the Social Security system survive? A 2007 U.S. Treasury report indicated that the gap between what Social Security is expected to pay in benefits and what it will raise in payroll taxes in coming years is an incredible $13.6 trillion. The report's proposed solution: raise taxes and lower benefits. Democrats objected to lowering benefits; Republicans objected to raising taxes. The White House took the middle road and announced, "The president is not advocating for tax increases or benefit cuts." Why are politicians treading so fearfully? The baby boomer generation on the verge of receiving Social Security (approximately 78 million Americans) is simply too big a voting bloc to offend. And that ballot power is the reason why many people believe that Social Security will be kept alive, although with some tweaks.

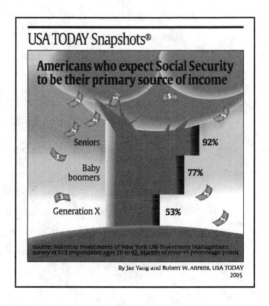

USA TODAY Snapshots®

Americans who expect Social Security to be their primary source of income

Seniors — 92%
Baby boomers — 77%
Generation X — 53%

Source: MainStay Investments of New York Life Investment Management survey of 515 respondents ages 26 to 82. Margin of error ±5 percentage points.

By Jae Yang and Robert W. Ahrens, USA TODAY
2005

Here's some more to consider. Social Security payouts are expected to exceed incoming payroll tax revenues around the year 2017. That's not a "cataclysmic" occurrence, according to research by the AARP, because incoming tax revenues combined with interest earnings are still expected to be enough to pay benefits. The so-called manure is not expected to hit the cooling device until about 2041 (even if no changes are made to the system). At that point, something will need to be done to extend Social Security's life.

What's the solution? One macabre proposal offered in Christopher Buckley's satire, *Boomsday*, is for seniors to voluntarily kill themselves in return for special predeath benefits (no estate taxes, free botox injections, etc.). The more realistic suggested solutions to the Social Security crisis include:

> *Thanks in large part to Social Security, the number of older Americans below the poverty line has dropped from almost 50% to only 8%.*

- raising (or eliminating) the cap on wages subject to Social Security (in 2008 individuals are taxed on income up to $102,000)

- raising the age at which retirees can claim full benefits

- reducing benefits for affluent retirees, and

- investing some of the Social Security surplus in higher-interest securities.

Although we're optimistic that Social Security will survive, you may disagree and believe that the system is heading off the rails. If so, calculate your needs (see Chapter 6) accordingly—that is, eliminate or cut your Social Security expectations when calculating your Number.

What About the Medicare Crisis?

The Medicare system may be facing greater challenges than Social Security. Consider these facts: Medicare's hospital fund now pays out more than it takes in. The fund is expected to run out of money in 2019. Fixing Medicare would require a 122% payroll tax hike or a 51% reduction in spending. Ouch! Even worse, Medicare's payments for doctors and prescription drugs are expected to rise faster than the nation's overall economic growth. At least the Congressional Budget Office is recognizing this threat, and has revamped Medicare's operation to find new ways to lower costs.

 "Social Security hits first wave of boomers," by Richard Wolf, October 9, 2007.

Beyond Social Security's retirement program

The Social Security Administration (SSA) does more than send monthly checks to retired persons. It's a collection of government programs that pays benefits to retired workers, disabled workers, or workers' dependent or surviving family members. Although we focus on retirement benefits in this chapter, let's take a moment to familiarize you with all four programs. After all, you may someday meet the eligibility rules for more than one—for example, you might become eligible for benefits based on your own retirement as well as that of your retired spouse. Check the SSA website for eligibility, but generally you can collect whichever one of these benefits is higher, but not both. Social Security's four programs are:

- **Disability benefits.** If you're younger than 65 but have met the work requirements and are considered disabled under the Social Security program's medical guidelines, you can receive disability benefits. The amount of these benefits will be roughly equal to what your retirement benefits would be.

- **Dependents benefits.** If you're married to a retired or disabled worker who qualifies for Social Security retirement or disability benefits, you and your minor or disabled children may be entitled to benefits based on your spouse's earning record. This is true whether or not you actually depend on your spouse for your support. Married recipients should determine whether they would receive a greater sum from the combination of one Social Security benefit and one dependent benefit or from two Social Security retirement benefits (assuming both partners are entitled to one). Each person may be awarded retirement or dependent benefits, but not both.

- **Survivors benefits.** If you are the surviving spouse of a worker who qualified for Social Security retirement or disability benefits, you and your minor or disabled children may be entitled to benefits based on your deceased spouse's earnings record.

- **Retirement benefits.** This is the program we'll be focused on in this chapter. It provides benefits to workers, regardless of financial need, based on how long they've worked and how much they've paid into the system.

RESOURCE

Looking for details? The information we provide about Social Security and pensions incorporates material from attorney Joe Matthews' excellent book, *Social Security, Medicare & Government Pensions: Get the Most Out of Your Retirement & Medical Benefits* (Nolo).

Retirement benefits: How much will you receive?

Assuming you've worked for approximately ten years in jobs covered by Social Security, you should be eligible for some level of retirement benefits. The question is, how much? Because predicting this is such a crucial first step in budgeting for retirement, the SSA periodically mails out a document called "Your Social Security Statement." If for some reason you've never received this estimate of how much money you'll receive each month after you retire, call 800-772-1213, contact your local Social Security office, or go to www.ssa.gov/mystatement to request a copy. If you're not comfortable sending information via the Internet, you may download the Social Security Statement request form (SSA-7004) and mail it in. Or you can estimate your benefits by going to www.ssa.gov/retire2/ and clicking on "calculators."

As a ballpark figure, expect the amount of your retirement benefits to be between 20% of your average income (if your income is high) and 50% (if your income is low). For a 65-year-old single person first claiming retirement benefits in 2007, the average benefit is about $1,000 per month; it's $1,700 for a couple. The highest earners first claiming their benefits in 2007 at age 65 receive about $2,100 per month, or $2,700 per couple. These benefits increase yearly with the cost of living.

Other factors that will affect the amount of your Social Security check include how much you earn over all the years you work until you retire, future cost-of-living adjustments to benefit eligibility amounts, your date of birth, the type of benefit (such as retirement or survivors benefits) you are eligible for, and the age at which you claim retirement benefits.

Who's Not Covered by Social Security?

Some state and local government employees, most federal workers hired before 1984, and railroad workers are covered under separate pension plans and not by Social Security. Of course, if these employees also worked for a sufficient length of time in another job covered by Social Security, they are eligible for dual benefits. For more information, see *Social Security, Medicare & Government Pensions: Get the Most Out of Your Retirement & Medical Benefits*, by Joseph Matthews (Nolo).

When should you claim retirement benefits?

Deciding the age at which you'd like to begin receiving Social Security retirement benefits is like making a game-show choice: Should you go for the lower-dollar option at age 62—an immediate sure thing—or should you wait until full retirement age and get bigger monthly checks for the years that remain? (See "What's Your Full Retirement Age?" below.) To help you estimate how much you'd qualify for at each age, the SSA offers online calculators at www.ssa.gov. See your Social Security Statement for a personalized comparison of retirement benefits at age 62, at full retirement age, and at age 70. Let's look at what you're owed at each of these three ages:

- **If you claim benefits before full retirement age.** Approximately three-quarters of retirees claim benefits as soon as they turn 62 (referred to as "early retirement"). If you claim early retirement, you'll receive less than you would have if you'd waited until full retirement age—approximately 20% to 30% less. Your benefits permanently increase 7% for each year between age 62 and your full retirement age. Imagine you were to retire at age 62 after earning an average of $75,000 a year. You'd receive $15,888 in Social Security annually from retirement until the end of your life (the amount wouldn't go up at your full retirement age, probably 66). If your full retirement age was 66, and you waited until then to start receiving benefits, you'd receive $21,181 annually. Curious about the totals? This would come out to $222,423 if you started at age 62 and lived to be 75, or $211,810 if you started at age 66 and lived to be 75. (These annual amounts may vary based on cost-of-living increases built into the payment system.)

Fix Errors in Your Social Security Statement

Employers make mistakes in wage reports about 4% of the time. The result is that one dollar out of every $100 reported to Social Security fails to be credited to the correct worker's record. Most of these mistakes occur when workers have used more than one name—such as women who've changed their name when they marry or divorce. So don't just take a two-second look at your statement before tossing it onto a pile of paperwork.

If you believe a mistake has been made, you can do something about it, even if it concerns wages from years past. Many errors are easy to spot—incorrect Social Security numbers or employer income that doesn't match what you reported on your income tax—but some may require more diligence to track, perhaps by contacting old employers.

When you have evidence that the SSA has made an error, call its helpline at 800-772-1213, Monday through Friday from 7 a.m. to 12 p.m. Eastern time. (This is the line that takes all kinds of Social Security questions, and it's often swamped, so be patient. It's best to call early in the morning or late in the afternoon, late in the week, and late in the month.) Have all your documents ready for when you speak with a representative.

> (!) CAUTION
>
> **Choose carefully:** Once you start claiming retirement benefits, you can't change your mind and stop.

What's Your Full Retirement Age?	
Year Born	Full Retirement Age
Before 1938	65
1938	65 years, 2 months
1939	65 years, 4 months
1940	65 years, 6 months
1941	65 years, 8 months
1942	65 years, 10 months
1943 - 1954	66 years
1955	66 years, 2 months
1956	66 years, 4 months
1957	66 years, 6 months
1958	66 years, 8 months
1959	66 years, 10 months
1960 or later	67 years

- **If you claim benefits at full retirement age.** In this scenario, you claim benefits at age 65 or higher, depending on the year in which you were born. (See "What's Your Full Retirement Age?" above.) Although this entitles you to "full" retirement benefits, you're actually given an incentive to wait even longer, as described next.

- **If you claim benefits after full retirement age.** From your full retirement age until you reach age 70, the SSA will increase your benefits by the percentage shown on the chart below. As you can see, baby boomers will earn a whopping 8% more for each year they delay until age 70. Remember the example above in which you could have received $15,888 annually if you retired at age 62 and $21,181 annually if you'd waited until age 66? Under that same set of facts, if you were to wait until age 70, you'd receive $28,821 annually, an 81% increase in monthly payments over claiming them at age 62.

You'll be in good company: Two-thirds of the people in human history who lived beyond age 65 are still alive today.

Increase Per Year in Benefits for Delayed Retirement After Full Retirement Age	
Year born	Percentage increase
1927 - 1928	4.0
1929 - 1930	4.5
1931 - 1932	5.0
1933 - 1934	5.5
1935 - 1936	6.0
1937 - 1938	6.5
1939 - 1940	7.0
1941 - 1942	7.5
1943 or later	8.0

Which approach is best? Should you take the money and run at age 62? Or hold out until you're 70—at the risk of poor health and an early death—in pursuit of the largest possible monthly retirement benefits check? Approximately 75% of people don't wait past age 62, usually because they need the money, are convinced that Social Security might collapse at a later date, or are fearful of a short life span.

Are you a good candidate for early retirement?

There are some people for whom it makes sense to claim early retirement, despite the permanent reduction in benefit amounts. The questions below will help you decide whether you're one of them.

- **Have you stopped working?** For some people, especially construction workers and other physical laborers, their bodies at age 62 can't take any more work though they don't qualify for disability. They may be good candidates for early retirement (between 62 and full retirement age). However, if you're still able-bodied and interested in working, you might want to avoid claiming early retirement benefits. If you're earning a high salary, you'll miss the opportunity to boost your Social Security payment amount. (Your monthly payments are fixed based on the average of your top 35 earning years. But once you elect to receive benefits, you can't continue to up your average based on later Social Security contributions.) Second, you'll lose one dollar in benefits for every two dollars you earn over the SSA's Earnings Limits ($12,960 in 2007). There are no such deductions if you work after reaching full retirement age. The SSA provides an online calculator to determine whether working will lower your retirement benefits; it's at www.ssa.gov/OACT/COLA/RTeffect.html. Also, we'll talk more about working after retirement in Chapter 10.

- **How's your health?** If you're convinced—either by genetics, research, or the amount of time you spend in doctors' offices— that you'll have a shorter lifespan than your peers, it doesn't make much sense to delay your retirement benefits. Of course, if you had a good idea of when you were to die, you could compare your total benefit payments under all three common scenarios—age 62, full retirement age, and age 70. Financial planners prefer to calculate your break-even point—that's the age at which two of your total lifetime benefit amounts become equal to each other— for example, when total lifetime benefits claimed beginning at age

62 equal total lifetime benefits claimed beginning at age 66. If you believe you'll live past your this age (referred to as the "break-even" age), you should delay claiming benefits until the later of the two dates, in order to give yourself an overall higher total. Find out this number using the SSA's Break-Even Age calculator (pictured below, and located by going to www.ssa.gov and searching for "break-even calculator").

Social Security Online	Benefit Calculators				Search	GO

Break-Even Age
Updated October 24, 2005

Introduction
At your break-even age, the accumulated value of higher benefits (from postponing retirement) will start to exceed the accumulated value of lower benefits (from choosing early retirement). To use this form, you will need benefit estimates, in today's dollars, for each age at which you may wish to retire. An excellent source for such estimates is your Social Security Statement.

Enter your information
Replace the example values with the numbers you want to use.

Enter the *earlier* retirement age: 62 years and 1 month(s)
Enter the corresponding monthly benefit amount: $ 900

Enter the *later* retirement age: 65 years and 10 month(s)
Enter the corresponding monthly benefit amount: $ 1251
(Compute)

Estimated break-even age
Your estimated break-even age is _____.
If you expect to live beyond this age, it would be to your advantage to delay your retirement.

Note: interest is not considered in the calculation.

Break-Even Table: Comparison Between Total Benefits When Claiming at Ages 62 or Full Retirement Age

Age When You Start to Claim Benefits	Amount of Monthly Benefit	How Much You Will Have Collected by Age 72	How Much You Will Have Collected by Age 75 Years and 7 Months (in this case, the break-even age)	How Much You Will Have Collected by Age 85
62	$1,315	$173,580	$213,245	$362,940
66	$1,860	$156,240	$213,900	$424,080

- **Are you married?** If one spouse has contributed far less to Social Security than the other, the greater-contributing spouse should ideally wait longer to claim benefits—at least until full retirement age. Then if the higher-earning spouse dies first, the survivor can claim the spouse's full benefit. For many couples, it pays for the wife to start collecting at 62 and for the husband to wait. This is because husbands are likely to die first; when that happens, the widow can collect based on his, typically higher, benefits. It's all probability, of course, and changing right along with other societal changes.

- **What will you do with the money?** Claiming early benefits makes sense if you need the money for necessities—though that's also a sign that you're not saving enough, and should, if you're physically able, continue working longer. But claiming early benefits simply to augment an already-comfortable annual income doesn't make much sense. If you planned to invest the money, your investments would need to earn more than 7% annually to equal what you'd make by delaying benefits until full retirement age.

- **Do you have dependents?** Your family's dependents and survivors benefits may be reduced if you claim early retirement benefits. Before deciding, investigate the effects at the SSA website (www.ssa.gov).

Will Your Social Security Benefits Be Taxed?

You'll have to pay taxes on Social Security benefits if your postretirement "combined income" falls within certain IRS guidelines. If it's between $25,000 and $34,000 and you're a single person, or between $32,000 and $44,000 and you file jointly as a married couple (in 2007), you may have to pay income taxes on 50% of your Social Security income. If your "combined income" exceeds these guidelines (more than $34,000 for a single person or $44,000 for a couple), you may have to pay tax on 85% of your Social Security income. Your "combined income" is your adjusted gross income, plus any nontaxable interest income, plus one-half of your annual Social Security benefits.

Employer Pension Plans

Many federal, state, and local government employees are in line for generous pensions. Private employers are another matter—many of them began dissolving their pension systems in the early 1990s, turning pensions in the private sector into an endangered species.

If you're eligible for a pension, how much you'll receive will, of course, depend on the details of your particular plan. The most important factors in determining the size of your monthly check tend to be how long you worked for the employer, how much money you made, and how you specify that your benefits will be paid—for example, as a lump sum, monthly payments during your life, or lower monthly payments during your life in exchange for continuing benefits for the life of a survivor. Ask your employer for a detailed description of your pension plan, including explanations of the participation rules and benefit amounts, how benefits accrue and become locked in (vested), payment options, and claims procedures. If you don't get good answers, talk to your pension plan administrator.

Basic questions to ask about your pension plan

Here's what you'll want to learn before factoring your pension into your retirement budget:

- **When does your pension vest?** Under most plans, you have no rights to a pension until you've worked for your employer (or another employer, if your pension rights are transferred) for a certain number of years. At that point, the pension vests, which means you have a legal right to receive benefits, commonly by a certain age. Often your right to at least a modest pension will vest after ten years of service, although some plans provide limited vesting after just five years. To receive a good-sized pension, you'll probably need to work for an employer for at least 20 or 30 years.

- **Will your pension be adjusted for inflation?** Many plans—especially for public employees—index the benefit levels to inflation, meaning that as the value of the dollar goes down, your pension amount goes up. Unfortunately, lots of pensions do not adjust for inflation, which means the purchasing power of the money you receive is likely to decrease if you live for many years after retirement.

- **Should you take monthly pension payments or a lump sum?** Some employers let you choose between taking monthly payments until death (similar to an annuity, described below) and receiving a lump sum payment when you retire. Since lump sum offers are often in the hundreds of thousands of dollars, this is a good time to consult a financial adviser. Your adviser may weigh several factors, including:

  - **Is the company's pension plan healthy?** Even if your plan is federally insured by the Pension Benefit Guaranty Corporation (most are), many companies underfund their pensions. (It's estimated that plans insured by the PBGC are underfunded by several hundred billion dollars). (Note: In the event that a plan goes under, the PBGC insures up to a maximum guaranteed annual benefit of $47,659 for a single life pension, payable as an annuity over the life of the participant.) You can request information about any funding shortfalls from your pension plan administrator.

  - **Can you do better by investing the lump sum payment?** The purchasing power of your fixed monthly payment would—with a 3% to 4% annual inflation rate—likely be halved after two decades. Could you earn more by investing the lump sum?

  - **Do you want to leave money to your heirs?** If you choose to receive monthly payments from your pension, the payments will stop when you die. But if you elect to take a lump sum instead, the remainder becomes part of your estate after death.

- **What about disabled veteran pensions?** There are two different benefits available to disabled veterans; you can collect only one of them. "Disability compensation" is available to veterans who are disabled as a result of active military service. Benefits range from $100 to $2,100 per month, depending on the degree of disability. In addition, pension-style payments are available to low-income, wartime veterans who suffer from a permanent and total disability not incurred during military duty. These pensions run about $800 per month ($1,000 for a veteran with a dependent child or spouse, and slightly higher for each additional dependent). For more information on eligibility and other rules, contact the U.S. Department of Veterans Affairs (www.va.gov) and refer to *Social Security, Medicare & Government Pensions*, by Joseph Matthews (Nolo).

Looking to retire and play golf? Maricopa County, Arizona, has more than 150 golf courses.

Can you receive both a pension and Social Security?

How does receiving a pension affect your right to Social Security? The answer to this question can be extremely complicated. In a nutshell:

- **Some pensions are completely separate from Social Security.** With these, you receive your entire pension check plus all Social Security benefits for which you're eligible, making for a potentially comfortable retirement. For example, consider Enid and Walter McDougal. Both work at jobs covered by pensions that are indexed to increase with inflation. Assuming both continue working for another ten years, their combined pension income will be about $38,000 per year. When combined with the approximately $21,000 they will receive each year from Social Security, the McDougals will have enough to cover their expected retirement expenses.

- **Some private pension plans are integrated with Social Security.** This means your monthly pension check will be reduced by all or some of the amount of your Social Security check. Integrated plans must, however, leave you with at least half of your pension check.

- **If you work for a state or local government, you may get a good pension but no Social Security.** For example, the State of California has its own pension system, and some employees do not pay into Social Security. In addition, most federal government employees hired before 1984 and most railroad workers are covered by separate plans. In this situation, you'll receive Social Security benefits only if you've also worked at other jobs for the total required length of time.

> **TIP**
> **Not getting the pension answers you need from your employer?** You can access information about and assistance with your legal rights from the Pensions Rights Center, www.pensionsrights.org.

Individual Retirement Savings Plans: IRAs and 401(k)s

By now, you may have concluded that neither the government nor your employer is going to provide you with a fully padded retirement cushion. That's the reason most workers rely instead on voluntary retirement savings plans, such as IRAs or 401(k)s. These plans offer tax breaks during the years you make contributions and provide retirement income in later years.

We'll talk about the various types of plans below, but let's start with one general piece of advice: Most retirement accounts ask you to choose among various places to invest your money, including mutual funds that then invest in a variety of stocks and bonds. One thing these funds usually have in common is that they charge fees. Unless you keep an eye on the fee amounts you're being charged, you could end up earning much less than you otherwise might have.

As USA TODAY reporter John Waggoner explains, "Suppose the Wombat fund earns 10% annually, but takes two percentage points a year in fees. The Bull Moose fund also earns 10% a year, but takes just one percentage point of that a year in fees. After 50 years, a $10,000 investment in the Wombat fund will grow to $469,000. Your Bull Moose fund investment will grow to $754,500—nearly $286,000 more."

401(k) and 403(b) plans

Many companies offer workers the opportunity to participate in a 401(k) plan (called a 403(b) if you work for a nonprofit organization). The big incentive to participate is that the money you contribute to your account is not taxed in the year it's earned. It continues to accumulate—with tax-free investment earnings—until you withdraw it, at any time after age 59½. Once you commence withdrawals, either

in installments or as one lump sum, you owe income tax on the money you receive at your current tax rate. This is often lower than the tax bracket you would have been in at the time you were making the contributions. Certain withdrawals aren't subject to these rules, and different rules apply to a 401(k) that you convert to a tax-deferred IRA. (Both are described more below.)

USA TODAY Snapshots®

Americans who expect a defined-contribution plan, such as a 401(k), to be their primary source of retirement income

71%
63%
45%

Generation X
Baby boomers
Seniors

Source: MainStay Investments of New York Life Investment Management survey of 515 respondents ages 26 to 82. Margin of error ±5 percentage points.

By Jae Yang and Dave Merrill, USA TODAY 2005

What's the savings advantage of a 401(k)? Over the years, the 401(k) tax incentives combine to allow you to save far more than would have otherwise been possible. But it gets better if, as is common, your employer makes a contribution to your account. For example, if your employer kicks in 50%, you'll receive an additional $50 for every $100 you have taken out of your paycheck, up to the plan (or the employer's) limits. For 2008, the IRS limits on employee contributions are $16,000 per year, or $21,000 if you're 50 or older. Over one third of all companies match 100% of employee contributions.

What if you're self-employed? You can set up a solo 401(k), to which you can contribute whenever you choose, up to certain limits.

How much money will you have in your 401(k) or 403(b) account when you retire? That depends on how much you contribute each year, how much (if anything) your employer contributes, how many years you make contributions for, whether you borrow money from your plan, and how well the investments you choose perform over the years. (We discuss choosing investments in Chapter 9.) See the table below for an example of how the savings can add up—and notice that the earlier you start, the better you'll do. This can be true even when your earlier investments don't fare as well.

Comparison of 401(k) Savings With Different Starting Ages (Contribution Amounts and Return Rates)				
Age at Which You Begin Contributing	Annual Contribution	Annual Employer match	Annual Return on Investment	What You'll have at Age 66
45	$5,000	$500	6%	$219,960
30	$4,000	None	4%	$310,393

How much should you deposit into your 401(k) account? For starters, don't miss out on the chance to collect your employer's matching amount, if any. After that, putting in as much as you can, while still paying your bills and meeting other financial goals, is an easy and practical way to prepare for retirement. Even if you get partway through the year and realize you're having too much taken from your paycheck, you can change your mind and reduce it. You can also do the opposite if you feel you're having too little withdrawn (but are you really going to remember to do that)?

> **CAUTION**
> **Don't cash out if you switch to a new job.** The moment your money leaves your 401(k) account—even if it's because you get a check in your name that you plan to deposit into your next employer's 401(k)—it's considered a distribution. Any distribution is subject to both income tax and a 10% penalty if you're under age 59½. Instead, make sure you do a "rollover," using a "trustee-to-trustee transfer." You can transfer the money directly into a new 401(k), or better yet, as USA TODAY's Sandra Block advises, into an IRA: "Your money will grow, tax-deferred, until you take withdrawals. And you'll have more investment options than those offered by your 401(k) plan." You can still open a new 401(k) at your new job.

Why not invest it all in your employer's stock? Ideally, your 401(k) plan should allow you to choose from a wide selection of top-quality stock, bond, and money market funds, including ones that charge low fees. Less ideal plans limit an employee to a few higher-fee investments. The worst plans, such as that of the infamous Enron, force employees to make substantial investments in the employer's own stock. That's a risky idea even if you work for a good company. As USA TODAY's John Waggoner explains, "You've already invested your biggest asset—you—in the company. Your future earnings and, therefore, your future investments are riding on your company already.... But more important, an individual stock is, by definition, riskier than the overall market of thousands of stocks."

Should a Married Couple Fund Two Separate 401(k)s?

If you and your spouse don't have enough spare cash to fully fund your two separate 401(k)s, it may make sense for you to combine your resources and fund one plan, and then not fund or only partially fund the other plan. This is particularly true if one of the 401(k) plans is substantially better than the other one. Instead of each spouse contributing $5,500 to his or her own plan, for example, they could contribute $11,000 to the plan that offers a better deal (such as a higher employer match, better investment choices, or lower fees).

One word of caution: Couples who have doubts about their marriage should contribute to their own retirement accounts. Even though pension plan assets are usually divided at divorce, it's always a good idea to keep as many assets as possible in your own name if your marriage is shaky.

Is it okay to borrow against a 401(k) before you retire? Approximately 50% of 401(k) plans permit you to make short-term loans (usually up to $50,000 or half of what's in your account, whichever is less) as a nontaxable distribution against your 401(k) before you retire. Some administrators limit these loans for medical, educational, or other purposes. These short-term loans are usually for a maximum of five years. Approximately 75% of 401(k) administrators allow long-term loans for home buying. These loans usually must be repaid in 15 years, though some plans give you as long as 30 years. Financial advisers advise against taking out these types of loans before you retire, because you must pay back pretax dollars using after-tax money. In addition, you'll lose the interest you could have earned in your retirement account. And if your purpose is to buy a home, the 401(k) loan makes even less sense, because the loan is not tax deductible. If you take a home equity loan instead, you can deduct the interest on your taxes. Finally, if you haven't repaid the loan by the time your share of plan assets is distributed to you, the loan amount will be subject to income tax. One other warning: Typically, if you lose your job after taking the loan, you'll have 30 to 90 days to pay it off.

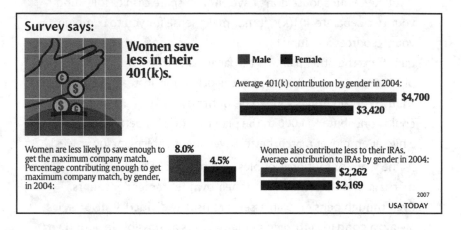

Survey says:

Women save less in their 401(k)s.

■ Male ■ Female

Average 401(k) contribution by gender in 2004:

$4,700

$3,420

Women are less likely to save enough to get the maximum company match. Percentage contributing enough to get maximum company match, by gender, in 2004:

8.0%

4.5%

Women also contribute less to their IRAs. Average contribution to IRAs by gender in 2004:

$2,262

$2,169

2007

USA TODAY

IRAs

In 1974, Congress passed the Employment Retirement Income Security Act (ERISA), and the world of retirement savings has never been the same. Among other things, ERISA established individual retirement arrangements (IRAs). Three decades later, one-quarter of this country's retirement investments—some three and a half trillion dollars—is kept in IRAs.

USA TODAY Snapshots®

Many rely on IRAs

Americans who expect IRAs to be their primary source of income:

Seniors **66%**

Baby boomers **61%**

Generation X **58%**

Source: MainStay Investments of New York Life Investment Management survey of 515 respondents ages 26 to 82. Margin of error: ±5 percentage points.

By Jae Yang and Karl Gelles, USA TODAY 2005

Like 401(k) plans, IRAs are retirement accounts that offer various tax benefits (depending on the type of IRA) and a variety of investment options within the account. However, instead of your employer administering it, you start your own IRA, through a trust company, bank, federally insured credit union, savings and loan association, or other IRS-approved entity. IRAs fall into several categories:

- **Traditional Contributory IRA.** A traditional IRA permits you to deposit up to $5,000 per year (2008 figures), or $6,000 if you'll reach age 50 by the end of 2008. You receive a tax deduction for the amount you contribute. However, your maximum deduction may be reduced if you contribute to your employer's 401(k) or other retirement plan.

- **Simplified Employee Pension (SEP) IRA.** Designed for small businesses and the self-employed, the SEP has higher contribution limits than a traditional IRA—as much as 25% of your annual compensation, up to a maximum contribution of $45,000 in tax year 2007 (subject to annual cost-of-living adjustments for later years). The amount placed in a SEP IRA is not taxed until you withdraw it.

- **SIMPLE IRA.** You might be offered this kind of IRA if you work for an employer with 100 or fewer employees. It permits you to have withdrawals taken from your salary up to $10,500 in tax year 2007 or $12,500 if you reach age 50 by the end of the year (subject to annual cost-of-living adjustments for later years). These are expected to increase to $11,000 and $13,500 respectively in 2008.

- **Roth IRA.** Unlike other IRAs, you must pay income tax on your money before depositing it into a Roth IRA . But here's why Roth IRAs have become increasingly popular: You won't pay tax on your eventual withdrawals (provided you are age 59½ and have held the account for at least five years), meaning you escape whatever high income tax rates may be imposed in the future. Also, you can continue contributing to a Roth IRA for as long as you earn income (unlike the 70½ year age limit for other IRA contributions). The annual contribution limits are the same as a traditional contributory IRA. However, there are income limits, as shown in the table below, based upon which the IRS begins to phase out your ability to make Roth IRA contributions.

Because of the advantages offered by Roth IRAs, converting your regular IRA to a Roth IRA can look like a wise move. But research the tax implications first—they can be thorny. For one thing, your taxation may be affected by the timing of the withdrawal from the original IRA and the subsequent withdrawal from the Roth IRA. To start your research, try using one of the many IRA-to-Roth IRA calculators on the Internet.

Phaseout of Roth IRA Contributions Based on Income Level (Modified AGI, or MAGI*)		
Filing status	MAGI at which Roth IRA phaseout begins (2007)	MAGI at which you cannot make a Roth IRA contribution (2007)
Married filing jointly or qualifying widow(er) and	$156,000	$166,000
Unmarried single filer	$99,000	$114,000

*Your modified AGI (MAGI) is your adjusted gross income plus various items including deductions for student loans, deductions for regular IRA contributions, and other tax breaks. Learn more about calculating your MAGI at the IRS website (type "Modified Adjusted Gross Income" into the search box at www.irs.gov).

Where to Invest the Money in Your IRA (Traditional or Roth)

We'll talk about investment strategies in Chapter 9, but here's some simple advice from USA TODAY's John Waggoner: "The more time you have before you retire, the more stocks and stock funds you should have in your IRA. This has nothing to do with taxes. Over a long period, stocks tend to fare better than bonds or risk-free investments, such as Treasury bills or bank CDs."

TIP

If your income is too high for a Roth, plan for 2010. That's the year in which everyone, regardless of income, will be allowed to convert traditional IRAs into Roth IRAs. The income limits for Roth conversions will be suspended from then until 2012. Although you'll pay income tax when you convert, it may be worth it to gain the tax savings in later years when you make withdrawals. Some experts advise putting money into a regular IRA now in anticipation of converting.

Withdrawing Money From Your 401(k), IRA, or Annuity

Yes, it's your money, but ... the government has created various incentives and disincentives to make sure you wait to use it for its intended purpose, namely your retirement. We'll alert you to those rules here, as part of explaining the pros and cons of each type of retirement plan. For a preview of what decisions you'll need to make when you're closer to retirement, see the advice from USA TODAY's Kathy Chu under "What to Withdraw First," below.

Rules and penalties for early withdrawals

To discourage you from removing money from your tax-deferred IRA, 401(k), annuity, or other qualified plan too soon, the IRS applies a 10% early-withdrawal tax. Any withdrawals you make before reaching the somewhat ripe age of 59½ are considered "early." In addition, any withdrawals from a Roth IRA before the money has been in the account for least five years are considered early. And if the 10% penalty isn't enough to keep your hands away from the cookie jar, remember that you will likely owe income taxes on the withdrawal (though not for qualified contributions to Roth IRAs). So if you're in the 25% tax bracket, you'd pay $350 in taxes for every $1,000 you withdrew under this system ($100 in early withdrawal tax plus $250 in income tax).

There is no 10% tax on funds you withdraw before age 59½ if:

- you are dead (that lets your heirs access the account)
- you are disabled, as defined in IRS rules
- you take substantially equal monthly installments (similar to an annuity) over your life (this is a complex exemption; review IRS guidelines before initiating it)
- you are over 55 and leave your job, in which case you can claim the benefits from that employer's 401(k) (but not from your IRAs)
- you use the money to pay for your (or certain family members') medical expenses, provided that the expenses exceed 7.5% of your adjusted gross income
- you receive a distribution of dividends from employer stock held in an Employer Stock Ownership Plan (ESOP)
- you use the money to pay child support or alimony as part of a divorce settlement, provided the divorce court has issued a Qualified Domestic Relations Order (QDRO); this rule does not apply to IRAs
- the IRS levies your retirement plan for back taxes (a last resort for the IRS)
- you receive a refund of a contribution to your retirement plan (usually because you contributed more than the law permits)
- you were unemployed (or recently unemployed) and you use the distribution to pay for health premiums (this applies only to IRAs)
- you use the money to pay higher education expenses for a spouse, child, or grandchild and the distribution doesn't exceed the amount of higher education expenses (this applies only to IRAs), or
- you use up to $10,000 for the acquisition, construction, or re-construction of your principal residence and you are a first-time home buyer (this applies only to IRAs).

What to Withdraw First

In what order should you tap your retirement assets? USA TODAY reporter Kathy Chu advises:

A general rule is to withdraw your taxable money before your tax-deferred accounts. The tax-advantaged money can then continue to grow, free of taxes, thereby boosting your retirement assets.

There are, however, exceptions. If you own appreciated stock in a brokerage account, you might plan to withdraw it last, rather than first. That way, if you never sell the stock, it will pass to your heirs once you die. And they'd have to pay tax only on the stock's gains after they'd received it.

Also, if you think income tax rates will rise in the future, you might consider tapping tax-deferred retirement accounts before brokerage assets, says Dallas Salisbury, chief executive of the Employee Benefit Research Institute.

True, you'd sacrifice tax-deferred growth. But you'd pay lower income tax on the retirement money than if you took it out after income tax rates had risen.

Or say you're working in retirement and are temporarily in a high tax bracket. In that case, consider withdrawing assets from a Roth IRA before you pull assets from a 401(k) account. Wait till you're in a lower bracket to tap the 401(k); you'll pay less tax on that money.

In a Roth, no matter when you pull your money, your withdrawals will be tax-free. You already paid tax on the contributions. The earnings are also tax-free.

 "Six steps you can take to financial prosperity," by Kathy Chu, September 24, 2007.

Withdrawal options at age 59½

Happy one-half birthday: On or after the day you reach age 59½, you can withdraw money from your IRA, 401(k), annuity, or other tax-deferred plan, without facing the 10% early withdrawal tax. However, there's more you need to know:

Special rules for Roth IRAs. Once you reach age 59½ and you've maintained the funds in your Roth IRA account for five years, you won't have to pay taxes on those funds or their gains (referred to as a "qualified distribution").

Special rules for 401(k)s. At age 59½, you'll probably be asked to make some decisions regarding your employee 401(k) program. Most plans offer such options as:

- **Converting your 401(k) holdings into an annuity.** Annuities provide some security but, as noted in our discussion of annuities below, their fixed monthly payments may not offer a hedge against inflation.

- **Keeping your money in the company's 401(k) plan.** You can then delay touching the money until at least age 70½ (when withdrawals are mandatory), if you wish.

- **Taking a lump sum payment of your 401(k) holdings.** This would allow you to get your hands on all the money, but of course you'd have to pay income taxes on the entire amount.

Mandatory withdrawals at age 70½

At age 70½, you're required to begin withdrawing money from all of your tax-deferred retirement plans, except your Roth IRA. You must take a series of annual "required minimum withdrawals" beginning in the year you turn age 70½. And—get ready to do some of that mental exercise we recommended in earlier chapters—you'll calculate the required minimum distribution for each year by dividing the IRA account balance as of December 31 of the prior year by the applicable distribution period in the Uniform Lifetime Table (below).

Uniform Lifetime Table			
For use by all IRA owners unless their sole beneficiary for the year is a spouse who is more than ten years younger.			
Age	Distribution Period	Age	Distribution Period
70	27.4	93	9.6
71	26.5	94	9.1
72	25.6	95	8.6
73	24.7	96	8.1
74	23.8	97	7.6
75	22.9	98	7.1
76	22.0	99	6.7
77	21.2	100	6.3
78	20.3	101	5.9
79	19.5	102	5.5
80	18.7	103	5.2
81	17.9	104	4.9
82	17.1	105	4.5
83	16.3	106	4.2
84	15.5	107	3.9
85	14.8	108	3.7
86	14.1	109	3.4
87	13.4	110	3.1
88	12.7	111	2.9
89	12.0	112	2.6
90	11.4	113	2.4
91	10.8	114	2.1
92	10.2	115 and over	1.9

No longer will you have the option of rolling money over into another plan or IRA. That's because the lawmakers who created these plans intended for you to deplete your retirement savings during retirement rather than leave it for your heirs.

RESOURCE

More information on taking money out of your retirement plans. There's more to know, particularly about exceptions to the rules, tax implications, and estate-planning strategies. Nolo's website contains good basic information, at www.nolo.com. Also see *IRAs, 401(k)s & Other Retirement Plans: Taking Your Money Out*, by Twila Slesnick and John Suttle (Nolo).

Savings and Investments

You may have also accumulated assets for retirement that are not in tax-deferred retirement accounts or tied up in home equity—for example, certificates of deposit, stocks and bonds, traditional interest-bearing savings accounts, and possibly cash in a strong box under your bed. We'll address where these assets fit into your retirement planning in Chapter 9.

Inheritances and Gifts

Many people preparing for retirement will receive money in the form of gifts or inheritances from family or close friends. Of course, no one can count on the generosity of another, nor on the timing of an inheritance—a topic that's not always pleasant to contemplate.

Is it worthwhile to discuss inheritances and gifts with your family? Or will your efforts trigger the types of dysfunctional family behavior you've been trying to avoid? Before deciding, read on.

Planning for inheritances

Though many Americans believe they will inherit or be given some amount of money, a substantial percentage don't work it into their retirement plans. After all, Dad might change the will after marrying a 40-something (and blow the inheritance), or Mom might need years of expensive nursing home care, depleting the estate.

For some people, not knowing how much they are likely to inherit makes little practical difference, anyway; they'd live their preretirement lives the same way regardless. But for others, ignoring inheritance prospects can affect their retirement decision making. If you're in the latter group, consider:

- **Should you talk to your parents?** This may be a touchy subject. Many parents dread this conversation, fearing the children will act poorly, bicker among themselves, or perhaps become slackers, awaiting an easy ride ahead. If these concerns stop your parents from making any plans, the biggest winners will be Uncle Sam and the lawyers who sort it out. Either one by one, or together with your siblings, it's worth approaching your parents. The tone of the discussion should be, "How can we work together, so that our family (and all its members) will have financial security?" (It's best not to start with the question, "How much will I get?") If any of your family members have evolved into good money managers, ask them to guide and counsel others. This approach may encourage matriarchs and patriarchs to openly discuss financials to ensure that their estate planning is done wisely.

- **What if your parents don't want to talk about it?** Despite your best efforts, some parents are masters at steering conversations away from the subject of money. But you've probably already made an educated guess as to how much you're likely to inherit. Since a substantial part of many older people's net worth is tied up in their fully paid-for house, estimating your parents' net worth often involves no more than checking how much comparable houses are selling for and then dividing that amount by the number of likely inheritors.

- **Will the estate be left more or less equally?** If your parents or grandparents are willing to disclose their finances, or have already done so, you should discuss whether they plan to leave the bulk of their property to their children more or less equally. Most will, but it's also common for a parent to provide a little extra for a child with health or financial problems, or to leave a bit less to a child who has already received a disproportionate amount of financial help or has become independently wealthy. And they may want to make sizable gifts to favorite charitable causes.

- **If a surviving parent remarries, will the inheritance automatically go to the new spouse?** If you (or either of your parents) is concerned with the issue, an estate attorney can help. A legal device known as a "bypass" or "AB trust" allows one spouse (or, in slightly different form, a living-together partner) to provide financial security for both a current spouse and any children from their marriage. With such a trust, one person can designate property for a spouse to use (a house or car), or to receive income from (a bank account or investments), during the surviving spouse's lifetime. At the death of the surviving spouse, the assets themselves go to named beneficiaries, usually the children or grandchildren of the person who established the trust.

- **What's the effect of estate taxes on your inheritance?** In 2008, the amount you can leave per estate without paying federal estate tax is $2 million. In 2009, it's $3.5 million. The federal estate tax miraculously disappears in 2010, but will reappear in 2011 with a threshold of $1 million unless Congress revises the law. These estate taxes can be hefty—as much as 45% in 2008. About one third of states also collect estate taxes (though at much lower rates), which is why some retirees move to Florida (which imposes no income or estate tax). Estate taxation provides another reason to discuss inheritances with your parents, since legal mechanisms such as trusts can lower or avoid estate taxes.

- **What if you inherit an IRA?** If you inherit an IRA plan (or plans), get assistance from a financial counselor or tax expert immediately. Your goal here is to avoid a nasty tax. Many issues arise, for example, based upon whether or not the deceased had reached the age of 70½. The age of the beneficiary (that's you) is also crucial as it affects the withdrawal rates and dates. Failure to take immediate action with an inherited IRA can have major tax consequences. For more information on withdrawing from inherited IRAs, see *IRAs, 401(k)s & Other Retirement Plans: Taking Your Money Out*, by Twila Slesnick and John Suttle (Nolo).

Edwina Shares Her Estate Plan

Ben and Sara are the only children of Edwina, a widow in her early 70s. Edwina, who recently sold the family pharmacy business, is not a person who gabs about how much she made when she sold her Microsoft stock. So although her children are pretty sure she is financially comfortable, they have no idea how much she is really worth or what her estate plan is. Ben and Sara, who are both married with two young children, are doing reasonably well financially, but each faces life choices that could be far better made if they had some idea of how much they might eventually inherit.

Sara is wondering whether she should go back to work full-time to save for the kids' college costs and her own retirement or whether she can continue to work three days a week and spend more time with her children, with the expectation that Edwina will help with college expenses. Ben, who lives in a big city with poor public schools, would like to send his children to a private school, but is concerned it would mean he couldn't fully fund his 401(k) plan, shortchanging his retirement savings.

Finally, after several false starts—Ben always becomes shy to the point of tongue-tied around his mother—Sara and Ben write Edwina a friendly one-page note. It raises some of their personal worries and asks if Edwina will take a few hours to discuss finances with them when they all get together over the Christmas holiday.

When Ben, Sara, and their families arrive at Edwina's that Christmas, they are pleasantly surprised. As soon as the children are off to bed, Edwina serves them coffee, pecan pie, and a complete list of her assets. It is immediately apparent to Ben and Sara that Edwina owns property worth about twice the amount they had guessed.

Edwina Shares Her Estate Plan, cont'd.

Edwina tells them she has decided to give both Sara's and Ben's children $10,000 every year for the foreseeable future, with the twin goals of decreasing her eventual estate-tax burden (for more on estate taxes, see "Tax benefits of gifts," below) and providing enough money so that all the kids will be able to afford the college of their choice. Edwina goes on to say that, at her death (which she laughingly says she intends to forestall as long as possible), she plans to divide her property equally between them, after giving about 15% of her estate to several charities she has supported for many years.

When the discussion is over and the tension has dissipated, Sara asks why Edwina hadn't shared her estate plan with them earlier. Edwina laughs and says she was waiting for the two of them to grow up enough to ask.

Tax benefits of gifts

Federal law (for tax years 2007 and 2008) permits unlimited tax-free gifts of up to $12,000 per recipient per year. (However, for gifts over $12,000, the giver must file a federal gift-tax return, and may ultimately owe gift tax if total lifetime gifts top $1 million.) In addition, another federal law allows one person to directly pay another's school and medical bills (regardless of amount) free of gift tax. Together, these tax exemptions permit large amounts of money to be transferred tax-free, while simultaneously reducing the size of the giver's estate and potential estate tax obligations. Another tax benefit to parental gifts is that, if the parents are in a higher tax bracket than their children, any interest and dividends generated by the gifts over time will be taxed at a much lower rate. (But if you're thinking about making such gifts yourself, don't forget the "Kiddie Tax." If your child is under age 18, your child's investment income over $1,700 may be taxed at the parent's tax rate unless the child is married and files a joint return.)

Early Retirement Incentives and Buyouts

Do you work for a corporation that's thinking of downsizing? In the last decade, many corporations trying to cut their payrolls have offered long-term employees the right to retire early, often with severance packages containing hefty lump-sum payments. For example, in 2006, General Motors offered nearly all of its 113,000 union-represented hourly workers incentives to retire early or leave, with payouts of up to $140,000. GM wanted to cut 30,000 manufacturing jobs by 2008, but hit their target two years early: Over 34,400 took the buyouts, according to reporter Stephanie Armour, writing in USA TODAY. In 2003, Verizon Communications made a buyout offer to 152,000 workers, and about 21,600 of them accepted. Also that year, 14,000 FedEx employees were offered early retirement or buyouts. About 25% accepted.

Here are some of the incentives you might look forward to in a corporate buyout:

- **Cash.** According to a study by benefits consultants Watson Wyatt Worldwide, cash is king in buyouts, with 43% of firms offering a cash severance payoff.
- **Enhanced health benefits.** One-third of firms responding to the Watson Wyatt survey offered enhanced retiree health benefits as part of their early-retirement plan.
- **Pension benefits.** Many companies offer pension benefits based on more years of service than an employee has actually worked.

Once a company makes a buyout offer, employees usually have 45 days in which to respond. As a condition of the buyout, the employee typically waives any rights to later sue the company.

Unfortunately, many people, including experienced executives and managers, feel like they've won the lottery and squander most of their buyout money instead of investing it for retirement. For that reason, many companies offer financial and career counseling as part of the package.

Only you can decide whether your company is making an attractive buyout offer. But don't be put off by fears that you won't find a new job.

Despite the myths, skilled workers in their late 40s, 50s, or even 60s can often find quality work if—and this is an important "if"—they are willing to take a moderate cut in pay. Experienced workers are in such high demand in many fields—for example in the health care, education, and legal professions—that a significant percentage of people who've been laid off as part of a major corporation's belt-tightening are able to find more interesting work in less than six months.

Reverse Mortgages

Even if you haven't saved an enormous nest egg, your house, if you own one, may have been doing some of the work for you. Thanks in part to the wonders of real estate appreciation, many retirees' homes are their most valuable asset—especially if they've paid off the mortgage. A 2007 report by the National Reverse Mortgage Lenders Association found that Americans 62 and older hold $4.3 trillion in home equity. Now it's just a matter of getting the money out of your house—which can be tricky, since you can't eat walls and plaster.

However, a solution has emerged in recent years, known as a reverse mortgage or home-equity conversion mortgage (HECM). It's available to any homeowner over the age of 62 whose mortgage is completely or nearly paid off. If the home is jointly owned, both owners must be at least 62.

Financial adviser James D. Pond, author of *You Can Do It: The Boomer's Guide to a Great Retirement*, refers to the reverse mortgage as a "late-life trump card." The idea is simple: You trade some or all of your equity in the house for tax-free income from a bank or other lender. The payments can be in the form of cash (a lump sum), monthly payments, or a line of credit you can draw on as needed (or a combination). The amount you can borrow is based on your home's value, current interest rates, and your age. And you can use the money for whatever you want, perhaps a recreational vehicle or travel, long-term care insurance, or in-home medical care.

While most reverse mortgages are adjustable-rate products, lenders are beginning to develop fixed-rate and larger-denomination loans. Additionally, many reverse mortgages don't require a credit or income test. Some states also require financial counseling.

When does the lender get paid back? The loan doesn't have to be repaid until you die (or sell the home or move out). After any of these occurrences, the lender is repaid (plus interest, of course). Whatever is left over goes to you or your heirs. If your total withdrawals end up exceeding the value of your home when it's sold, no need to shed tears for the lender; it will be protected against loss by FHA insurance. (Note: One common misconception about FHA-insured reverse mortgages is that the government owns your home—not true!)

USA TODAY Snapshots®

Do you plan to sell your home and use the proceeds as retirement income?

— **75%** No
— **20%** Yes
— **5%** Don't know

Source: TIAA-CREF survey of 1,001 investors age 30 and older who help make household financial decisions. Margin of error ±3 percentage points.

By Jae Yang and Sam Ward, USA TODAY 2006

How much of your house's value can you draw out using a reverse mortgage? It's possible to withdraw substantial amounts of money for years and still not bump up against the reverse mortgage maximum, which will be around 80% of your equity interest. The government sets annual upper limits on your total borrowing based on where you live. The range in 2007 was between $200,160 and $362,790 (no matter how much more than that the house is worth). There's also a good chance that (unless the United States goes into a deep and lasting recession) your house's value will increase over time, meaning that the amount you'll be able to draw against will also likely go up.

What should you watch out for? Since the closing costs on a reverse mortgage tend to be high, and the mortgage terminates when you move or sell your home, getting one obviously won't make financial sense if you think you might move in a year or two. USA TODAY columnist Sandra Block explains that, "Unlike with conventional mortgages, which are based on the loan amount, fees for reverse mortgages are based on the value of your home or the limit on federally insured reverse mortgages in your area. So even as rising home values have increased the amount that homeowners can borrow through a reverse mortgage, they've also raised the costs." Once title searches, appraisals, and other expenses are included, closing costs can exceed 5% of the home's value.

> *Feeling old? Maybe that's because approximately one-third of the world's population is under 15.*

Who does a reverse mortgage benefit the most? Retirees whose incomes are low but whose houses are valuable can significantly improve their lives using a reverse mortgage. Consider Edna, age 78, who owns her house outright. The house is worth about $500,000, but Edna's savings are almost exhausted and her Social Security income barely pays enough to cover her personal expenses—with nothing left over to cover the costs of maintaining and insuring her house. Edna's two children have offered to provide whatever income she needs, but even though they will recover it when they ultimately inherit her house, Edna is determined not to be a burden. She eventually solves her liquidity problem by participating in Fannie Mae's reverse mortgage program. Edna immediately borrows $10,000 so that she can replace her deteriorating roof, and then arranges to receive a payment of $1,000 per month. Even allowing for loan costs and interest, and assuming Edna lives into her mid-90s, she will not come close to exhausting her $500,000 in equity. Her equity may even increase if the value of her house goes up faster than the amount of her modest withdrawals.

RESOURCE

Shopping for a reverse mortgage? For a list of lenders (and to get help in finding one that will fit you like a glove, not a handcuff), check www.aarp.org/revmort. You'll also want to look at www.fanniemae.com. Enter "reverse mortgage" in the home page search box to find a long list of relevant articles.

Renting Space in Your Home

Got a spare room you're not using much? Your home may provide a source of rental income. Many people shy away from the idea of renting space in their homes, out of fear of losing privacy or getting a troublesome tenant. But by using the good planning and screening techniques developed by many senior organizations, it's possible to comfortably rent surplus space. Especially if you live near a college, resort area, or community that is growing fairly rapidly, it may be fairly easy to bring in substantial monthly income by renting one or more rooms. In addition, many states and municipalities are establishing programs to match older people who need good affordable housing with other retirees who have space to rent. In many cases, organizations and government programs subsidize some rentals by voucher, bonds, or other funding.

You can find out about this at websites such as Senior Resource (www.seniorressource.com/hsoa.htm). For assistance on choosing the right tenants, see *Every Landlord's Guide to Finding Great Tenants*, by Janet Portman (Nolo).

Immediate-Fixed Annuities

If you're confident you'll live a long life—so confident you're willing to put money on it—an immediate-fixed annuity might appeal to you. The principle is simple. You pay an insurance company a lump sum—say $200,000—and the insurance company sends you monthly payments for the rest of your life. With an immediate-fixed (also referred to as an "income-fixed" annuity), the payments start right away (that's the "immediate" part). The payment amounts and duration—like Social Security payments—are permanent at the time you sign the contract (that's the "fixed" part). When you die, the insurance company keeps what's left.

What you're really doing with an immediate-fixed annuity is betting against the house odds. If you die soon after buying the annuity, you lose. If you outlive the actuarial tables, you win. (At least that's the way it traditionally goes, except that the life insurance industry has retooled annuities for a new generation and now also offers survivor benefits and other options—for example, you can buy an annuity that, in the event of your death, will continue to pay your beneficiary the monthly payments for a fixed period of time.)

Immediate-fixed annuities aren't the only offerings in town. Something similar called a deferred annuity allows you to invest money in a tax-deferred account and then withdraw it at a later date. The payments are either monthly or lump sum, or you can roll the money into an immediate-fixed annuity. Another option, called a variable annuity, pays amounts that depend upon the performance of selected mutual funds.

Whatever route you take regarding annuities, play it safe: Avoid placing more than 20% to 25% of your retirement assets into an annuity.

Options for a $200,000, Immediate-fixed Annuity by a 65-Year-Old Man (with 60-Year-Old Wife)	
Type of Annuity	**Monthly Payment**
Lifetime monthly income; no payments after death.	$1,312
Lifetime monthly income; if the man dies before 20th policy year, beneficiary receives monthly amount until 20th policy year.	$1,143
Lifetime monthly income; if the man dies before receiving an amount equal to premium ($200,000), beneficiary receives monthly amount until full $200,000 premium has been reached.	$1,234
Lifetime monthly income for as long as both spouses are living. After the last person has died, no payments are made to beneficiaries.	$1,074
Lifetime monthly income for as long as both spouses are living; if both spouses die before receiving an amount equal to premium ($200,000), beneficiary receives monthly amount until full $200,000 premium has been reached.	$1,068

What are the downsides to annuities? They do provide security by guaranteeing your income. However, one obvious drawback is that you may die soon after investing in one. You can deal with this by choosing annuities with fixed time periods or survivor benefits. Another negative may be that the annuity doesn't keep up with inflation. The solution may be to choose one of the inflation-enhanced annuity policies that offer lower monthly payments. And if you're concerned that the insurance company will disappear before you do, do some homework on your company. Though there's no 100% guarantee of an insurance company's longevity, you'll always have more security with a Triple-A or similarly rated insurance company. You can find insurance ratings online at companies such as A.M. Best Company, Standard & Poors, Weiss Research, Duff & Phelps, and Moody's Investor Service.

For more information on how annuities work, check out Immediate Annuities (www.immediateannuities.com), where you can calculate your estimated monthly income. Or, if you want to combine charitable giving with an annuity, talk to your favorite nonprofit. Many large or established nonprofits offer charitable gift annuities, in which you make a tax deductible gift to the nonprofit, then receive annuity payments for life. ●

9

Growing and Protecting Retirement Assets

The Safe Withdrawal Approach_____178

What Are Your Investment Choices?_____184

Cash: Lowest Risk, Low Returns _____184

Bonds: Low to Moderate Risk, Low to Moderate Returns___186

Individual Stocks: High Risk, Varying Returns_____188

Mutual Funds: Varying Risks, Varying Returns_____190

Making Choices, and Sticking by (Some of) Them_____198

Investing in and Profiting From Real Estate_____201

   What's the best type of property to invest in?_____201

   Downsides to real estate investing_____202

Getting Help: Financial Planners, Advisers, and Brokers_____204

   Checking credentials_____204

   How you'll pay: Flat fee, commission, or percentage fee__205

   What the adviser will do for you—and only for you_____206

nvestor Warren Buffet once said, "Predicting rain doesn't count; building arks does." In other words, your ability to forecast general economic trends won't do you much good if you don't shield yourself from potential economic storms. In this chapter, we'll attempt to help you fashion your "ark"—a financial plan that will protect and serve your assets. Our core principle is simple: Make smart and prudent financial choices that consistently outpace inflation and maximize your retirement nest egg while limiting your potential for loss.

The right formula—and it differs based upon personality and nest egg—involves a mix of caution and risk. As USA TODAY columnist John Waggoner puts it, "Once you're retired, you probably won't have fresh income to make up for investment losses, so you have to be especially prudent." But, he says, "Don't be too cautious, either. In addition to income-producing investments, such as bonds, you need stocks, too. In the long term, stocks tend to outperform bonds or bank CDs. And retirement could last longer than you imagine."

The Safe Withdrawal Approach

If you're like most people, your major financial concern for retirement is having enough money to live on comfortably for the rest of your life—that is, without outliving your savings. One common approach for achieving this is what's called the "safe withdrawal system." The idea is that you use your nest egg to generate a return (say 6% to 7% per year in interest or profits) and withdraw a fixed percentage of the egg (commonly 4% to 5% each year) as your "harvest." By withdrawing less than you're earning, you protect the principal from depletion. You then use this extra annual income as your major source of income or as a means to augment Social Security or pensions.

The safe withdrawal system, popularized by retirement experts like Bob Clyatt, author of *Work Less, Live More* (Nolo), seeks to keep your portfolio intact. Assuming you can maintain a solid fixed group of assets (the "principal"), you will never outlive your savings. In fact, your principal should remain the same (or grow) until your death.

Obviously, the bigger the nest egg (and the wiser the portfolio management), the better the annual harvest. And keep in mind that this system presumes a return on investment of at least 7%. Below are a few examples of how this might play out based on:

Annual and Monthly Income Using Withdrawal Rates of 4% and 5%			
Amount of Nest Egg ("Principal")	Rate of Withdrawal	Annual Harvest	Monthly Harvest
$150,000	4%	$6,000	$500
	5%	$9,000	$750
$250,000	4%	$10,000	$833
	5%	$12,500	$1,041
$500,000	4%	$20,000	$1,666
	5%	$25,000	$2,083
$750,000	4%	$30,000	$2,500
	5%	$37,500	$3,125
$1,000,000	4%	$40,000	$3,333
	5%	$50,000	$4,166
$1,250,000	4%	$50,000	$4,166
	5%	$62,500	$5,208

In order for this 4% withdrawal plan to work, you need to consider a few things:

- **What withdrawal rate is right for you?** We use a 4% withdrawal rate since most studies show retirees can take out 4% to 5% of their portfolio each year with little fear of running out. However, that's assuming a 30-year retirement and earnings higher than 4%. If you take out more than 7% a year—which you might have to do if high inflation struck—you risk running out of cash someday. That's not necessarily a disaster if your goal is to die without leaving an inheritance.

Common Investment Possibilities for Retirement

NOTE: The "rate of return" provided below is an average, usually compiled from the last few years. As with all such calculations, there is no guarantee that these rates will continue and there is always the possibility that they may deviate substantially, based upon changes in the economy.

Type of asset or investment product

Savings account. Savings accounts are the classic interest-bearing accounts offered at a bank, credit union, or savings and loan, from which the account holder can make periodic deposits and withdrawals.

Money market account (MMA). An MMA earns interest at a rate set by the bank and usually limits the customer to a fixed number of transactions within a stated time period, after which penalties may apply.

Certificate of deposit (CD). A CD earns interest if the money remains in the account for a fixed period of time, usually from six months to ten years. Penalties are commonly assessed for early withdrawals.

U.S. Treasury bills (T-bill). T-bills are an alternative to bank CDs. They are generally issued in denominations of $10,000 or more, and are available for three, six, nine, and 12-month maturities. They do not pay interest as such; instead, they are issued at an appropriate discount from their face value (depending on current interest rates), but pay their full value at maturity. An added benefit is that profits are free of state income tax.

U.S. Treasury bond. When you purchase a treasury bond, you are lending money to the federal government. Like T-bills, U.S. government treasury bonds are a good choice for conservative investors in states with a high income tax (since income is free of state tax). Because the rate of inflation affects the value of existing bonds, buying them is not risk-free. If you need to sell a bond quickly at a time when inflation has gone up substantially, you'll receive less than what you paid for it.

Treasury inflation protected securities (TIPS). These inflation-protected U.S. government securities (the principal value rises with the Consumer Price Index) lock in a decent return with low risk.

Municipal bonds. When you buy a municipal bond, you are lending money to a city government. Investing in tax-free municipal bonds makes good sense for people in higher federal tax brackets, especially those who live in states with relatively high income taxes. Although interest rates may be low for some bonds, the payoff can be deceptive. For example, even though a municipal bond might pay an interest rate of only 3%, a taxpayer in the highest federal income tax bracket who lives in a high-income-tax state would normally have to earn between 5%–6% on a taxable investment to net as much.

* For maximum FDIC protection, avoid keeping more than $100,000 in a single institution.

** Bond risk is generally low (for higher-quality bonds) but may be riskier (always check the bond ratings).

Rate of return	Risk level
Between 2% and 4%, depending on balance requirements.	Lowest risk.*
Between 2.5% and 5%, depending on balance requirements.	Very low risk.*
Between 5% and 6%, depending on length of term.	Very low risk.*
Approximately 4%.	Low risk.
Between 4% and 5%, depending on length of maturity.	Low risk.
Between 2% and 3.5% (plus increases in CPI), depending on length of maturity.	Low risk.
Between 3.5% and 4.5% for Triple A rated municipal bonds, depending on term (up to 30 years).	Low to moderate risk.**

Common Investment Possibilities for Retirement, cont'd.

NOTE: The "rate of return" provided below is an average, usually compiled from the last few years. As with all such calculations, there is no guarantee that these rates will continue and there is always the possibility that they may deviate substantially, based upon changes in the economy.

Type of asset or investment product

Corporate bonds. These are loans to corporations. Their ratings are usually tied to the solvency of the company. The highest-rated bonds of top companies pay much lower rates of interest than lower-rated bonds (but still more than those paid by the U.S. government).

Mutual funds: index funds. Generally the highest performing class of mutual funds, with little active management (and therefore low fees) and with stock choices set to match stock indexes such as the S&P 500.

Mutual funds: target funds. These mutual funds invest in stocks, bonds, and money funds, based on when you plan to retire or close the account (the "target"). Managers rebalance investments as you near the target date.

Exchange-traded funds (ETFs). ETFs track an index, nation, area, or industry such as biotech or commodities. ETFs are traded like regular stocks on an exchange, going through price changes throughout the day.

Individual stocks. These include any individual purchase of company stock (that is, not as part of a mutual fund purchase).

Real estate investments. These includes individual and group purchases of real estate as well as REITs, which are trusts that operate like a real estate mutual fund to pool investors' contributions and invest them in commercial and residential real estate.

+ High quality (highly rated corporate bonds) are considered a low risk; junk bonds (lower rated) are a moderate to high risk.

^ Mutual funds have varying risks. Large company stock funds and high quality stocks are a lower risk than small and midsize company stock and international stock funds.

- **What type of portfolio do you have to maintain for this to work?** Any system that generates approximately 7% a year should work. To achieve that, financial advisers commonly recommend a diversified, low-volatility portfolio that mixes conservative, dividend-paying stocks and high-quality bonds. You may also need to adjust or "rebalance" the mix of investments in your portfolio periodically to guarantee performance. We'll talk more about this in our discussion of mutual funds. (For a detailed explanation of investment strategies and portfolio management, see *Work Less, Live More,* by Bob Clyatt.)

Rate of return	Risk level
Between 3.5% and 6%, depending on ratings and term. The weighted average interest rate (CBWI) is between 5% and 6%.	Low to high risk.+
Depends on the matching index. S&P index funds (2002-2007) averaged between 15% and 16%, but these returns were much better than historical averages.	Low to moderate risk.^
Vary widely. The recent five year average (2002-2007) was between 13% and 15%, but these returns were much better than historical averages..	Low to moderate risk.^
Varies widely from 5% to 50% or more.	Low to moderately high risk.^
Varies too widely to calculate.	Low to very high risk.
Home prices have increased an average of 10% to 11% over the past five years. Historically home price declines are rarely more than 4%-5% in any year.	Moderate to high risk.

- **At what point can you tap your principal?** Whenever you tap your principal, you lower its earning power and shrink your nest egg. On the other hand, if you have no desire to leave a bundle to your inheritors, there may come a point—based on your own predictions of life expectancy—when you feel comfortable tapping into the principal.

- **What about money for emergency needs?** You shouldn't place all of your money into your investment-generating nest egg. Whenever you invest in bonds, stocks, or funds, you may suffer a downturn. For example, if you're investing mainly in stock mutual funds, keep in mind: Although stocks have historically outperformed other investments, they may fall dramatically in darker financial times. For that reason, you should put aside a cash emergency fund that can tide you through six to 12 months, to buy food and supplies, or to bail you out of minor (or major) emergencies. Of course, there are other emergency cash sources you may be able to tap, including credit cards and life insurance policies, but a cash emergency fund enables you to get through the downturn without touching your principal assets or racking up high-interest debt.

What Are Your Investment Choices?

With inflation nipping at your savings, you'll need to take steps to preserve and grow your retirement income. Below is a preview of common investments and their relative returns and risks. We discuss them in more detail later in this chapter.

Cash: Lowest Risk, Low Returns

The rate of return for money in cash accounts—savings accounts, money market accounts (MMAs), and certificates of deposit (CDs)—is much less than if you invest in stocks, bonds, mutual funds, or other financial products. But what you may lose in profits, dividends, or interest income, you gain in security. The risks are very low when your money is in a cash account, because these accounts are usually insured by the FDIC (see "How the FDIC Backs You Up," below). Note: only bank money market accounts are insured by the FDIC; money market mutual funds are not insured by the FDIC.

Still, you probably won't want to put the majority of your retirement nest egg into cash accounts. The interest rates are also relatively low (usually under 4%), sometimes even lower than the inflation rate.

How the FDIC Backs You Up

The Federal Deposit Insurance Corporation (FDIC) is a federal agency that oversees banks and savings and loans and insures deposits up to $100,000 per depositor per insured bank.

Note that the amount is not $100,000 per account. In other words, if you and your family have more than $100,000 spread among various deposit accounts at one institution, you will still only be insured up to $100,000 per person. To protect yourself, it's best to spread your accounts among several institutions so that you never have more than $100,000 at any one FDIC-insured institution at a time. Certain retirement accounts, such as IRAs, are insured up to $250,000 per depositor per insured bank.

What types of accounts are insured? The FDIC insures traditional cash deposit accounts—checking, savings, trust, certificates of deposit (CDs), and bank money market deposit accounts (as well as some IRA retirement accounts consisting of cash on deposit at a bank or savings and loan)—at all FDIC-insured institutions. To check whether your bank or savings association is insured by FDIC, call toll-free 877-275-3342, or use "Bank Find" at www.fdic.gov/deposit/index.html.

What is not insured? Even if your bank is FDIC insured, that protection will not extend to investment products offered by the bank such as mutual funds, annuities, life insurance policies, stocks, and bonds. Such nondeposit investment products, whether offered by a bank or other institution, are not insured by the FDIC. In addition, mutual funds—even those comprising short-term CDs—are not FDIC protected. However, if you buy a specific bank's CD via a broker—for example, an FDIC-protected bank's CD through Fidelity.com—you will receive FDIC protection.

Bonds: Low to Moderate Risk, Low to Moderate Returns

As USA TODAY writer John Waggoner explains, "A bond is a long-term IOU issued by a company, a state or local government, or the U.S. government. You collect the interest until the bond matures, at which point you get your principal back."

Why are bond risks lower than stock risks? Because: (1) the interest rates are usually fixed and not subject to the dips and dives of the stock market; and (2) the institutions making these loans—with the exception of lower-rated so-called "junk bonds"—are stable entities such as cities, states, and large corporations. Government bonds—such as U.S. Treasury bonds (with minimum investments of $1,000, and minimum terms or "maturities" of ten years or more)—are considered the lowest risks, primarily because they're backed by the U.S. government. Some municipal bonds are insured and are also considered very low risk. In addition, interest income generated by most municipal bonds is exempt from federal income taxes, and—if you're a resident of the state of issuance—exempt from state taxes as well.

Of course, regardless of how low the risk, there is a potential for default on any bond—that is, the government entity or corporation may not be able to repay the amount borrowed. (It's worth pointing out, though, that the U.S. government has never defaulted on its principal or interest payments.) Another choice for conservative investors is Treasury Inflation-Protected Securities (TIPS). These are guaranteed to pay a fixed premium above the annually adjusted Consumer Price Index. For example, if inflation is running at 2%, TIPS might yield 5%.

How can you determine the riskiness of a bond? All bonds receive ratings—a grade indicating their credit quality. The higher the risk, the lower the rating. Bonds are rated by agencies like Moody's and Standard & Poor's (S&P), with AAA (S&P) or Aaa (Moody's) the best. Most experts advise against investing in anything rated below BBB. (Note: Even AAA-rated corporate bonds aren't immune to default—as the

2007 credit crunch taught us—since those bonds might contain more risk than the agencies that rated them had realized.)

What's the best way to acquire bonds? Although you can buy bonds directly, most people entering the bond market buy into a bond fund, a mutual fund that invests primarily in bonds or similar debt securities. There are many variations on these mutual funds. For example, you could invest in a government bond fund, a mortgage-backed bond fund, a global bond fund, a high-yield bond fund, or a municipal bond fund, to name a few. The advantage of the fund is convenience: You can rely on someone else (the fund manager) to manage the bond selection decisions for you.

The tradeoff with bond funds is that you have less certainty than if you'd bought a bond directly and held onto it. USA TODAY writer John Waggoner provides this example: "Suppose ... you'd bought a ten-year T-note (a note issued by the U.S. Treasury) that yielded 15% back in 1981. By 1986, yields on newly issued T-notes had tumbled to about 7.5%. Suddenly, your 15% T-note would have looked very attractive to other investors—so much so that they would pay more for your T-note than you did. Quite a bit more." In addition, Waggoner cautions, mutual funds have to "calculate the value of their bonds every day. When bond prices fall, so will your fund's share price. If you own a bond fund, your principal losses in a bear market will erode your fund's income. Inflation will, too."

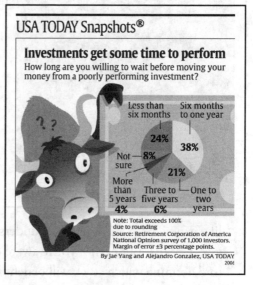

USA TODAY Snapshots®

Investments get some time to perform
How long are you willing to wait before moving your money from a poorly performing investment?

Less than six months **24%**
Six months to one year **38%**
Not sure **8%**
One to two years **21%**
Three to five years **6%**
More than 5 years **4%**

Note: Total exceeds 100% due to rounding
Source: Retirement Corporation of America National Opinion survey of 1,000 investors. Margin of error ±3 percentage points.

By Jae Yang and Alejandro Gonzalez, USA TODAY 2006

You can purchase bonds or bond funds directly from their sources (for example, see www.treasurydirect.gov for U.S. Treasury bonds and securities) or through brokers such as Vanguard or Fidelity. Another good source of information is www.investinginbonds.com.

Individual Stocks: High Risk, Varying Returns

As you're probably aware, a share of stock is an ownership interest (or "equity interest") in a corporation. Owners of stock make money when the value of the stock exceeds what was paid for it, or if the company issues a periodic dividend. As you're also aware—and as evidenced by the burst of the dot-com bubble in March 2000—there's no guarantee of any return on a stock at all (or as the warning goes, "past performance is no guarantee of future results").

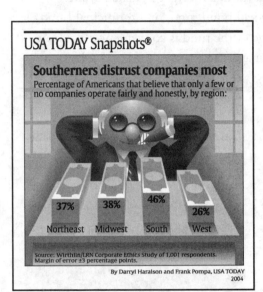

USA TODAY Snapshots®

Southerners distrust companies most
Percentage of Americans that believe that only a few or no companies operate fairly and honestly, by region:

Northeast 37% Midwest 38% South 46% West 26%

Source: Wirthlin/LRN Corporate Ethics Study of 1,001 respondents. Margin of error ±3 percentage points.
By Darryl Haralson and Frank Pompa, USA TODAY 2004

Is playing the stock market really so risky? The challenge with buying individual stocks is figuring out what's going to explode (or implode) before any one else. In that sense, guessing about the success of individual stocks is not much different than guessing cards at Texas Hold-em. Sure there may be some skill involved. Experienced gamblers, like experienced stock analysts, understand statistical probability and can assess trends. But even if you're aware of economic trends, you still need to determine which stock will benefit from (or survive) that trend. And if you're wrong, you can lose your entire investment.

What's the best stock-buying strategy? If you're asking this question, you shouldn't be buying individual stocks. As businessman Norm Augustine once put it, "If stock market experts were so expert, they would be buying stock, not selling advice." Nowadays, many of the best stock analysts work as fund managers for well-known mutual funds. So before embarking on a career as a stock market player, you may want to ask, "Can I do a better job than the fund managers at Fidelity or Vanguard?" If the answer is "no," better pass on purchasing individual stocks and proceed to our section on mutual fund investments. If you still feel the urge to gamble on the market, here are some suggestions:

- **Use a small portion of your nest egg to buy the shares of several individual companies.** As long as you don't speculate with more than 10% of your savings, you're unlikely to seriously dent your retirement. Also avoid putting more than 3% of your retirement savings into the stock of one company. If you come out momentarily ahead, you can parlay those profits into more successful investing. In any event, do not invest in individual stocks if you're carrying credit card or other debt, whose high interest is likely to negate any profits you might simultaneously earn.

- **Purchase investments you understand.** Most stock market gurus recommend taking advantage of personal and professional insights that arise from your knowledge and experience within an industry. If you have the time and inclination to read financial magazines, do so to gain more information about companies and industries you're already familiar with—not to find tips about companies you know little or nothing about. If you're tempted to speculate on a certain industry, you'll almost always be better off purchasing a good mutual fund specializing in that area.

- **Diversify.** No matter how blue the chip, it's always risky to invest all your money in one, or even two, stocks. As discussed later in this chapter, a mix of investments is always the best approach. If you feel positive that an entire industry is poised to do well, consider buying stock in several leading companies to be sure you get the real winner.

- **Pick stocks you plan to hold for an extended period.** If you buy and sell frequently, taxes and trading costs will almost surely make your return less than if you'd simply purchased an index mutual fund.

- **Avoid day trading.** Day trading is when you buy and sell a stock or other investment within a single day. It's practiced by investors who attempt to make money off small movements of stocks, and never hold a stock past the close of trading on the day they bought it. Day trading generally involves the purchase of expensive software. After you figure in all the costs, the chances of netting a profit are slim.

- **Avoid buying stocks on margin.** "Margin" is a fancy term for investing with borrowed money—usually loaned by a broker—to buy a security. Someone buying on margin can often borrow up to 50% of the stock's purchase price. Obviously, paying relatively high rates of interest to borrow money, and then using that money to speculate on stocks, is a risky and dangerous approach to managing your retirement nest egg.

Can Your Savings Survive Another Great Depression?

Firecalc (www.firecalc.com) is an innovative calculator that asks the question: How long will your money last after you retire? Firecalc looks at how your retirement savings would have panned out historically using the assumption that "if your retirement portfolio would have withstood the worst ravages of inflation, the Great Depression, and every other financial calamity the United States has seen since 1871, then it is likely to withstand whatever might happen between now and the day you no longer have any need for your retirement funds."

Mutual Funds: Varying Risks, Varying Returns

A mutual fund pools money from many investors and invests it in stocks, bonds, cash, or a combination of these asset types. Funds make money for investors by generating income from fund assets (dividends or interest earned by cash assets or bonds) or by generating profits (capital gains from stocks or bonds that the fund has sold or that have gone up in value). The fund managers are buying and selling investments all the time. To invest in a mutual fund, you buy shares of the fund. Like the price of an individual stock, the price of a share in a mutual fund fluctuates daily, depending upon the performance of the underlying investments.

Every mutual fund has a manager, who makes investments to meet the particular fund's goals. These goals may vary depending on the fund—for example, some funds focus on slow, long-term growth with little volatility; some focus on rapid, short-term growth. You can find a mutual fund for just about any kind of company you want to invest in and at any risk level you're comfortable with.

The major benefits of mutual funds are:

- **Ease of use.** It's simple to invest in a fund, to move your money from one fund to another, or to move from one investment company to another—whether online, by mail, or over the phone.

- **Professional guidance at low cost.** You get a professional managing your money, for less than you'd pay a traditional stockbroker fund or financial adviser.

- **Diversification.** Funds spread money among various assets, thereby reducing risk.

The downsides of funds are similar to those of all investments.

- **Risks and money march hand in hand.** There's no guarantee that a mutual fund will make money, that the value of your shares will go up, or that the fund will be immune from economic downturns.

- **Fees can reduce profits.** Although fund fees are generally reasonable, they can sneak up high enough to take a measurable bite out of your profits. Avoid funds that charge more than 1.5% of your assets each year (1.5% is the average). Also look for "no-load" funds, in which you're not charged an up-front commission (which can eat up around 3% to 6% of your investment). It's easy to compare funds' costs online.

Who are the major mutual fund players? Three of the leading mutual fund companies, are Vanguard (www.vanguard.com), T. Rowe Price (www.troweprice.com), and Fidelity (www.fidelity.com), all of which offer many different funds. You can choose one or more funds to invest in and buy shares from the fund company directly or through a broker. Similarly, your 401(k) or IRA will offer you a wide selection of mutual funds.

Types of Mutual Funds	
Cap funds (as in "small-cap" or "mid-cap" fund)	Cap funds are sometimes categorized as large-cap, mid-cap, small-cap, or mixed-cap. The "cap" refers to the market capitalization (or value) of each company within the fund. A large-cap (LC) fund is one that includes only companies with a market value of more than $5 billion. A mid-cap (MC) fund has companies with less than $5 billion value. A small-cap (SC) fund includes companies with a capitalization of less than $1 billion. Multicap (ML) refers to funds with a mixture of varying size companies—for example multicap growth (MLG); multicap value (MLV); multicap core (MLC).
Core funds	Core funds buy securities that they plan to hold for a long time—primarily companies with strong growth and value strategies. These are sometimes classified as large-cap core (LCC); mid-cap core (MCC); small-cap core (SCC); multicap core (MLC). International funds are preceded by an I, as in ILC, for international large-cap core. Global funds are preceded by a G.
Equity-income funds (EI)	EI funds are commonly composed of bonds and stocks with steady growth potential, particularly stocks that provide dividends.
Growth funds	These funds invest in companies whose earnings are expected to grow aggressively—that is, faster than the general economy. Growth fund classifications include large-company growth (LCG); mid-cap (MCG); small-cap (SCG); and multicap (MLG).
Index funds	Index funds are a type of mutual fund that instead of being actively managed, are set up to match, or track, the stocks in a market index such as the S&P 500. (That's a Standard & Poor's measurement of the stock prices of 500 large-cap, blue-chip, low-risk, mostly U.S. corporations.) The only time the fund manager buys or sells a stock is when the index itself changes.
Value funds	These funds buy undervalued stocks—that is, shares in out-of-favor companies selling for low prices relative to earnings. Value classifications include: large-company value (LCV); mid-cap value (MCV); small-cap value (SCV); and multicap value (MLV).
Target funds	Target funds invest in a mix of stocks, bonds, and money funds, based on when you plan to retire or close the account (the "target"). The fund will periodically rebalance your investments and shift to more conservative funds as you near the target date. Target funds that seek to maximize income as you approach the target date are known as MXX funds. (The XX represents the target year; for example, M40 funds have a target retirement date of 2040.)

Types of Mutual Funds, cont'd.	
Exchange-Trade Funds (ETFs)	These are not, technically, mutual funds, but they're a close cousin, so we include them here. Most ETFs track an index that is designed to change with economic conditions or cover a niche area such as biotech or commodities. ETFs are traded like regular stocks on an exchange, going through price changes throughout the day. In buying and selling ETFs, you have to pay broker commissions just as with any ordinary stock. Their advantage: They require little management (managers aren't constantly trading their holdings, but instead simply tracking an index) and costs are low.
Socially Responsible Investing (SRI) Funds	SRI funds invest in companies that either seek to do positive things or at least avoid doing negative things. Some funds monitor social issues (human rights, labor relations, environmental practices, etc.) and some seek investor strategies such as community investments and shareholder advocacy.
Income Replacement Funds	These are funds that generate consistent monthly payouts while seeking to extend your income until your chosen "termination" date. They act like "safe withdrawal" funds, paying out at rates between 3% to 7% and handling management chores such as portfolio rebalancing.

What does it cost to get in the game? Most mutual fund companies want you to invest a minimum of $1,000 to open an account. You can also buy into funds (often for less than $1,000) through brokers. However, as USA TODAY's John Waggoner points out, "There are two drawbacks with broker-sold funds, at least from the point of view of a small investor. The first is the sales commission, or load, which will consume up to 5.75% of your initial investment. In theory at least, you'll get a broker's specialized advice in return for that sales commission. Which brings us to our second drawback: 5.75% of $500 won't buy you much of a broker's attention. On the other hand, small investors may not need a lot of investment advice, which is why no-load funds are generally a good deal. No-load funds don't charge a sales fee, or load, and they don't give you investment advice. If you know where you want to invest, you can put more of your money to work in a no-load than in a load fund."

Where can you get information about specific funds? In addition to the mutual fund companies mentioned above, some popular sites for help include:

- Morningstar (www.morningstar.com). You have to pay for some of Morningstar's information, but you can find much excellent advice there for free.

- FundAlarm (www.fundalarm.com). This is a favorite site among USA TODAY reporters, who state, "Ask most people in the fund industry when to sell a fund, and they'll say never. FundAlarm disagrees: Kick that sucker out when its performance lags behind its peers for the past one, three, and five years. FundAlarm's list of most alarming funds is a terrific guide to the very worst funds."

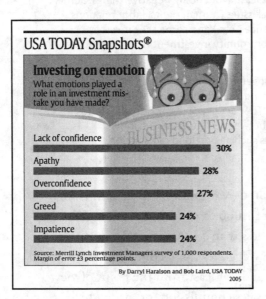

USA TODAY Snapshots®

Investing on emotion
What emotions played a role in an investment mistake you have made?

Lack of confidence — 30%
Apathy — 28%
Overconfidence — 27%
Greed — 24%
Impatience — 24%

Source: Merrill Lynch Investment Managers survey of 1,000 respondents. Margin of error ±3 percentage points.

By Darryl Haralson and Bob Laird, USA TODAY 2005

What's the best fund for someone who doesn't want to learn about investing? If you're not interested in learning about investments, put your money in an index fund and leave it there. Index funds have a record of outperforming most actively managed mutual funds. Since index funds are set up to match, or track, the stocks in a market index, you're guaranteed a performance that mirrors the stock market in general, or at least a corner of it. For example, an S&P 500 index fund will generally guarantee a return similar to the results affecting the stock of the nation's largest 500 companies. The only time the fund manager buys or sells a stock is when the index itself changes. With index funds there is less guessing by managers and the fund does less buying and selling (so it owes less capital gains tax).

Of course, not all index funds are created equal. Although each fund chooses an index to guide its investments and then sticks with it (regardless of what the market does), the choice of index itself can reflect very different investment allocations. Some index funds invest partly in bonds, to lower the risk. Some have introduced a bit of active management. Others specialize, for example, by choosing only socially responsible investments within a major index. The result is that different index funds present different levels of risk and potential returns. See John Waggoner's tips for choosing an index fund, below.

What's the difference between exchange-traded funds (ETFs) and index funds? ETFs are not mutual funds and were created primarily for professional investors. However, they've begun filtering down to consumers and are even offered to some 401(k) plan participants. ETFs are like index funds in that they track a group of stocks, commodities, or other investments. The risk is different than an index fund in that you're not betting on all the companies in the NASDAQ or S&P 500; instead ETFs are built around a specific industry (like pharmaceutical or aerospace stocks) or a region or country (for example, only Chinese stocks). ETFs are a popular choice among investors who like to make large lump-sum investments (for example, in a retirement account). Also like index funds, ETFs are considered a "buy and hold" investment.

Are target funds the best choice for those heading for retirement? Some financial advisers say that a well-rounded retirement portfolio should include at least two target funds. Target funds are aimed at a "target" year—usually the year of your retirement—and are based on the principle that you can accept less risk as you age. John Waggoner explains, "Because stocks typically fluctuate more than bonds, they can produce bigger short-term losses. If you're 30, you can afford to ride out bear-market losses. But if you're 55, a downturn in stocks can deliver a serious dent to your retirement plans. Target funds make those decisions for you—they reallocate your mix of stocks and bonds in the fund as you age."

Choosing an Index Fund

As USA TODAY reporter John Waggoner describes it, science-fiction writers in the 1950s used to fret that machines would replace humans. Lately, their worries seem to be coming true. Supercomputers have clobbered chess masters. Copy machines have replaced monks. And unmanaged index funds have steamrolled fund managers.

That's why you should have at least part of your stock fund portfolio invested in index funds. But bear in mind, too, that not all index funds are alike—nor are all good investments.

Some index funds just don't make much sense. Consider QQQ, an exchange-traded fund that tracks the Nasdaq 100. That index measures the performance of the 100 largest stocks traded on the Nasdaq stock exchange.

Logically, however, it doesn't make much sense to buy stocks simply because they are traded on the Nasdaq. Where a stock is traded doesn't really have anything to do with its prospects. There's no similar fund that buys the 100 largest stocks on the New York Stock Exchange. Why? Because that would be dumb.

What kind of index fund should you choose? If you just want exposure to the stock market, buy a fund that tracks the broad-based Wilshire 5000 index or the Russell 3000. You'll get large and small stocks, all in one fund. Want big stocks only? Buy one that tracks the S&P 500.

You could create an entire portfolio of index funds, and there's nothing wrong with that. But if you still have some faith in humanity, consider keeping half your stock portfolio in an index fund. Use the rest for the actively managed funds. If your managers fail, you'll lag behind the index slightly. If your managers win, you might be able to buy that robot you've been eyeing.

 "Index funds' low cost makes them a solid place to start," by John Waggoner, February 27, 2004.

How do target funds allocate (or rebalance) your assets? Usually the closer you get to retirement, the more bonds are added into your fund, lowering your risk. What you need to watch in a target fund is its "glide path"—or as John Waggoner explains, "how quickly a fund moves from stocks to bonds. Just how the fund family arrives at the glide path is a mixture of mathematics and philosophy. Putnam's RetirementReady funds, for example, use a mathematical formula to determine their glide paths. The formula considers a person's earning power and financial assets as two parts of one portfolio." Some funds move out of stocks fairly quickly as retirement approaches, while others take a more aggressive approach, seeking to have the stock portion of the portfolio significantly boost overall returns. One more thing to consider: Target funds charge fees. The higher the fees, the less you keep.

What is socially responsible investing? Socially Responsible Investing funds (SRIs) screen the companies in which they invest based on social, environmental, labor, human rights, or related concerns. Some SRIs may emphasize product focus (for example avoiding alcohol, tobacco, or firearms companies) and some may emphasize shareholder advocacy or local investing. There are over 200 SRI funds, so you'll need to make some choices about which match your personal and performance criteria. Two places to begin your research are Social Funds (www.socialfunds .com) and the Social Investment Forum (www.socialinvest.org). Also be aware that some investors disfavor these funds: Traditionally, SRIs do not perform as well, as a class, as index funds; their costs are higher (usually attributed to the higher research costs); and some SRIs are not as pure as they sound. For example, a company known to pollute may offer stellar child care, qualifying it for inclusion in some funds.

How many funds should I invest in? Keep it simple. As John Waggoner advises, "Simplicity is a virtue, especially in investing. You can build a simple and powerful portfolio with no more than five funds."

Can You Invest When the Market Is Tanking?

According to USA TODAY's John Waggoner, the bull market (when stocks rise), now roaring into its fifth year, leads some investors to assume the party will run forever. For others, a long-running bull market just means a bear market (when stocks fall) is lurking nearby.

If you want to bet your money on a bear market, the mutual fund industry has rolled out dozens of funds that rise only when the stock market tumbles.

Just beware: It's best not to bet your retirement account on a bear market. Consider instead using a small portion of your non-retirement portfolio to buy any of dozens of bear-market funds of a wide variety, including bond funds.

 "Bear funds unfurl when market's cloudy," by John Waggoner, July 6, 2007.

Making Choices, and Sticking by (Some of) Them

Okay, you've studied your options. So what's next?

How should you divvy up your money? Ask yourself how much risk you're willing to take on, and how many years you have before retirement. If you still have many years in which to catch up from downturns in high-risk investments, you can take more chances, betting on higher returns. However, the closer you get to retirement, the more conservative you need to be. You don't want all your money in volatile investments when you might need to take it out soon. John Waggoner advises, "If you have ten years or more before retirement, most of your money should be in stocks, which usually return more than bonds over the long haul. One rule of thumb: Subtract your age from 125. The remainder is the amount you should have in stocks. So if you're 50, you should have 75% of your assets in stocks, with the rest in bonds."

How often do you have to reexamine your choices? Even after choosing your funds, you'll need to revisit your choices regularly, and do some "rebalancing." USA TODAY's Sandra Block explains, "Suppose your strategy is to invest 60% in stocks and 40% in bonds. If the stock market fares well for several years, you could end up with 70% in stocks and 30% in bonds. That might be a riskier portfolio than you want." Most planners suggest rebalancing once a year or if your allocation falls more than five percentage points out of whack. That way, as one analyst explained, "You're giving yourself some leeway to let your winners run but not taking on too much risk."

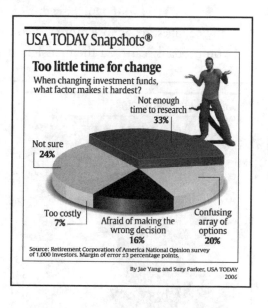

USA TODAY Snapshots®

Too little time for change

When changing investment funds, what factor makes it hardest?

Not enough time to research
33%

Not sure
24%

Too costly
7%

Afraid of making the wrong decision
16%

Confusing array of options
20%

Source: Retirement Corporation of America National Opinion survey of 1,000 investors. Margin of error ±3 percentage points.

By Jae Yang and Suzy Parker, USA TODAY 2006

There are some shortcuts around rebalancing. Some 401(k) plans offer automatic rebalancing, rebalancing the portfolio each quarter. Or, an easier option is to invest in a target fund, described above.

How can you make sure you're choosing funds with low fees? As John Waggoner explains, "Funds, like any other business, incur expenses. A fund has to pay for prospectuses, managers, and teak-paneled conference rooms. To pay those expenses, the average fund charges about 1.5% of assets each year in fees, which reduces your returns. Over time, fees add up. Suppose your fund earned 11.5% before expenses. A $1,000 investment would become $26,000 in 30 years. But you actually earned 10%, after your fund took its 1.5 percentage points, so your $1,000 became $17,500—an $8,500 difference. Rather than holding a dozen average funds, you'd be better off owning a single highly diversified low-cost index fund as your core holding."

To find out what fees a mutual fund is charging, check a document called its "prospectus," where federal law requires its fees and expenses to be disclosed. Your employer probably won't hand you a stack of these if you're investing through your 401(k), but you can normally find fund prospectuses online.

How do you avoid panicking during downturns? If you're like many novice investors, whose money is controlled by distant fund managers, you probably can't. At the first sign of a downturn, you may find yourself selling any fund that goes down in value, or madly shifting holdings into one that goes up. But this short-term approach will often lead only to higher transaction costs and a loss of long-term profits.

USA TODAY Snapshots®

Retirement philosophies differ

Which is more important: to protect your retirement savings or to grow savings, despite the risk of loss?

Protect, but being able to grow — 49%

Grow — 24%

Protect — 22%

Source: ING survey of 500 adults ages 40 to 59. Margin of error ±5 percentage points

By Jae Yang and Robert W. Ahrens, USA TODAY 2006

As John Waggoner counsels, "The stock market's ups and downs are one reason that, over time, it produces higher returns than, say, ultrasafe Treasury bills. Risk and reward are two sides of the same coin. Your best bet, if you're a long-term investor, is to try to ignore the market's short-term ups and downs. Over long periods of time—ten years or more—you'll get your best returns from stocks."

The key is to keep your eyes on the long term. As someone who is working toward future goals, you actually have an advantage over those investors who may need to get in and out of the market quickly. You can hang on through down times, potentially reaping greater rewards than those who buy in only when they realize that the market is already on the rise.

Investing in and Profiting From Real Estate

Our discussion about investing wouldn't be complete without consider-ing real estate investments, in particular rental properties and real estate investment trusts (REITS). After all, real estate has sometimes looked like a safer bet than the stock market lately—although, in a 25-year comparison made between the start of 1980 and the end of 2004, home sale prices increased 247% and the stock market (as measured by the S&P 500) went up more than 1,000%. Nevertheless, that's a national average for real estate—the numbers may differ in your location. What's more, the comparison doesn't factor in tax breaks and other income-generating revenue from real estate (rental income, reverse mortgages, etc.). In a short-term analysis, for example, home prices never seem to fall more than 5% in one year, whereas the stock market is capable of 20% drops (or more).

So should you put your money into real estate or the market? If you want a hands-on investment that you can see and touch and that will likely prove time-consuming, you should consider local real estate investments, provided you are familiar with the market. There are two potential sources of revenue from real estate investments: rental income and appreciation of property value (with no capital gains taxes until the property is sold). For that reason, real estate investments make for a popular back-up investment for retirees. But if you want to avoid the hassle of maintaining or improving a structure and dealing with tenants, then keep your money in mutual funds or bonds. Below is some more information to help you decide.

What's the best type of property to invest in?

Your main choices in the world of real estate investments will include:

- **Commercial property.** It's probably best to rule out investments in commercial real estate unless the property is small and you are extremely familiar with the area. Otherwise, the risk usually outweighs the rewards for office buildings, malls, and industrial real estate investments—or for forming partnerships that invest in these types of properties.

- **Residential property.** Condos and single family homes can be challenging investments, because if you plan to rent the property, the rental income must exceed the mortgage payments, property taxes, and management costs—an increasingly difficult task given that mortgage payments alone exceed average rents in many parts of the United States. Multifamily properties are usually a better, though pricier investment. One solution: sell your own home and move into one of the units of a multiunit property.

- **Real estate investment trusts (REITs).** If you believe real estate prices may outperform other types of investments, you can participate in a REIT, a trust that operates like a kind of real estate mutual fund to pool investors' contributions into commercial and sometimes residential real estate. REITs were high-flying investments in the past few years. (In 2006, REIT shares shot up 34.4% on average.) But in the fourth quarter of 2007, with the subprime crisis, REITs finally ran out of steam, hitting a 1.7% return (ouch!). Still. REITs have consistently outperformed the S&P index in the past five years, and are particularly strong in foreign markets. For more on REITs, consult the National Association of Real Estate Investment Trusts (www.nareit.com).

Downsides to real estate investing

Just a few years ago, many real-estate investors thought they were onto a no-lose proposition, but time proved many of them wrong. Watch out for these negatives:

- **Lack of diversification.** If you're like most people, you already own a house, condo, or co-op apartment. So you should think twice about putting more of your eggs in this investment basket. It may be far safer to diversify by purchasing stock and bond mutual funds.

- **Your lack of experience.** Since there's no daily market to help you determine a reasonable price for local real estate—as there is with stocks and bonds—casual investors often rely on the advice of local real estate people anxious to get a commission. The too-frequent result is that they pay too much for property and sometimes sell for too little.

- **Demands on your time.** If water pours through a tenant's skylight after a rainstorm, the owner is out in the middle of the night (or at the latest by the next morning) with a ladder to do something about it. If this doesn't sound like you, put your money someplace drier. Hiring a property manager is a possibility, but that means paying one more fee.

- **Potential liability.** Owners of real estate are perceived as wealthy targets for tenants, visitors, or even a trespasser who claims to be injured. You may need pricey insurance or to form a corporation or limited liability company to protect your personal assets.

- **Property tax obligations.** You must pay property taxes each year you hold the property, awaiting that ultimate profit.

- **Having to deal with partners.** Many people with extra money form a joint venture with family members, friends, or work colleagues in order to buy property. What happens if several of the other investors want out of the deal when the market is down? You'll likely be forced to either sell at a loss or raise money to buy the others out. No fun either way.

TIP
What about using your own home to generate revenue?
Besides being your castle, your home is also a potential revenue generator. We discuss ways to earn revenue from your home, such as reverse mortgages and rental income, in Chapter 8.

Getting Help:
Financial Planners, Advisers, and Brokers

There may come a time when you decide it's not worth your energy to invest your retirement assets on a do-it-yourself basis. If so, you may be confused by the choices of professionals—or pseudoprofessionals—available to help you. Financial advice-givers fall into three categories:

- **Financial planners,** who look at all aspects of your financial life, from investments to tax to retirement, and come up with a plan to coordinate them. The best ones are "fiduciaries," meaning they have a legal obligation to put your interests first (especially important if they earn commissions on your stock trades).

- **Investment advisers,** who give investment advice about stocks, bonds, or mutual funds. They're also legally obligated to act solely in your best interests, as fiduciaries.

- **Brokers (or stockbrokers),** who are licensed to buy and sell securities (stocks, bonds, or mutual funds) for you. They're not fiduciaries, but must choose investments that are "suitable" or "appropriate" for you.

Checking credentials

When choosing someone to give you financial advice, look for:

- **a college and graduate degree** (such as a Ph.D., MBA, or JD) with a concentration in finance, investing, tax, or estate planning

- **several years in the business**—preferably at least five

- **training and membership credentials.** A Certified Financial Planner (CFP) designation is, says USA TODAY's Sandra Block, "widely considered the gold standard for those who give financial advice." Other excellent credentials include the ChFC (Chartered Financial Consultant), PFS (Personal Financial Specialist), and NAPFA-registered financial adviser (NAPFA is the National Association of Personal Financial Advisors). You can double-check the person's credentials by contacting the appropriate organization.

- **registration with a government body,** such as the SEC (federal Securities and Exchange Commission), a state regulatory body, or FINRA (the Financial Industry Regulatory Authority, which is the largest nongovernmental U.S. regulatory organization for securities brokers and dealers). If the adviser isn't registered with anyone, walking away is your safest route, because no one is overseeing the adviser's activities. If registered with the SEC, ask to see a copy of the adviser's "ADV Form," which describes the person's background, fee arrangements, and more. Or look for the form on the SEC's website (at www.sec.gov; click "Check out Brokers and Investment Advisers").

How you'll pay: Flat fee, commission, or percentage fee

How fees are charged is a bigger deal than it sounds. Historically, advisers and brokers charged a commission on every transaction made on an investor's behalf. But complaints arose that this model created an incentive to move your money around for little reason other than to charge you more. That led many advisers to try out new fee models. "Fee-only" is a highly regarded one, meaning the advisers' charges are based on either the size of your portfolio under management, an hourly rate, a flat-fee basis, or a combination. "Fee-based" advisers charge a hybrid of commission and fee. Below are USA TODAY reporter Kathy Chu's tips on how to pay for advice.

"Which fee structure you choose will ... depend on the level of advice you're looking for," says James Barnash, president of the Financial Planning Association in Denver. If you have some investment knowledge and have identified a specific area where you need help, such as buying an individual stock, then commissions or hourly fees might be appropriate. If you need ongoing advice about reaching your financial goals, you might consider a fee-based adviser who charges a flat annual fee, a percentage of the assets being managed, or even a mix of commissions and fees.

"Paying a percentage of assets under management can 'align the interests of the adviser and the investor better because there's no incentive to churn,' or trade excessively to generate commissions," says Mary Schapiro, FINRA's chief executive. Asset-based fees typically range from 0.75% to 2% of assets. When the value of your investment portfolio rises, your adviser gets greater compensation.

You should also realize that not all advice in fee-based accounts is equal. If you're in a brokerage account, the advice you're getting is generally considered 'solely incidental' under securities laws. This means a broker has to make suitable recommendations, but doesn't have to do what's in your best interest.

The net effect could be that the broker puts you into a mutual fund that meets your risk tolerance and investment needs, and also pays him or her well. But it might not be the best choice of the options available.

What the adviser will do for you—and only for you

As Kathy Chu states, "Fees are only a starting point in evaluating an adviser. Make sure you also understand the individual's approach and areas of specialty." Don't just rely on the names they call themselves. Ask for a detailed rundown of what the person will do for you.

For example, the adviser's services might include goal setting, planning a budget, developing personalized tax, investment, estate, and insurance strategies, helping implement your plans (for example, by having authority to trade your assets), providing continuous oversight and advice, and more.

As part and parcel of evaluating the adviser's services, you'll need to examine whether the person will be serving your interests first and foremost (in a fiduciary relationship) or whether this person can also act as a salesperson for certain products. Everyone will tell you that they'll give you advice that's good for you—but that may not be enough. USA TODAY reporter Kathy Chu found that, with brokerage houses in particular, you may be steered in the direction of the house's own products, while, "Independent advisers who don't work at large financial-services companies have less incentive to push in-house products that might not be right for you."

For these reasons, it's best to look for advisers who have a fiduciary duty to you; in other words, who must put your interests first and foremost, even when your interests conflict with the adviser's. All registered investment advisers have this duty. For other financial planners, NAPFA suggests asking them to sign a "Fiduciary Oath," which you can find at www.napfa.org.

RESOURCE
To find a local financial planner or adviser, contact:
• National Association of Personal Financial Advisors, at www.napfa.org
• Financial Planning Association, www.fpanet.org
• American Institute of Certified Public Accountants/Personal Financial Planning Division, www.aicpa.org, or
• Society of Financial Service Professionals, www.financialpro.org.

Working After Retirement

Start Planning Now_____211

   Use your existing skills_____214

   Try a new job_____215

   Create a new venture_____217

   Buy an existing business_____220

Whether to Work and Collect Social Security_____221

Legal Rules Protecting Older Workers_____222

What happens if you reach retirement age and don't want to (or feel you can't) stop working? Will you be a working retiree? It may sound like an oxymoron, but in 2006, approximately 30% of Americans ages 65 to 69 were working (up from 18% in 1985). And nearly half of the people who participated in a 2007 survey (ages 44 to 64) said that they planned to work after age 65. These trends led Annika Sundén, director of Boston College's Center for Retirement Research, to tell USA TODAY that, "the new retirement age is probably between 68 and 70."

USA TODAY Snapshots®

Working past 65
Do you plan on working past 65 years old?
Yes 54%
No 45%
1% Don't know

Source: Ipsos Public Affairs and Aetna survey of 517 adults ages 45 to 64. Margin of error ±1 percentage

By Jae Yang and Sam Ward, USA TODAY 2006

Consider Horatio "Ray" Jenkins. Back in 1971, when Ray was 65, he was forced to retire from his job at IBM. After a decade or so of retirement, Ray went to work for his son at the Champlain Valley Exposition maintenance department in Vermont. In 2007, at age 101, Ray Jenkins was still working maintenance for the county fair—even though he'd promised his family he would retire at 100.

You don't have to be America's oldest worker to understand the desire or need to continue working after reaching the "age of retirement." Here are the three most common reasons:

- **You can make up for shortages in your retirement savings.** Working after age 65 allows you to substantially reduce the gap between expenses and your fixed income from Social Security, investments, and pensions.

- **You'll stay active, busy, and connected to others.** Around 30% of adults preparing for retirement who planned to keep working said their main reason was "to stay busy." In addition, working gives you social contact with fellow employees, customers, or clients, as well as elusive social perks. As one retiree confided, "No matter what your age, there is always a little low-level flirting that goes on [at the job]."

- **You're having too much fun to stop.** Some people love their jobs. Roderic Duncan, a California Superior Court judge in his 70s who works a few days a week on temporary judicial assignments, told us, "Being a judge is always an important job and, for me, on many days, a wonderful life-affirming role to be in."

If you have a traditional view of retirement—"I'm done working!"—and no desire to keep punching a time clock any longer than you have to, skip this chapter. But if you're interested in cashing paychecks as a senior, we provide some suggestions and rules below.

USA TODAY Snapshots®

When we expect to retire
Age group, Average age:

18 to 28	29 to 39	40 to 57	58 or older
62.7	63.6	64.6	66.5

Source: MSN, Media Contacts, Compete survey of 3,788 respondents. Margin of error ±3 percentage points.

By Jae Yang and Alejandro Gonzalez, USA TODAY
2006

Start Planning Now

There a few reasons to start thinking about postretirement work now. First, finding a job in the future may be trickier than you think. Since 43% of 45-to 64-year-olds plan to work either full- or part-time in retirement, you may be facing considerable competition for your dream job. Second, you may need training or experience. Third, the sooner you prepare, the easier your job search. Finally, you may not know exactly what will appeal to you in your later years, and the more you can investigate now, the happier you'll be with your choice.

In his helpful book, *Encore*, Marc Freedman sees three flavors of work for people in the second half of life:

- **Career recyclers.** These are older workers who transition from one job to another related position—for example, from a truck driver to a driver for the disabled.

- **Career changers.** These are older workers who hunger for something different than what they previously did—for example, an executive who longs to manage a movie theater.

- **Career makers.** These are people who create their own new ventures or reinvent themselves, usually based on some lifelong interest.

Consider Betty: part career-changer and part career-maker. After three decades of teaching junior high school English, Betty wanted to work part time, in a field that truly interested her—book publishing. Instead of waiting until after her retirement, Betty began exploring the possibilities as soon as her youngest child was in college. She spoke with small publishers in her area and learned that there was a continuing demand for people with computer graphics and layout skills.

Betty signed up for a desktop publishing course at a nearby community college, invested in a reasonably priced Macintosh computer and page layout software, and after six months of classroom and self-study (still two years before her retirement), called two publishers and inquired about summer freelance work. Both companies offered her "tryout" projects: one incorporating revisions for a bed and breakfast guidebook, the other a "favorite recipes" book commissioned by a local children's shelter.

Both publishers were pleased with Betty's work and told her she could have more whenever she wanted it. Later, Betty celebrated by taking her children to a local bookstore, where she proudly showed them the books, with her name on the back of the title page under the heading "Graphics and Production."

The moral of Betty's story: You can jump-start your dreams of trying something new in retirement by investing time, energy, and a little money in developing the skills and contacts necessary *beforehand*. Gerontologist Sandra Timmermann, who directs MetLife's Mature Market Institute, told USA TODAY, "Rather than have that linear life path of 'I went to school, got a job, and then we retired,' we see people go back and forth. They go to school. They work. They go back to school, retire and decide to go back to school and go back into the workforce again."

Professor Grout Is Born

Alan, a smart guy from a poor family, had a limited education and spent most of his working life as a school maintenance man and maintenance supervisor. He didn't hate his work, but after 30 years, he didn't love it either. Alan's dream had always been to run his own business. At age 55, with his kids out of the house, Alan decided that if he was ever going to change his career, it was time to begin. But without a lot of money to invest in buying or starting a business, and no obviously bankable skills, he was at a loss as to what his new work should be.

Alan's personal epiphany came one day as he was fixing some broken tiles in the kitchen of the teacher's lounge. It dawned on him that tile grout was always falling apart, and what the world truly needed was more people expert at replacing it. Alan checked out the local tile scene and found that most tile contractors preferred bigger jobs—such as tiling new bathrooms and kitchens—not small fix-it jobs like patching a few broken tiles or replacing old grout.

Alan perfected his skills: He purchased every type of grout concoction on the market, scavenged a bunch of broken tiles, and before long, was a master at matching and patching old tile and ready to market his new service.

His first ad in a penny-saver newspaper yielded five calls. Within a year, Alan, who now called himself Professor Grout, had retired from the school district (he was eligible for a decent pension) and was happily and profitably embarked on his new career.

Below we discuss three common work strategies for those over 65.

Use your existing skills

What skills do you have from previous employment—assuming you can't continue your job there—that you can use (or adapt) to another job? We're not necessarily referring to specific skills that you can apply directly, but rather skills upon which you can build—to become what author Marc Freedman referred to as a career recycler.

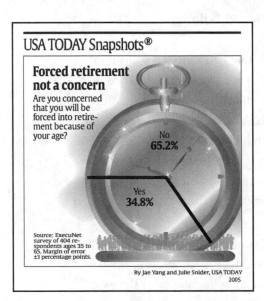

USA TODAY Snapshots®

Forced retirement not a concern

Are you concerned that you will be forced into retirement because of your age?

No
65.2%

Yes
34.8%

Source: ExecuNet survey of 404 respondents ages 35 to 65. Margin of error ±3 percentage points.

By Jae Yang and Julie Snider, USA TODAY 2005

Stan's a good example. He'd spent 33 years in the U.S. Navy and later worked as a law librarian with the federal government. Retiring at 65 with a solid pension, he looked forward to doing lots of volunteer work and plenty of fishing. But Stan found that he missed the activity and intellectual challenge of work. He contacted the publisher of this book, Nolo, about a job. Although his initial position with Nolo did not use his legal research skills—he was hired as a receptionist—four years later, he moved to the editorial department, where he helps Nolo editors with a wide variety of research tasks (including some for this book). Stan explained, "Somewhere along the line, I got over the urge to retire. Going to work keeps me active and interested and keeps my mind off aging."

As Stan's situation demonstrates, patience is required when starting your search. Sometimes, you must accept an entry-level position and then work your way into a position that better utilizes your skills.

Try a new job

According to the AARP, certain jobs are ideal for seniors—for example, bank tellers ("banks like older workers"), floral assistants, tour guides, customer greeters, security screeners, and home care assistants. Many seniors find job satisfaction, benefits, and some enjoyment working in these and similar service-related positions.

If this type of work sounds like a step down for you, consider Michael Gates Gill, a former advertising executive for J. Walter Thompson. Having suffered through business failures and a brain tumor, at age 63 he accepted an entry-level job at Starbucks (whipping up iced macchiatos for $10.50 an hour). The experience changed his life, as he later wrote in, *How Starbucks Saved My Life: A Son of Privilege Learns to Live Like Everyone Else*. Gill wrote that he had fallen into a job "where people could be nicer and the work environment better than I had ever believed possible." In short, you may not know which job is ideal for your retirement until you test the waters.

USA TODAY Snapshots®

Older workers, younger bosses

Are you comfortable reporting to a manager who is younger than you?

Yes 84%

Don't know 2%

No 14%

Source: OfficeTeam survey of 567 workers. Margin of error ±4 percentage points.

By Jae Yang and Adrienne Lewis, USA TODAY 2007

To give you an idea of what might be available, here are three careers with low entry hurdles and high self-satisfaction levels:

- **Home health aide.** You may need state certification (in the form of an associate medical degree) and you may need a personal bond (check your state's laws). Most aides work at a client's home and earn $20,000 or more per year, part time. You can work for yourself or (like most aides) work for an agency.

- **Personal chef.** This fast-growing field usually involves moving among two or three clients or preparing dinners for delivery. Usually these chefs have a culinary degree and earn $30,000 or more on a part-time basis.

> *The first woman senator was eighty-seven-year old Rebecca Felton.*

- **Graphic designer.** Most designers work from home on a range of projects from ads to websites, and often earn more than $35,000 a year. You may need a graphic design degree. You'll definitely need experience with a wide range of design programs.

RESOURCE
For more ideas of what's available In the senior job market, check these resources:

- The retirement portion of the AARP website (www.aarp.org.), which contains a "Money & Work" section with helpful work ideas and tips.
- Experience Works (www.experienceworks.org), a website that helps seniors get the skills they need to compete in the marketplace.
- Workforce50.com (www.workforce50.com) (formerly known as the Senior Job Bank), which helps older workers find employment opportunities. Their motto: "No pastures here."
- Retirement Jobs (www.retirementjobs.com), which has a program to certify employers such as Borders, Marriott, and Staples that are considered "Age-Friendly."
- Dinosaur Exchange (www.dinosaur-exchange.com), which has an international approach to matching older workers (dinosaurs) with those seeking them (the dinosaur hunters).
- Seniors4Hire (www.seniors4hire.com), billed as being "for those 50 and older and the companies that want to recruit them."
- Monster (www.monster.com), the Internet's leading job database.

Create a new venture

Your "encore" years may be the perfect time to commence a venture based on a lifelong interest. If you run a business right now, then you already know what's required to be your own boss. But if you're planning to start a new business or to buy an existing business or franchise as a retirement project, ask yourself the following questions:

- **Do you like doing the actual, day-to-day work involved?** If you hate the smell of coffee or would get bored by floral arranging, opening a shop that offers those services makes no sense. Even if you plan to manage other employees, you'll have your best chance of success if you love (or at least like) thinking about, handling, and otherwise being in contact with your business's core products or services. A small business can be all-consuming, and your work may alternate between crisis and boredom. Only your love for your business and what it does will carry you through.

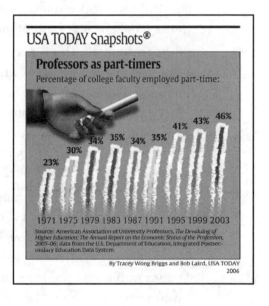

USA TODAY Snapshots®

Professors as part-timers

Percentage of college faculty employed part-time:

1971: 23%
1975: 30%
1979: 34%
1983: 35%
1987: 34%
1991: 35%
1995: 41%
1999: 43%
2003: 46%

Source: American Association of University Professors, *The Devaluing of Higher Education: The Annual Report on the Economic Status of the Profession, 2005-06*; data from the U.S. Department of Education, Integrated Postsecondary Education Data System

By Tracey Wong Briggs and Bob Laird, USA TODAY 2006

- **Are you good at what you do?** It's not enough to love what you do; you also need to be good at it. How do you honestly assess this? Ask yourself whether, if you were hiring someone to run your business, you'd hire yourself. If you were in an interview for this position, what within your resume could convince someone to give you the job? What's your training? Do you have experience in this industry or business? Have you successfully run a similar business before? If you're having trouble hiring yourself, then perhaps you should fire yourself now, before making a big mistake.

- **Are you good with people?** Commerce requires an ability to deal with people, whether they're vendors, employees, or customers. If you're not a "people person," running your own business may not be the best new adventure for you.

- **Is there a market demand?** Business guru Peter Drucker says that businesses exist to create customers. If you can't create customers, your business will end. If you're unsure whether market demand exists (or whether current demand will continue), you'll need to do some market research. That means collecting facts about your potential industry, customers, area, and type of business. Your efforts should include both primary and secondary research.

  - **Primary research.** This is research that no one has done for you, and that answers specific questions about the demand for your business—for example, you survey local residents about whether they'd pay to have monograms painted on the sides of their cars. For more how-to advice, we suggest reading *The Market Research Toolbox*, by Edward F. McQuarrie, or Jim Nelens's *Research to Riches: The Secret Rules of Successful Marketing*.

  - **Secondary research.** This means pulling together information that's already been gathered about a business or industry. The easiest method is to dig through Internet data or search at your local library. You're looking for demographics in your area, trends within your industry, and economic forecasts. When you're done, you should be able to answer questions such as, "How many parents of small children live in San Diego?" or "Is there a national market for vegan desserts?" Common sources for secondary research are trade associations, trade publications, government websites (for example, the U.S. Department of Commerce, www.commerce.gov, or the U.S. Census Bureau, www.census.gov), and business directories (for example, Big Yellow (www.bigyellow.com).

- **Can you market your business?** Many people who have worked for an employer—whether a corporation, the government, or a school or college—haven't a clue about how to market services to a wider world. If this describes you—and especially if you plan to work as a self-employed consultant or service provider—you'll need to learn a thing or two about how it's done. For an up-close tutorial, see whether you can arrange to work with someone who is already successfully running a small business. Also start thinking now about who among your business friends and colleagues could help you market your business later (or become customers). With a few years of planning and thought, you should be able to develop a powerful contact list. In addition, consider joining networks for business contacts such as LinkedIn (www.linkedin.com).

- **Can you master basic business skills?** Many people get interested in opening a business as a way of expanding on their favorite hobby, such as designing gardens or training animals. But to turn a hobby into a business, you'll probably need to master a basketful of small-business skills. The good news is that there are many resources to help—some specialized for your field and some geared toward running a small business. On the other hand, if you're the kind of person who has trouble handling tax returns, keeping track of household spending, and meeting deadlines, you might want to think twice before jumping into entrepreneurship.

- **Are you prepared for the potential liability?** There's a reason why businesses acquire insurance or incorporate—to shield the owners from personal liability. If you're operating a business that involves the public—for example, a used-clothing store or a scuba diving school—your risks may be greater. Before beginning any business, review your risks and assess how to best shield yourself. (Nolo, the publisher of this book, offers a wide range of books and resources to help you, at www.nolo.com.)

Buy an existing business

If the entrepreneurial life appeals to you, but you're not ready for the initial push (and probably low income) of starting a business from the ground up, there's another possibility. You might be able to buy a small business from a current owner who wants to move on. That's what Bob did after he was forced from his job as an executive at a music retail chain in Sacramento, when the company was acquired. In his mid-50s, and not ready to retire, Bob researched local business trends and locations and hit on the idea of buying a copy shop. He researched the costs and potential profits, and talked to owners of other copy shops in neighboring towns. When Bob finally understood the economics and was certain that he could handle the business details—he already had 25 years experience with customers, employees, and marketing—he waited for the right opportunity in his town.

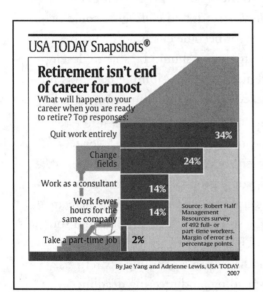

USA TODAY Snapshots®

Retirement isn't end of career for most
What will happen to your career when you are ready to retire? Top responses:

Quit work entirely 34%
Change fields 24%
Work as a consultant 14%
Work fewer hours for the same company 14%
Take a part-time job 2%

Source: Robert Half Management Resources survey of 492 full- or part-time workers. Margin of error ±4 percentage points.

By Jae Yang and Adrienne Lewis, USA TODAY 2007

When a copy shop came up for sale, Bob researched its finances and physical assets and then bought the shop—which has continued to clear a profit since opening. Bob's success can be traced to the fact that he took most of the preparatory steps recommended in attorney Fred Steingold's *The Complete Guide to Buying a Business* (Nolo), which offers in-depth advice on things like checking out the business's financial picture, debts and lease obligations, and more, and on creating and signing the appropriate legal paperwork.

You can begin scouting for the perfect business to buy right now, close to home. For instance, if you're currently employed by a small business you like, find out whether the present owner would consider selling. Or, ask business associates and friends for leads on similar businesses that may be put on the market soon. Many of the best business opportunities surface by word of mouth—and are snapped up before their owners ever list them for sale.

Whether to Work and Collect Social Security

Of course, we haven't forgotten that, for some people, the very definition of retirement is starting to collect Social Security. All those years of putting in and finally you get something back! But wait, the system actually offers some incentives to continue working after retirement:

- **You can permanently raise the amount of your Social Security retirement check by waiting until you're past full retirement age to start collecting benefits.** What's your full retirement age? It's somewhere between 65 and 67, depending on the year in which you were born (for example, it's age 66 for Americans born between 1943 and 1954; see Chapter 8 for details). The amount of the benefits to which you'll be entitled will go up slightly for each year you wait until you reach age 70. By the same token, you would permanently lower the amount of your check if you retired early, which you can do as early as age 62. The calculators at the Social Security website will help you figure out what retirement age makes more financial sense for you, at http://ssa.gov/planners/calculators.

- **You can start collecting Social Security retirement benefits and keep working.** If you've already reached full retirement age, working will have no effect on your Social Security benefits. However, if you retire early, Social Security will subtract one dollar for every two dollars you earn over the "earned income limit," a number that increases each year. (In 2007, it was $12,960.) The table below will give you a couple of examples:

Reduction in Social Security Income for Workers Who Claim Benefits Before Reaching Full Retirement Age			
Amount of earned income claimed by retiree in 2007	2007 earned income limit	Difference between amount earned and earned income limit	Amount subtracted from Social Security for 2007
$15,000	$12,960	$2,040	$1,020
$50,000	$12,960	$37,040	$18,520

- **You can collect Social Security retirement and unemployment benefits.** So if you're working and lose your job and subsequently qualify for unemployment benefits, you can collect them in addition to retirement benefits.

For more on Social Security retirement benefits, see Chapter 8.

Legal Rules Protecting Older Workers

After all those years of working, you may have gained a certain level of respect in your current job. But how will you be treated in your new job, especially since gray hair doesn't have the cachet it once did?

It's important to realize that you are protected by laws against age discrimination. Age discrimination occurs when employers favor younger workers (under 40) over older workers, whether the employer is drafting help-wanted ads, interviewing, hiring, compensating, promoting, disciplining, evaluating, demoting, training, giving out job assignments, or terminating an employee. Not only does federal law prohibit employers from discriminating against older workers in favor of those who are younger than 40, but it also prohibits employers from discriminating among older workers. For example, an employer cannot hire a 43-year-old over a 53-year-old simply based on age. The federal law that prohibits age discrimination is the Age Discrimination in

Ronald Reagan was, at age 69, the oldest American elected president.

Employment Act (ADEA, 29 U.S.C. §§ 621-634; find it online by typing "Age Discrimination in Employment Act" into your search engine).

Here are some common question and answers regarding age discrimination:

- **Does the federal law (ADEA) apply to all employers?** No, the ADEA applies only to private employers with 20 or more employees and to federal and local governments. It also applies to state governments, although their employees cannot sue them directly for age discrimination. Many state laws also prohibit discrimination on the basis of age. Although some of these laws essentially mirror federal law and protect only people older than 40, other state laws are broader and protect workers of all ages. State laws tend to apply to employers with fewer

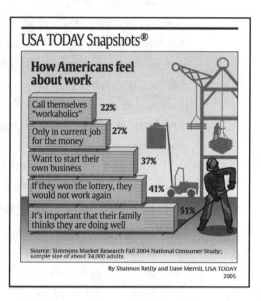

than 20 employees, so your employer might have to comply with your state law even if it isn't covered by federal law. However, really small businesses—for example, those with only one to three employees—usually don't have to follow age discrimination laws.

- **Can you be forced to retire based on your age?** No, not if your employer is governed by the ADEA, unless:

  - you're an executive or policy maker and would receive annual retirement benefits worth $44,000 or more

  - you're among certain categories of police and fire personnel

  - you're a tenured faculty member of a university

- you're a federal employee in the field of law enforcement or air traffic control, or

- you're in any job, such as piloting an airplane, where age is a bona fide occupational qualification. However, an employer that sets age limits on a particular job must be able to prove that the limit is necessary because the worker's ability to adequately perform that job does, in fact, diminish after the age limit is reached. This is difficult for most employers to do.

• **Can my employers use my age as a basis for discrimination in benefits and retirement?** No, the federal Older Workers Benefit Protection Act (OWBPA) amended the ADEA to specifically make it illegal for employers to use age as a basis for discrimination in benefits and retirement. Such discrimination might, for example, include reducing older employees' health or life insurance benefits or stopping their pensions from accruing if they work past the normal retirement age. The OWBPA protects people who are at least 40 years old. The Act also discourages businesses from targeting older workers when cutting staff.

• **Where can I learn more about these laws?** To find out more about the ADEA, the OWBPA, and age discrimination law in your state, including how to file an age discrimination complaint, contact your local field office of the Equal Employment Opportunity Commission (EEOC; contact information is available at www. eeoc.gov) and your state fair employment office. For a good summary of the federal Age Discrimination in Employment Act (ADEA), see *Your Rights in the Workplace*, by Barbara Kate Repa (Nolo). Also, the American Association of Retired Persons (AARP) publishes several good pamphlets on age discrimination. Check out AARP's AgeLine Database at www.aarp.org, where you can search out references to books, journal and magazine articles, and videos. You can also write to AARP, 601 E Street NW, Washington, DC 20049, or call 800-424-3410.

Index

A

AARP (American Association of
Retired Persons)
  adult education options, 96
  age discrimination information, 224
  online retirement calculator, 101
  work ideas and tips, 216
AB or bypass trusts, 166
Activities, engaging and enjoyable,
84–96
  doing what you always meant to
  do, 93–94
  friendships developed through, 71,
  79
  importance of, 2, 11–12, 65, 84
  for men, 17
  with spouse, 63–64
  survey of top leisure activities, 68
  turning into businesses, 12
  volunteering, 84–92
Acupuncture, to stop smoking, 23
ADEA (Age Discrimination in
Employment Act), 222–224
Adjustable-rate mortgages
  monthly payment amount, 131
  prepayment penalties, 130
  reverse mortgages, 171
Affluence, loneliness and, 70
Age 55, IRA or 401(k) early
withdrawals, 10, 160
Age 59½ , IRA or 401(k) withdrawals,
10, 124, 152, 160, 162

Age 62
  reverse mortgage availability, 170
  See also Early retirement
Age 65
  first country with more than one-
  fifth population over, 14
  Social Security benefits at, 9,
  141–144, 221–222
Age 70, delaying retirement until, 9,
143–144
Age 70½, mandatory IRA or 401(k)
withdrawal, 10, 157, 162–164, 166
Age discrimination, 222–224
Age Discrimination in Employment
Act (ADEA), 222–224
Aging Well (G. Vaillant), 62
Alcohol and alcoholism
  impact on family, 25, 59, 60
  preventing substance abuse by
  children, 51
  stress and, 42
Alimony, 401(k) withdrawals to pay,
160
Alzheimer's, brain-stimulating
hobbies and, 95
American Association of Retired
Persons. *See* AARP
American Cancer Society
  smoking cessation strategies, 23
  smoking cost calculator, 24
American Institute of Certified
Public Accountants, contact
information, 207

Annuities
  charitable gift annuities, 175
  early withdrawals from, 159–161
  FDIC protections, 185
  immediate-fixed, 173–175
  See also Pension plans
Antidepressants, for smoking
  cessation, 21
Antismoking products, 23
Arthritis
  by gender, 35
  number of people with, 43
  obesity and, 25, 26, 28
  yoga for, 38
Artistic activities, 93
Asthma, yoga for, 38
Athletes, older, 36
Atkins diet, effectiveness of, 28

B

Baby boomers (born 1943-1954)
  benefits of delayed retirement,
    143–144
  preparations for retirement, 135
  reliance on IRA income, 156
  retirement age, 9, 10
  social networking sites, 74
  Social Security benefits, 137
  work-life balance, 51
Balance, yoga to improve, 38
Bank accounts
  debit cards, 125
  See also Savings accounts
Bankruptcy, 126

Big Yellow, business directories, 218
Biomarkers: The 10 Keys to
  Prolonging Vitality (W. Evans), 33
Blogger website, 58
Blogging
  family websites, 58
  virtual social networking through,
    73
Blood tests, 43
Bonds
  bond ratings, 186–187
  corporate, 182–183
  index funds, 195
  junk, 186
  municipal, 180–181, 186
  purchasing, 187
  rates of return and risks, 186–187
  vs. stocks, 158, 198–199
  U.S. Treasury, 180–181, 186
  See also Mutual funds; Securities
Bone density scans, 43
Boomertown website, 74
Boomj website, 74
Boomsday (C. Buckley), 138
Born 1943-1954. *See* Baby boomers
Born after 1954
  retirement age, 10
  Social Security benefits, 104
Born after 1960 (Generations X and
  Y)
  retirement age, 9, 10
  Social Security benefits, 104
  work-life balance, 51
Born before 1943, retirement age, 10

Brains
  challenging through learning,
    95–96
  See also Mental health; Mental
    illness
Break-even age, 145–146
Breathing exercises, to control blood
  pressure, 30
Brittle bones, preventing, 41, 43
Brokers. *See* Stockbrokers
Budgets, shortcomings of, 116
Business directories, 218
Businesses
  buying existing, 220–221
  starting new, 12, 217–219, 218
Business skills, requirements for, 219
Business-wardrobe expense, 103
Buyouts, early retirement, 136,
  169–170
Bypass or AB trusts, 166

C

Calcium, to prevent brittle bones,
  41
Calories
  burning, exercise and, 37
  product label information, 40–41
Cancer
  number of people with, 43
  obesity and, 26
  skin, 41
  smoking and, 22, 23, 24
Cap funds, 192
Capital gains taxes, on mutual fund
  distributions, 194

Career changers, 212
Career makers, 212
Career recyclers, 212
Car payments
  avoiding, 117–119
  car leases, 118
  payment priority, 122
Cash. *See* Savings accounts
Certificates of deposit (CDs), rate
  of return and risk, 158, 180–181,
  184–185
Certified financial planners (CFPs),
  204
Charge accounts. *See* Credit card
  debt; Debt reduction
Charitable gift annuities, 175
Chartered Financial Consultants
  (ChFCs), 204
Chef (personal), as postretirement
  work, 216
Child abuse, protecting family
  members from, 61
Child care, by grandparents, 56
Children
  expense of raising, 103, 109, 134
  making time to be with, 50–54
  substance abuse prevention, 51
  volunteering to work with, 88–90,
    91
  See also Grandchildren
Children, adult
  care and monitoring role, 48
  inheritances and gifts to, 136,
    164–168
Child support, 401(k) withdrawals
  to pay, 160

Cholesterol
  blood (serum), 31
  HDL vs. LDL, 28, 30–32
  nutritional role, 30
  in oils, 32
  screening, 31, 43
Choose to Save Ballpark Estimate,
  EBRI, 101, 102
Civic Ventures program, 90
Combined income, taxes on Social
  Security benefits, 147
Commercial property, investing in,
  201–202
Commuting
  expenses reduced when
    employment ends, 103
  extreme commuters, 52
  flextime and, 51–52, 54
  telecommuting, 52
The Complete Guide to Buying a
  Business (F. Steingold), 220
Computers
  blogging, 58, 73
  learning to use, 75
  See also Internet resources
Consumer Credit Counseling
  Service, 126
Core funds, 192
Corporate bonds, rate of return and
  risk, 182–183
Corporations, public distrust of, 188
Credit card debt, 119–127
  advantages of paying off, 121,
    131–132
  dangers of, 119–120, 125
  vs. debit cards, 124

interest on, 116, 119–121, 123, 131
payment priority, 122
statistics, 120
support groups, 125
tips for breaking credit habit,
  122–125
See also Debt reduction
Cultural activities, participation in,
  69, 84

D

DASH (Dietary Approaches to Stop
  Hypertension Diet), 29
Day trading, 188
Death
  of friends, 75–76
  impact on family relationships, 55,
    58
  IRA or 401(k) withdrawals after,
    160
  leading causes after 100, 8
  reverse mortgage repayment after,
    171
  Social Security survivors/dependents
    benefits, 139, 146–147
  of spouse, loss of friends and, 78–79
  See also Estate planning; Life
    expectancy
Debit cards, vs. credit cards, 124
Debt problems
  coping with overdue debts, 126
  trouble controlling spending, 125
Debt reduction, 116–132
  bankruptcy and, 126
  car payments, avoiding, 117–119,
    126–127

vs. prepaying mortgage, 131–132

before retirement, 7, 99

See also Credit card debt

Delayed retirement

advantages of, 145–146

necessity for, 7

Social Security benefit amount and, 143–144, 221–222

statistics, 9

Dementia, obesity and, 26

Dependents benefits, Social Security, 139, 147

Depression

exercise and, 34

obesity and, 25

stress and, 42

Depressions (economic), impact on retirement funds, 190

Diabetes

number of people with, 43

obesity and, 25, 26, 28

Die Broke (S. M. Pollan), 134

Diet

aging and, 31

to control blood pressure, 29

fat types, 32, 40

perimeter shopping, 40–41

to prevent ailments, 42

to prevent brittle bones, 41

principles of good, 38, 40–41

to reduce stress, 42

replacing sugary drinks with water, 27

smoking cessation and, 23

See also Obesity; Weight loss

Dietary Approaches to Stop Hypertension Diet (DASH), 29

Diets, comparing, 28

Dinner

entertaining guests, 77

family togetherness, 50–51

Dinner with Dad: How I Found My Way Back to the Family Table (C. Stracher), 50

Dinosaur Exchange, 216

Disability benefits, Social Security, 139

Disabled veterans, pensions, 150

Discrimination, age, 222–224

Divorce

401(k)s and, 154, 160

extended families and, 55

families disrupted by, 61, 62

impact on men, 17

pension plan shares/retirement savings and, 15

QDROs, 15, 160

Do-it-yourself retirement calculator, 107–114

how much to save, 110–114

how much will be needed, 107–109

Domestic violence, protecting family members from, 61

Dot-com bubble, 188

Drug abuse

families disrupted by, 59, 60

preventing substance abuse by children, 51

stress and, 42

E

Early retirement, 9, 10
  break-even point, 145–146
  candidates for, 144–147
  incentives and buyouts, 136, 169–170
  Social Security benefit amount and, 141–142, 145, 221–222
Eating out, caution against, 40
EBRI, Choose to Save Ballpark Estimate, 101, 102
Education
  in computer literacy, 75
  IRA early withdrawals for, 160
  part-time professors, 217
  paying for another's education, 128–129, 168
  postretirement, 65, 94–96
EEOC (Equal Employment Opportunity Commission), 224
Emergency funds, 132, 183–184
Employer Stock Ownership Plan (ESOP), 160
Employment
  401(k) loans and job loss, 156
  ADEA and, 222–224
  business travel, 53
  cashing out 401(k)s when changing jobs, 154
  commuting, 51–52, 54
  contributions to 401(k)s, 152, 153
  cutting hours, 53
  early retirement incentives and buyouts, 136, 169–170
  family-friendly companies, 53

flextime, 51–52, 54
  making friends outside work, 77
  part time, 65, 71, 79, 103, 136, 217
  telecommuting, 52
  using skills obtained from previous, 214
  work-life balance, 51
  See also Pension plans; Postretirement work; Tax-deferred accounts
Employment Retirement Income Security Act (ERISA), 156
Encore (M. Freedman), 212
Entrepreneurs
  buying existing businesses, 220–221
  creating new ventures, 217–219
  turning interests into businesses, 12
Eons website, 74
Equal Employment Opportunity Commission (EEOC), 224
Equity-income funds, 192
Equity interest, stock shares as, 188
Estate planning
  inheritances and gifts as income, 136, 168
  leaving no inheritance, 179
  Number calculation and, 106
  talking to beneficiaries about, 164–168
  trusts, 166
Estate taxes, 166, 168
Every Landlord's Guide to Finding Great Tenants (J. Portman), 173
Exchange-traded funds (ETFs), 182–183, 193, 195

Exercise, 33–38
  benefits of, 8, 28, 33–34, 42
  for brittle bone prevention, 41
  cardiovascular exercises, 37
  cholesterol control and, 32
  establishing regular program, 33, 35
  high blood pressure and, 29
  insomnia and, 43
  mistakes to avoid, 39
  muscle strength lost through immobility, 33
  reasons for avoiding, 34
  sample program, 36–37
  with spouse, 64
  strength and endurance exercises, 38
  stretching and flexibility exercises, 38
  walking dogs, 80–81
  for weight loss, 22, 27
Expenses, estimating preretirement, 107–108
Expenses, postretirement
  for cars, 117–119
  cutting back on, 99, 103, 111, 113, 116–117
  estimating, 102–103
  gap between income and expenses, 110–114
  See also Number, money needed through retirement
Experience Works, 216
Extended families, forging links within, 54–57

F

Facebook website, 74
Family relationships, 48–65
  family leadership role, 57–58
  importance of, 2, 8–9, 48–49
  inheritances and gifts, 164–168
  joint real estate investments and, 203
  links with extended family, 54–57
  making everyone feel welcome, 59–62
  making time to be with children, 50–54
  for men, 17
  strength of, 49–50
  travel with family, 56
  work-life balance, 51–54
  See also Marriage
Fannie Mae, reverse mortgages, 172
Fathers at Work, 54
Fats
  mono- and polyunsaturated, 32, 40
  in restaurant food, 40
  trans, 32, 40
Fearcasts, 4
Federal Deposit Insurance Corporation (FDIC), 184–185, 186
Federal laws
  Age Discrimination in Employment Act, 222–224
  ERISA, 156
  Older Workers Benefit Protection Act, 224
Felton, Senator Rebecca, 216

FHA insurance, for reverse mortgages, 171

Fidelity, mutual funds, 187, 188, 191

Financial Industry Regulatory Authority (FINRA)

  online retirement calculator, 101, 102

  stockbrokers registration, 205

Financial planners

  checking credentials, 204–205

  information resources, 207

  payment options, 205–206

  role of, 204, 206–207

Financial Planning Association, contact information, 207

Firecalc, 190

Fixed-rate reverse mortgages, 171

Flashbulb moments, for smoking cessation, 22

Flexibility and stretching exercises, 38

Flextime, 51–52, 54

Food Politics (M. Nestle), 40–41

Forgiveness, within families, 60–61

401(k)s and 403(b)s, 151–164

  advantages of, 153

  cashing out when changing jobs, 154

  contributions by employer, 152, 153

  contributions, excess, 160

  contributions, gender differences, 156

  converting to IRAs, 152

  early withdrawals from, 124, 128, 159–161

  estimating amount in account, 153

  expectation of income from, 152

  how much to deposit, 154

  information resources, 164, 167

  investment options, 151–152, 153, 154, 195

  overview, 151–152

  for self-employed persons, 153

  separate accounts for married couples, 154

  withdrawals at age 59 ½, 10, 124, 152, 160, 162

  withdrawals at age 70 ½, 162–164

  See also Tax-deferred accounts

Friends, defined, 69

Friendships, 68–81

  art of forming, 70–72

  assessing current relationships, 9

  death of friends, 75–76

  importance of, 2, 8–9, 68–69

  joint real estate investments with friends, 203

  making friends outside work, 77

  making younger friends, 75–76

  with pets, 80–81

  renewing relationships, 8–9

  separate from marriage, 78–79

  travel with friends, 56

  virtual social networking, 73–74

Fruits, benefits of eating, 38

FundAlarm, 194

Funding for retirement

  age started, 6, 7, 10

  baby boomer preparations, 135

  calculating money set aside, 104

  common methods for, 136

converting debt to savings, 116–132

vs. cutting work hours, 53

early retirement and, 147

estimating amount needed, 110–114

how long money will last after retirement, 190

late beginnings, 134

oversaving, 100

renting space in home, 173

savings lost by divorcing women, 15

vs. vacations, 8

working to make up for shortages, 210

See also Annuities; Inheritances and gifts; Investments; Number, money needed through retirement; Pension plans; Reverse mortgages; Savings accounts; Social Security retirement benefits; Tax-deferred accounts

Fund managers

to buy and sell bonds, 187

for index funds, 194, 196

for mutual funds, 191

stock analysts as, 188

G

Gather website, 74

Gay or lesbian relationships

families disrupted by, 59–60

family support groups, 60

Generations X and Y (born after 1960)

retirement age, 9, 10

Social Security benefits, 104

work-life balance, 51

Gifts. *See* Inheritances and gifts

Gift taxes, 168

Global funds, 192

Going Broke: Why Americans Can't Hold on to Their Money (S. Vyse), 122

Golf courses, number of, 150

Government workers, state and local

ADEA and, 223

forced retirement, 224

pension plans, 148–149, 151

Social Security retirement benefits, 141, 151

Grandchildren

impact of divorce on, 62

importance of contact with, 55, 56, 61

joys of, 48

leaving money for college to, 106

Graphic designer, as postretirement work, 216

Groups

friendships developed through, 71–72, 79

See also Activities, engaging and enjoyable; Support groups

Growth funds, 192

H

HDL (high-density lipoprotein)

Atkins diet and, 28

benefits of, 31

cholesterol screening to determine levels, 31

effect of diet on, 28

trans fats and, 32

Health
  brittle bone prevention, 41
  cholesterol levels, 8, 28, 30–32, 43
  creating healthy habits, 7
  four conditions to treat now, 20
  impact of health habits on spouse, 25
  importance of, 2, 6–8
  medical tests, 43
  relaxation and, 96
  stress management, 42–43
  See also Diet; Exercise; High blood pressure/hypertension; High cholesterol; Smoking cessation; Weight loss
Health care needs. *See* Medical care; Medical costs
Heart attacks
  cholesterol control and, 30–31
  HDL/LDL and, 30, 31, 32
  obesity and, 26
  smoking cessation and, 24
  visits to emergency rooms for, 30
Heart disease
  cardiovascular exercises, 37
  cholesterol control and, 30–31
  diet to reduce, 42
  high blood pressure and, 30
  LDL and, 30, 32
  number of people with, 43
  obesity and, 28
  salt intake and, 29
  smoking cessation and, 24
  stress and, 42

HECMs (home-equity conversion mortgages). *See* Reverse mortgages
High blood pressure/hypertension
  ailments associated with, 28–29
  benefits of controlling, 30
  number of people with, 28, 43
  obesity and, 25, 26
  strategies for controlling, 8, 28–30, 38
High cholesterol
  benefits of reducing, 32
  HDL vs. LDL, 28, 30–32
  number of people with, 43
  strategies for reducing, 8, 31–32
Hobbies. *See* Activities, engaging and enjoyable
Holiday parties, attendance at, 76
Home buying
  income-producing rentals, 103, 202
  IRA early withdrawals for, 160
  by women, 16
  See also Mortgages
Home equity loans
  to pay off credit cards, 123
  tax deductions for, 155
Home equity, reverse mortgages and, 170–173
Home health aide, as postretirement work, 215
Housing costs
  for rented vs. owned homes, 16
  selling or downsizing home to reduce, 111
Hypertension. *See* High blood pressure/hypertension
Hypnosis, to stop smoking, 23

I

Imagining retirement, 4

Immediate Annuities, 175

Immediate-fixed (income-fixed) annuities, 173–175

Income, postretirement, 103–104, 134–175

estimating, 103–104, 107–109, 111

gap between income and expenses, 110–114

growing and protecting, 178–207

safe withdrawal system, 178–184

See also Annuities; Funding for retirement; Inheritances and gifts; Investments; Number, money needed through retirement; Pension plans; Reverse mortgages; Savings accounts; Social Security retirement benefits; Tax-deferred accounts

Income, preretirement

age of peak income, 134

to calculate Number, 102

caps, for Social Security taxes, 138

estimating, 107

limits for specific IRA categories, 157, 159

modified adjusted gross, 158

Social Security benefits based on, 140

Income replacement funds, 193

Index funds

benefits of, 194

distinguished from ETFs, 195

overview, 192

rate of return and risk, 182–183

tips for choosing, 195–196

Inflation/inflation rate

bond value and, 187

Number calculation and, 104, 112–113

pension plans adjusted for, 149, 150

savings withdrawals adjusted due to, 110–111, 179

Ingredient lists, on food products, 40–41

Inheritances and gifts

charitable gift annuities, 175

as income, 136, 164–168

IRAs, inherited, 166

Insomnia

cures for, 43

obesity and, 25

stress and, 42–43

Insurance

car insurance, 117, 122

FDIC, 184–185

FHA, for reverse mortgages, 171

immediate-fixed annuities, 173–175

importance of buying, 132

life insurance, 185

long-term care, 44–45

medi-gap, 105

Interest rates/payments

vs. amount of principal, 179, 183

amount saved by prepaying mortgage, 127–132

for cars, 117–119

for common types of investments, 180–183

for credit card debt, 116, 119–121, 123, 126–127

on home equity loans, 123

mortgage prepayment and, 128–132

rates on nest egg, 178

reducing through debt reduction, 116–117

rescheduling debts at lower rate, 126

for reverse mortgages, 171

savings through reducing, 121, 125–127

tax write-offs for, 128

Internet

ages of people who use, 74

cost to use, 75

free access at libraries, 74

learning to use, 74, 75

virtual social networking, 73–75

Internet resources

AARP, 96

age discrimination information, 224

business research, 218

cholesterol control information, 31

credit card interest rates, 123

credit card payment calculators, 123

family websites, 58

financial advisor information, 205, 207

job market resources for seniors, 216

life expectancy calculators, 106

long-term care information, 45

mortgage payoff calculators, 129

mutual fund information, 194

retirement age calculators, 141, 145, 221

retirement Number calculators, 98–99, 100–102, 190

social networking sites, 74

Social Security Administration, 103, 140

USA TODAY website, 18

Investment advisers

checking credentials, 204–205

information resources, 207

payment options, 205–206

role of, 204, 206–207

Investments

choosing when to buy and sell, 198–200

early retirement benefit money for, 147

from early retirement incentives, 169

emotions and, 194

in employer's stock, 154, 160

growing and protecting, 178–207

income from, 134, 164

increasing amount put into, 117, 121

in IRAs and 401(k)s, 151–152, 153, 158

from lump sum pension payments, 149

vs. prepaying mortgage, 128–129

rates of return vs. risk, 104, 180–183, 198–200

by women, 16

See also Businesses; Mutual funds; Real estate investments; Securities; Tax-deferred accounts

Inward view, 14

IRAs, 401(k)s & Other Retirement Plans: Taking Your Money Out (T. Slesnick and J. Suttle), 167

IRAs (Individual Retirement Accounts), 156–164
  converting 401(k)s to, 152
  converting traditional to Roth, 158–159, 163
  early withdrawals from, 128, 155–156, 159–161
  excess contributions to, 160
  expectation of income from, 156
  information resources, 164, 167
  inherited, 166–167
  investment options, 151–152, 158, 191
  overview, 151–152, 156–157
  Roth, 157, 159, 162
  SEP, 157
  SIMPLE, 157
  traditional contributory, 157
  Uniform Lifetime Table, 162–163
  withdrawals at age 59 ½, 10, 124, 157–158, 162
  withdrawals at age 70 ½, 162–164, 166
  See also Tax-deferred accounts
Isolation. See Loneliness and isolation

J
Japan, age demographics, 14
Joint problems
  arthritis, 25, 26, 28, 35, 43
  obesity and, 25, 26
  yoga for, 38
Joint ventures, real estate investments, 203

Junk bonds, 186
Junk foods, avoiding, 38, 40–41

K
Kiddie Tax, 168

L
Label information, on food products, 40–41
Landlords
  information resources for, 173
  See also Rentals (home)
LDL (low-density lipoprotein)
  benefits of reducing, 32
  cholesterol screening to determine levels, 31
  diseases/death caused by, 30
  trans fats and, 32
LEARN diet, effectiveness of, 28
Leasing cars, 118
Legal resources for older workers, 224
Lesbian relationships. See Gay or lesbian relationships
Liability, personal
  for business ventures, 219
  for real estate investments, 203
Libraries, free Internet access, 74
Life expectancy
  vs. amount of money needed in retirement, 98–99, 113
  break-even age, 145–146
  extended, 11, 136
  forecasting, 106

high blood pressure and, 28

for men, 10, 17, 106

obesity and, 26

online calculators, 106

vs. retirement age, 98, 144, 145

smoking cessation and, 24

statistics, 10, 48, 76, 144

for women, 10, 17, 106

Lifestyles

vs. amount of money needed in
  retirement, 98

cutting back on expenses, 6, 99,
  103, 111, 113, 116–117

families disrupted by disputes over,
  59

postretirement expectations, 116

unhealthy, damage created by, 6

Living to 100: Lessons in Living to
Your Maximum Potential at Any
Age (D. Perls), 7

Load funds, 193

Loans

to buy stocks, 190

on cars, 117–119

home equity, 123, 155

to repay overdue debts, 126

student, 128–129, 132

from tax-deferred accounts, 124,
  128, 155–156

See also Debt reduction; Mortgages

Loneliness and isolation

affluence and, 70

coping with, 14

dangers of, 68

following loss of spouse, 78–79

pets to reduce, 80–81

Longevity. See Life expectancy

Long-term care

calculating cost of, 105

impact on inheritances, 136

Long-Term Care: How to Plan and
Pay for It (J. Matthews), 44–45

Long-term care insurance, 44–45

Luxury, definition of, 63

M

Margin buying, of stocks, 190

The Market Research Toolbox (E. F.
McQuarrie), 218

Marriage, 15–16

benefits for men, 17

couples power, 62–64

creating space for yourself, 12

early retirement and, 146–147

impact of health habits on spouse,
  25

one spouse retires before the other,
  12, 15, 64–65

remarriage and extended families,
  55

remarriage of surviving parent,
  estate planning and, 166

separate 401(k)s, 154

separate friendships, 78–79

separate interests, 84

Social Security dependents
  benefits, 139

Social Security survivors benefits,
  139, 146–147

statistics for people over 55, 62

statistics for people over 85, 64
tips for successful, 62–64, 78
travel with spouse, 56
Medical care
to lower cholesterol, 32
for smoking cessation, 21
Medical costs
vs. benefits of good health habits, 7
enhanced benefits for early retirees, 169
estimating future, 103, 105, 109
health care premiums for unemployed, 160
high blood pressure and, 28
impact on inheritances, 136
insecurity about, 99
IRA or 401(k) withdrawals to pay, 160
long-term care insurance for, 44–45
Medicare to pay, 10, 99, 105, 138
obesity and, 26
paying for another's medical costs, 168
prescription drug costs, 105, 109
Medical tests, importance of scheduling, 43
Medicare
age of qualification for, 10
calculating future health care costs, 105
confusing information about, 99
payments to doctors, 138
Medications
antidepressants, 21
antismoking products, 23

for blood pressure control, 29
for cholesterol reduction, 31, 32
drug abuse, 42, 51, 59, 60
for insomnia, 43
paid by Medicare, 138
prescription drug costs, 105, 109
stress and, 42
Medi-gap insurance policies, 105
Meditation, to control blood pressure, 30
Men
401(k) savings rate, 156
arthritis and, 35
average life expectancy, 10, 76, 106
creating space in home, 12
HDL risk levels, 31
loss of self-esteem after retirement, 12, 17
over 85 living with spouse, 64
preparation for retirement, 17
Mental health
alcoholism, 25, 42, 51, 59, 60
domestic violence and abuse, 61
drug abuse, 42, 51, 59, 60
exercise and, 34, 36
loneliness and isolation, 14, 68, 70, 78–81
maintaining a healthy marriage, 63–64
obesity and, 25, 26
of people with pets, 80–81
Modified AGI (MAGI), calculating, 158
Money
disputes over, 59

how much is enough, 5–6

importance of, 2, 5

Money market accounts (MMAs), rate of return and risk, 180–181, 184–185

Monounsaturated oils, 32

Monster.com, 216

Moody's bond ratings, 186–187

Morningstar, 194

Mortgages

  15- vs. 30-year, 132

  interest as tax deductible, 128, 130

  paying off, 103, 109, 116, 127, 128

  payment priority, 122

  prepaying, 116, 127–132

  reverse mortgages, 111, 134, 136, 170–173, 202

Moving at retirement

  pros and cons, 48, 56, 65, 99

  statistics, 48

MSN TV box (Web TV), 75

Multiply website, 74

Municipal bonds, rate of return and risk, 180–181, 186

Mutual funds, 190–198

  bear market investments, 198

  benefits of, 191

  bond funds, 187

  costs of, 193, 197, 199

  FDIC protections, 185

  fund managers, 187, 188, 191, 194, 196

  how many to invest in, 197

  index funds, 182–183, 192, 194, 195–196

  information resources, 194

  for IRA and 401(k) investments, 151–152, 191

  leading companies, 187, 188, 191

  overview, 190

  prospectuses, reading, 200

  target funds, 182–183, 192, 195–197

  types of, 192–193

MySpace website, 74

N

Name changes, Social Security benefits and, 142

NAPFA-registered financial advisers, 204

Nasdaq stock exchange, funds that track, 196

National Association of Personal Financial Advisors (NAPFA), 204, 207

National Cancer Institute, smoking-cessation programs, 22

National Cholesterol Education Program, 31

National Clearinghouse for Long-Term Care Information, 45

National Institute of Health (NIH)

  DASH program, 29

  National Cholesterol Education Program, 31

Needlework (knitting and crocheting), 95

Nicotine Anonymous, 22

No-load funds, 193

Nonprofit organizations. See Volunteer (nonprofit sector) activities

The Number (L. Eisenberg), 102

Number, money needed through retirement, 98–114
choices and variables, 102–106
defined, 98
do-it-yourself calculator, 107–114
insecurity about, 98–99
online retirement calculators, 98–99, 100–102
people confident they will have enough, 98
percentage of people who have calculated, 101
See also Funding for retirement; Income, postretirement

Nursing homes
calculating cost of, 105, 136
long-term care insurance for, 44–45
obese people sent to, 26
people with high blood pressure sent to, 28

O

Obesity
ailments associated with, 25–26, 28, 29
defined, 26
impact on retirement, 26
statistics, 25–26
trans/saturated fats and, 40
See also Diet; Weight loss

Older Workers Benefit Protection Act (OWBPA), 224

Ornish, Dean, Eat More Weigh Less Diet, 28, 42

Osteoporosis, 41

Outward view, 13–14

P

Pap smears, 43

Parents and Friends of Lesbians and Gays, 60

Pension Benefit Guaranty Corporation (PBGC), 149

Pension plans, 148–151
benefits for early retirees, 169
for disabled veterans, 150
estimating payments from, 103–104, 110, 148
health of company plan, 149
income from, 134, 136
inflation adjustments, 149, 150
information resources, 151
monthly vs. lump-sum payments, 149
payout age, 10
shares lost by divorcing women, 15
Social Security benefits in addition to, 150–151
vesting age, 148
See also Annuities

Personal Financial Specialists (PFSs), 204

Pets, as friends, 80–81

Pied Piper of Bikes, 91

Politics
friendships developed through, 69, 77
Gather website, 74

involvement in, 12
of Social Security, 137, 138
Polyunsaturated oils, 32
Postretirement work, 1, 210–224
  buying existing businesses, 220–221
  creating new ventures, 217–219
  forced retirement, 214, 223–224
  part time, 65, 136
  percentage of people who expect, 200, 210, 211
  planning for, 211–221
  reasons for, 7, 96, 134, 136, 210–211
  Social Security benefit amount and, 221–222
  trying new jobs, 215–216
  types of, 212–213
  using existing skills, 214
  See also Delayed retirement
Postretirement work, age issues
  Age Discrimination in Employment Act, 222–224
  job market resources for seniors, 216
  jobs that are ideal for seniors, 215–216
  Older Workers Benefit Protection Act, 224
  working for younger managers, 215
Prehypertension, ailments associated with, 28–29
Preparation for retirement, 1–2, 4–18
  inward view, 14
  by men, 17
  outward view, 13–14

requirements, 2, 5–13
by women, 15–16
Prepaying mortgages, 127–132
  15- vs. 30-year, 132
  benefits of, 116, 127, 128–129
  vs. investing elsewhere, 128–129
  vs. paying off other debts, 131–132
  procedure, 131
Prepayment penalties
  on cars, 119
  on mortgages, 130
Principal, living off, 178, 183
Professor Grout, 213
The Promise of Sleep (Dement, W.), 43
Property taxes, 203
Property value, appreciation of, 103
Prospection, defined, 4
Prospectuses, mutual fund, 200
Prostate exams, 43

Q

Qualified Domestic Relations Orders (QDROs), 15, 160
Quit Day, smoking cessation, 21

R

Reagan, President Ronald, 222
Real estate investments, 201–203
  commercial property, 201–202
  property value appreciation, 201
  rate of return and risk, 182–183, 202–203
  for rental income, 103, 201

residential property, 202

Real estate investment trusts (REITs), 201, 202

Rebalancing securities portfolios, 199

The Recovery Book (Mooney, Eisenbert, and Eisenberg), 60

Relaxation, wellness and, 96

Religion
families disrupted by disputes over, 59
friendships developed through, 69, 79, 92
most satisfying religious experiences, 87
stress and, 42
volunteering for religious institutions, 92

Rentals (home)
income-producing, 103, 202
renting space in home, 173, 203
by women, 16

Repetitive stress injuries, yoga for, 38

Required minimum withdrawals, from tax-deferred retirement plans, 162–164

Research to Riches: The Secret Rules of Successful Marketing (J. Nelson), 218

RESPeRate, 30

Restaurants, caution against eating in, 40

Retired Brains, 92

Retirement
forced, 214, 223–224
how affluent adults *see*, 48
number of years spent in, 1, 106, 113
of only one spouse, 12, 15, 64–65
possibility of, 1

Retirement age
break-even point, 145–146
expectations, by age group, 211
full retirement age, 9, 10, 141–144, 221–222
statistics, 9, 210
table, 10
vesting age for pension plans, 148
for women, 15
See also Delayed retirement; Early retirement; Social Security retirement benefits

Retirement Jobs, 216

Retirement plans. *See* Annuities; Pension plans; Social Security retirement benefits; Tax-deferred accounts

Reverse mortgages (home-equity conversion mortgages), 170–173
fees, 171–172
income from, 111, 134, 136, 202
information resources, 172
likely candidates for, 172
loan repayment, 171
overview, 170–171
withdrawing money from, 171

Rezoom website, 74

Rollovers between retirement plans, 154

Rollovers, between retirement plans, 163

Roth IRAs, 157–158, 159, 162

Royalties, income from, 103
Russell 3000 index, 196

S

Safe withdrawal system, 178–184
Salt, high blood pressure and, 29
Satisfaction Factor, 102–103
Saturated fats, 32, 40
Savings accounts
  certificates of deposit, 158, 180–181, 184–185
  for emergencies, 132, 183–184
  FDIC protections, 184–185
  as income, 136, 164
  money market accounts, 180–181, 184–185
  rate of return and risk, 180–181, 184–185
  withdrawals from, 110–111, 178–184
  See also Funding for retirement; Number, money needed through retirement
Securities
  allowing time to perform, 187
  calculating income from, 104
  day trading, 188
  of employers, investing in, 154
  FDIC protections, 185
  increasing amount put into, 121
  for IRA and 401(k) investments, 151–152, 153, 158, 160, 191
  rates of return vs. risk, 180–183, 198–200
  rebalancing portfolios, 199

TIPS, 180–181, 186
  withdrawals, 161
  See also Bonds; Mutual funds; Stocks
Securities and Exchange Commission (SEC), 205
Self employment, 401(k)s and, 153
Senior Job Bank (Workforce50.com), 216
Seniors4Hire, 216
SEP (Simplified Employee Pension) IRAs, 157
Shopping the perimeter, 40–41
Sigmoidoscopies and colonoscopies, 43
SIMPLE IRAs, 157
Simple Living Investments for Old Age (M. Phillips and C. Campbell), 76
Skin cancer, 41
Sleep
  amount of time spent in, 110
  insomnia, 25, 42–43
Smoking
  cost of, 24
  diseases/death caused by, 20
  states with lowest percentage of smokers, 20
Smoking cessation, 20–25
  antismoking products, 23
  benefits of, 8, 24
  high blood pressure and, 29
  impact on spouse, 25
  relapse avoidance, 23
  strategies that don't work, 23
  support groups, 22

tips, 20–22
weight gain and, 22
Social Funds, 197
Social Investment Forum, 197
Socially Responsible Investing (SRI) funds, 193, 197
Social networks. *See* Family relationships; Friendships; Support groups
Social Security
  dependents benefits, 139
  disability benefits, 139
  survivors benefits, 139, 146–147
Social Security Administration (SSA)
  contacting about errors, 142
  retirement age calculator, 141, 145
  Your Social Security Statement, 103, 140, 142
Social Security, Medicare & Government Pensions: Get the Most Out of Your Retirement & Medical Benefits (J. Matthews), 141
Social Security retirement benefits, 137–147
  for baby boomers, 137
  confusing information about, 99
  delayed retirement, 9, 143–144, 145–146
  dependents benefits and, 139
  early retirement and, 10, 141–142, 145
  estimating amount of, 103–104, 110, 136, 140–141
  full retirement age, 9, 10, 141–144, 145–146
  investing surplus in securities, 138

for low- vs. high-income households, 135
  outlook for survival, 104, 137
  pensions and, 150–151
  reducing for affluent retirees, 138
  solutions to crisis, 138
  taxes on, 147
  unemployment benefits and, 222
  when to claim, 141–144
  who is not covered by, 141
  for widows/widowers, 10
  working after retirement and, 221–222
Society of Financial Service Professionals, contact information, 207
Solitude
  benefits of, 68
  vs. loneliness, 68
  vs. traveling with others, 56, 65
Solve Your Money Troubles: Get Debt Collectors Off Your Back & Regain Financial Freedom (R. Leonard), 126
Space, creating in marriage, 12
Sports
  ice skating, 94
  for older athletes, 36–37
  volunteer opportunities, 88–90
SRI (Socially Responsible Investing) funds, 193, 197
SSA. *See* Social Security Administration
Standard & Poor's (S&P)
  bond ratings, 186–187

index funds that track, 194

State laws
against age discrimination, 223
estate taxes, 166
information resources, 224
usury laws, 120

Stockbrokers (brokers)
checking credentials, 204–205
for mutual funds, 193
payment options, 205–206
role of, 204, 206–207

Stocks
vs. bonds, 158, 198–199
individual, rate of return and risk, 182–183, 188–190, 200
margin buying, 190
rebalancing portfolio, 199
tips for buying and selling, 188–190, 198–200
See also Mutual funds; Securities

Stress
exercise to reduce, 36
pets to reduce, 81
smoking as response to, 22
tips for managing, 42–43

Stretching and flexibility exercises, 38

Stroke
ailments associated with, 42
cholesterol control and, 30–31
LDL and, 32
obesity and, 26, 28
salt intake and, 29
smoking cessation and, 24

Strong Women, Strong Hearts, 37

Stumbling on Happiness (D. Gilbert), 4

Support groups
to control spending, 125
to encourage exercise, 35, 39
family websites, 58
friendships developed through, 69, 79
Parents and Friends of Lesbians and Gays, 60
smoking cessation, 21–22

Survivors benefits, Social Security, 139, 146–147

T

Target funds, 182–183, 192, 195–197

Tax deductions
for 401(k) loans, 155
charitable gift annuities, 175
for home equity loans, 123, 155
for home mortgage interest, 128, 130
for real estate, 103
for specific IRA categories, 157–158

Tax-deferred accounts, 151–164
benefits of, 136
early withdrawals from, 124, 128, 155–156, 159–161
excess contributions to, 160
income from, 104, 134
increasing amount put into, 116–117, 121, 126–127, 128–129, 132
information resources, 164, 167

withdrawals at age 59 ½, 10, 152, 160, 162

withdrawals at age 70 ½, 162–164

See also 401(k)s and 403(b)s; IRAs

Taxes

on 401(k) loans, 156

capital gains, 194

on inheritances and gifts, 136, 166, 168

Kiddie Tax, 168

payroll, Social Security payouts and, 137, 138

property, 203

on Roth IRA funds, 157–158, 159

on Social Security retirement benefits, 147

unpaid, IRS levies on retirement plans, 160

Tax penalties, for early withdrawals from tax-deferred accounts, 154, 159–161

T-bills (U.S. Treasury bills), rate of return and risk, 180–181, 200

Telecommuting, 52

Television, cable/satellite, 122

ThirdAge website, 74

Traditional contributory IRAs, 157

Traffic accidents, sleep deprivation and, 43

Trans fats, 32, 40

Transitioning, 1, 13–14

Travel

business travel, 53

European countries most want to visit, 86

with others vs. alone, 56

by retired spouse, 65

Treasury inflation protected securities (TIPS), 180–181, 186

T. Rowe Price

mutual funds, 191

online retirement calculator, 101

Trusts

bypass or AB, 166

to reduce estate taxes, 166

REITs, 201, 202

U

Unemployment benefits, Social Security benefits and, 222

Unemployment, health premiums and, 160

Uniform Lifetime Table, for IRAs, 162–163

USA TODAY

annual weight loss challenge, 27

website, 18

U.S. Census Bureau, information resources, 218

U.S. Treasury bills (T-bills), rate of return and risk, 180–181, 200

U.S. Treasury bonds

purchasing, 187

rate of return and risk, 180–181, 186

vs. stocks, for IRA investments, 158

Usury laws, charge accounts exempt from, 120

V

Vacations, vs. saving for retirement, 8

Value funds, 192

Vanguard, 187, 188, 191

Vegetables, benefits of eating, 38

Vesting age, for pension plans, 148

Veterans, pensions for disabled, 150

Vitamin D, to prevent brittle bones, 41

Volunteer Match, 92

Volunteer (nonprofit sector) activities, 84–92

  benefits of, 12, 84, 86–87, 90

  examples, 88–90, 91

  problems associated with, 87–90

  starting before retirement, 90, 92

  statistics, 84

Volunteer Solutions, United Way, 92

W

Walking, benefits of, 22, 27, 37

Water, replacing sugary drinks with, 27

Web TV (MSN TV box), 75

Weight gain, smoking cessation and, 22

Weight loss

  benefits of, 8, 28

  high blood pressure and, 29

  tips, 26–27

  See also Diet

Weight, maintaining healthy, 22, 25–28, 32

Weight training (strength and endurance), 37, 38

Widows/widowers, Social Security benefits, 10

Wilshire 5000 index, 196

Women

  401(k) savings rate, 156

  activities of retired, 84

  arthritis and, 35

  average life expectancy, 10, 17, 76, 106

  HDL risk, 31

  home ownership by, 16

  investments by, 16

  loss of pension plan shares, 15

  over 85 living with spouse, 64

  preparation for retirement, 15–16

Workforce50.com (Senior Job Bank), 216

The Work From Home Handbook (D. Fitzpatrick and S. Fishman), 54

Work Less, Live More (B. Clyatt), 10, 53, 178, 182

Y

Yoga, benefits of, 38

You Can Do It: The Boomer's Guide to a Great Retirement (J.D. Pond), 170

Your Rights in the Workplace (B. K. Repa), 224

Your Social Security Statement (SSA), 103, 140, 142

Z

Zone Diet, effectiveness of, 28

CATALOG
...more from Nolo

BUSINESS	PRICE	CODE
Business Buyout Agreements (Book w/CD)	$49.99	BSAG
The California Nonprofit Corporation Kit (Binder w/CD)	$69.99	CNP
California Workers' Comp: How to Take Charge When You're Injured on the Job	$34.99	WORK
The Complete Guide to Buying a Business (Book w/CD)	$24.99	BUYBU
The Complete Guide to Selling a Business (Book w/CD)	$34.99	SELBU
Consultant & Independent Contractor Agreements (Book w/CD)	$29.99	CICA
The Corporate Records Handbook (Book w/CD)	$69.99	CORMI
Create Your Own Employee Handbook (Book w/CD)	$49.99	EMHA
Dealing With Problem Employees	$44.99	PROBM
Deduct It! Lower Your Small Business Taxes	$34.99	DEDU
Effective Fundraising for Nonprofits	$24.99	EFFN
The Employer's Legal Handbook	$39.99	EMPL
The Essential Guide to Family and Medical Leave (Book w/CD)	$39.99	FMLA
The Essential Guide to Federal Employment Laws	$39.99	FEMP
The Essential Guide to Workplace Investigations (Book w/CD)	$39.99	NVST
Every Nonprofit's Guide to Publishing (Book w/CD)	$29.99	EPNO
Form a Partnership (Book w/CD)	$39.99	PART
Form Your Own Limited Liability Company (Book w/CD)	$44.99	LIAB
Home Business Tax Deductions: Keep What You Earn	$34.99	DEHB
How to Form a Nonprofit Corporation (Book w/CD)—National Edition	$49.99	NNP
How to Form a Nonprofit Corporation in California (Book w/CD)	$49.99	NON
How to Form Your Own California Corporation (Binder w/CD)	$59.99	CACI
How to Form Your Own California Corporation (Book w/CD)	$39.99	CCOR
How to Write a Business Plan (Book w/CD)	$34.99	SBS
Incorporate Your Business (Book w/CD)	$49.99	NIBS
Investors in Your Backyard (Book w/CD)	$24.99	FINBUS
The Job Description Handbook (Book w/CD)	$29.99	JOB
Legal Guide for Starting & Running a Small Business	$34.99	RUNS
Legal Forms for Starting & Running a Small Business (Book w/CD)	$29.99	RUNSF
LLC or Corporation?	$24.99	CHENT
The Manager's Legal Handbook	$39.99	ELBA
Marketing Without Advertising	$20.00	MWAD
Music Law: How to Run Your Band's Business (Book w/CD)	$39.99	ML
Negotiate the Best Lease for Your Business	$24.99	LESP
Nolo's Quick LLC	$29.99	LLCQ
Patent Savvy for Managers: Spot and Protect Valuable Innovations in Your Company	$29.99	PATM
The Performance Appraisal Handbook (Book w/CD)	$29.99	PERF
The Progressive Discipline Handbook (Book w/CD)	$34.99	SDBH
Small Business in Paradise: Working for Yourself in a Place You Love	$19.99	SPAR
The Small Business Start-up Kit (Book w/CD)	$24.99	SMBU
The Small Business Start-up Kit for California (Book w/CD)	$24.99	OPEN
Starting & Building a Nonprofit: A Practical Guide (Book w/CD)	$29.99	SNON
Starting & Running a Successful Newsletter or Magazine	$29.99	MAG
Tax Deductions for Professionals	$34.99	DEPO
Tax Savvy for Small Business	$36.99	SAVVY
Whoops! I'm in Business	$19.99	WHOO
Working for Yourself: Law & Taxes for Independent Contractors, Freelancers & Consultants	$39.99	WAGE
Working With Independent Contractors (Book w/CD)	$29.99	HICI
Your Limited Liability Company: An Operating Manual (Book w/CD)	$49.99	LOP
Your Rights in the Workplace	$29.99	YRW

Prices subject to change.

CONSUMER

	PRICE	CODE
How to Win Your Personal Injury Claim	$29.99	PICL
Nolo's Encyclopedia of Everyday Law	$29.99	EVL
Nolo's Guide to California Law	$24.99	CLAW
Your Little Legal Companion (Hardcover)	$9.95	ANNI

ESTATE PLANNING & PROBATE

	PRICE	CODE
8 Ways to Avoid Probate	$19.99	PRAV
The Busy Family's Guide to Estate Planning (Book w/CD)	$24.99	FAM
Estate Planning Basics	$21.99	ESPN
The Executor's Guide: Settling a Loved One's Estate or Trust	$34.99	EXEC
Get It Together: Organize Your Records so Your Family Won't Have To (Book w/CD)	$21.99	GET
How to Probate an Estate in California	$49.99	PAE
Make Your Own Living Trust (Book w/CD)	$39.99	LITR
Nolo's Simple Will Book (Book w/CD)	$36.99	SWIL
Plan Your Estate	$44.99	NEST
Quick & Legal Will Book (Book w/CD)	$19.99	QUIC
Special Needs Trust: Protect Your Child's Financial Future (Book w/CD)	$34.99	SPNT

FAMILY MATTERS

	PRICE	CODE
Always Dad: Being a Great Father During & After a Divorce	$16.99	DIFA
Building a Parenting Agreement That Works	$24.99	CUST
The Complete IEP Guide	$34.99	IEP
Divorce & Money: How to Make the Best Financial Decisions During Divorce	$34.99	DIMO
Divorce Without Court: A Guide to Mediation & Collaborative Divorce	$29.99	DWCT
Do Your Own California Adoption (Book w/CD)	$34.99	ADOP
Every Dog's Legal Guide: A Must-Have for Your Owner	$19.99	DOG
Get a Life: You Don't Need a Million to Retire Well	$24.99	LIFE
The Guardianship Book for California	$34.99	GB
A Judge's Guide to Divorce (Book w/CD)	$24.99	JDIV
A Legal Guide for Lesbian and Gay Couples (Book w/CD)	$34.99	LG
Living Together: A Legal Guide for Unmarried Couples (Book w/CD)	$34.99	LTK
Nolo's Essential Guide to Divorce	$24.99	NODV
Nolo's IEP Guide: Learning Disabilities	$29.99	IELD
Parent Savvy	$19.99	PRNT
Prenuptial Agreements: How to Write a Fair & Lasting Contract (Book w/CD)	$34.99	PNUP
Work Less, Live More: The Way to Semi-Retirement	$17.99	RECL
The Work Less, Live More Workbook: Get Ready for Semi-Retirement (Book w/CD)	$19.99	RECW

GOING TO COURT

	PRICE	CODE
Beat Your Ticket: Go To Court & Win—National Edition	$21.99	BEYT
The Criminal Law Handbook: Know Your Rights, Survive the System	$39.99	KYR
Everybody's Guide to Small Claims Court—National Edition	$29.99	NSCC
Everybody's Guide to Small Claims Court in California	$29.99	CSCC
Fight Your Ticket & Win in California	$29.99	FYT
How to Change Your Name in California	$34.99	NAME
Legal Research: How to Find & Understand the Law	$39.99	LRES
Nolo's Deposition Handbook	$34.99	DEP
Represent Yourself in Court: How to Prepare & Try a Winning Case	$39.99	RYC
Win Your Lawsuit: A Judge's Guide to Representing Yourself in California Superior Court	$39.99	SLWY

HOMEOWNERS, LANDLORDS & TENANTS

	PRICE	CODE
Buying a Second Home (Book w/CD)	$24.99	SCND
The California Landlord's Law Book: Rights & Responsibilities (Book w/CD)	$44.99	LBRT
The California Landlord's Law Book: Evictions (Book w/CD)	$44.99	LBEV
California Tenants' Rights	$29.99	CTEN
Deeds for California Real Estate	$27.99	DEED
Every Landlord's Legal Guide (Book w/CD)	$44.99	ELLI
Every Landlord's Guide to Finding Great Tenants (Book w/CD)	$19.99	FIND
Every Landlord's Tax Deduction Guide	$34.99	DELL
Every Tenant's Legal Guide	$29.99	EVTEN

	PRICE	CODE
For Sale by Owner in California (Book w/CD)	$29.99	FSBO
How to Buy a House in California	$34.99	BHCA
Leases & Rental Agreements (Book w/CD)	$29.99	LEAR
Neighbor Law: Fences, Trees, Boundaries & Noise	$26.99	NEI
Nolo's Essential Guide to Buying Your First Home (Book w/CD)	$24.99	HTBH
Renters' Rights: the Basics	$24.99	RENT

IMMIGRATION

	PRICE	CODE
Becoming A U.S. Citizen: A Guide to the Law, Exam and Interview	$24.99	USCIT
Fiancé & Marriage Visas	$34.99	IMAR
How to Get a Green Card	$29.99	GRN
U.S. Immigration Made Easy	$39.99	IMEZ

MONEY MATTERS

	PRICE	CODE
101 Law Forms for Personal Use (Book w/CD)	$29.99	SPOT
Chapter 13 Bankruptcy: Repay Your Debts	$39.99	CHB
Credit Repair (Book w/CD)	$24.99	CREP
How to File for Chapter 7 Bankruptcy	$29.99	HFB
IRAs, 401(k)s & Other Retirement Plans: Taking Your Money Out	$34.99	RET
Lower Taxes in Seven Easy Steps	$16.99	LTAX
The New Bankruptcy: Will It Work for You?	$21.99	FIBA
Nolo's Guide to Social Security Disability (Book w/CD)	$29.99	QSS
Solve Your Money Troubles	$19.99	MT
Stand Up to the IRS	$29.99	SIRS
Surviving An IRS Tax Audit	$24.95	SAUD

PATENTS AND COPYRIGHTS

	PRICE	CODE
All I Need is Money: How to Finance Your Invention	$19.99	FINA
The Copyright Handbook: What Every Writer Needs to Know (Book w/CD)	$39.99	COHA
Getting Permission: How to License & Clear Copyrighted Materials Online & Off (Book w/CD)	$34.99	RIPER
How to Make Patent Drawings	$29.99	DRAW
The Inventor's Notebook	$24.99	INOT
Legal Guide to Web & Software Development (Book w/CD)	$44.99	SFT
Nolo's Patents for Beginners	$24.99	QPAT
Patent, Copyright & Trademark: An Intellectual Property Desk Reference	$39.99	PCTM
Patent It Yourself	$49.99	PAT
Patent Pending in 24 Hours	$34.99	PEND
Patent Savvy For Managers: Spot & Protect Valuable Innovations in Your Company	$29.99	PATM
Profit from Your Idea (Book w/CD)	$34.99	LICE
The Public Domain	$34.99	PUBL
Trademark: Legal Care for Your Business and Product Name	$39.99	TRD
What Every Inventor Needs to Know About Business & Taxes (Book w/CD)	$21.99	ILAX

SENIORS

	PRICE	CODE
Long-Term Care: How to Plan & Pay for It	$19.99	ELD
Social Security, Medicare & Goverment Pensions	$29.99	SOA

SOFTWARE Call or check our website at www.nolo.com for special discounts on Software!

	PRICE	CODE
LLC Maker—Windows	$89.95	LLP1
Patent Pending Now!	$119.99	PP1
PatentEase—Windows	$349.00	PEAS
Personal RecordKeeper 5.0 CD—Windows	$59.95	RKD5
Quicken Legal Business Pro 2008—Windows	$109.99	SBQB8
Quicken WillMaker Plus 2008—Windows	$79.99	WQP8

Special Upgrade Offer: Save 35% on the latest edition of your Nolo book

Because laws and legal procedures change often, we update our books regularly. To help keep you up-to-date, we are extending this special upgrade offer. Cut out and mail the title portion of the cover of your old Nolo book and we'll give you 35% off the retail price of the New Edition of that book when you purchase directly from Nolo. This offer is to individuals only. Prices and offer subject to change without notice.

Get the Latest in the Law

Nolo's Legal Updater
We'll send you an email whenever a new edition of your book is published! Sign up at **www.nolo.com/legalupdater**.

Updates at Nolo.com
Check **www.nolo.com/update** to find recent changes in the law that affect the current edition of your book.

Nolo Customer Service
To make sure that this edition of the book is the most recent one, call us at **800-728-3555** and ask one of our friendly customer service representatives (7:00 am to 6:00 pm PST, weekdays only). Or find out at **www.nolo.com**.

Complete the Registration & Comment Card ...
... and we'll do the work for you! Just indicate your preferences below:

Registration & Comment Card

NAME _____ DATE _____

ADDRESS _____

CITY _____ STATE _____ ZIP _____

PHONE _____ EMAIL _____

COMMENTS _____

WAS THIS BOOK EASY TO USE?   (VERY EASY)   5   4   3   2   1   (VERY DIFFICULT)

☐ Yes, you can quote me in future Nolo promotional materials. *Please include phone number above.*

☐ Yes, send me **Nolo's Legal Updater** via email when a new edition of this book is available.

Yes, I want to sign up for the following email newsletters:

    ☐ **NoloBriefs** (monthly)
    ☐ **Nolo's Special Offer** (monthly)
    ☐ **Nolo's BizBriefs** (monthly)
    ☐ **Every Landlord's Quarterly** (four times a year)

☐ Yes, you can give my contact info to carefully selected partners whose products may be of interest to me.

NOLO

US-RICH1

Nolo
950 Parker Street
Berkeley, CA 94710-9867
www.nolo.com

YOUR LEGAL COMPANION